Number Thirty-seven
Number Thirty-eight
Number Thirty-nine
Number Forty

Edited by
Wayne Rice
and
Paul Thigpen

Illustrations by
Corbin Hillam

ISBN 0-910125-34-1 (Ideas Combo 37-40)
ISBN 0-910125-00-7 (Ideas Library)
© 1985, 1986, 1990 by Youth Specialties
1224 Greenfield Drive, El Cajon, CA 92021
619/440-2333

Ideas in this book have been voluntarily submitted by individuals
and groups who claim to have used them in one form or another
with their youth groups. Before you use an idea, evaluate it for
its suitability to your own groups, for any potential risks, for
safety precautions that must be taken, and for advance
preparation that may be required. Youth Specialties, Inc., is not
responsible for, nor has it any control over, the use or misuse of
any of the ideas published in this book.

Ideas Combo 37–40

CONTENTS

CHAPTER FIVE

SERVICE 147

CHAPTER SIX

SPECIAL EVENTS 154

CHAPTER SEVEN

YOUTH GROUP LEADERSHIP 170

CHAPTER EIGHT

HOLIDAY IDEAS 188

There are lots more ideas where these came from.

This book is only one of an entire library of **Ideas** volumes that are available from Youth Specialties. Each volume is completely different and contains tons of tried and tested programming ideas submitted by the world's most creative youth workers. Order the others by using the form below.

Combo Books

52 volumes of **Ideas** have been updated and republished in four-volume combinations. For example, our combo book **Ideas 1-4** is actually four books in one—volumes 1 through 4. These combos are a bargain at $19.95 each (that's 50% off!).

The Entire Library

The **Ideas** library includes every volume and an index to volumes 1-52. See the form below for the current price, or call the Youth Specialties Order Center at 800/776-8008.

SAVE UP TO 50%!

IDEAS ORDER FORM (or call 800/776-8008)

COMBOS
($19.95 each)
- ❑ Ideas 1-4
- ❑ Ideas 5-8
- ❑ Ideas 9-12
- ❑ Ideas 13-16
- ❑ Ideas 17-20
- ❑ Ideas 21-24

- ❑ Ideas 25-28
- ❑ Ideas 29-32
- ❑ Ideas 33-36
- ❑ Ideas 37-40
- ❑ Ideas 41-44
- ❑ Ideas 45-48
- ❑ Ideas 49-52

SINGLES
($9.95 each)
- ❑ Ideas 53
- ❑ Ideas 54
- ❑ Index to volumes 1-52

❑ **Entire Ideas Library**—54 volumes and Index (volumes 1-52) for only $199.95 (regularly $289-save over 30%!)

PAYMENT METHOD:

❑ Check or money order enclosed. (CA residents add 7% sales tax; SC residents add 5% sales tax.)

❑ Credit card: ❑ Visa ❑ MasterCard   Acct. # _____

Name on card:_____ Exp. _____

❑ Please bill me. (Shipping charges plus a 5% billing fee will be added to the total.)

SHIPPING CHARGES	
ORDER SUBTOTAL	ADD
$ 1.00- 9.99	$3
$ 10.00- 24.99	$4
$ 25.00- 49.99	$6
$ 50.00- 74.99	$7
$ 75.00- 99.99	$9
$ 100.00 AND UP	$10

NAME _____

CHURCH OR ORG. (IF APPLICABLE) _____

STREET ADDRESS _____

CITY _____ STATE _____ ZIP _____

DAYTIME PHONE (_____) _____

Clip and mail to Youth Specialties, P.O. Box 4406, Spartanburg, SC 29305-4406
or call 800/776-8008

Prices subject to change.

Your Idea May Be Worth $100

It's worth at least $25 if we publish it in a future volume of **Ideas**. And it's worth $100 if it's chosen as the outstanding idea of the book it appears in.

It's not really a contest, though—just our way of saying thanks for sharing your creativity with us. If you have a good idea that worked well with your group, send it in. We'll look it over and decide whether or not we can include it in a future **Ideas** book. If we do, we'll send you at least 25 bucks!

In addition to that, the **Ideas** editor will select one especially creative idea from each new book as the outstanding idea of that particular book—and send a check for $100 to its contributor.

So don't let your good ideas go to waste. Write them down and send them to us, accompanied by this form. Explain your ideas completely (without getting ridiculous) and include illustrations, diagrams, photos, samples, or any other materials you think are helpful.

FILL OUT BELOW

Name _____

Address_____

City_____ State __ Zip _____

Phone (____) _____

I hereby submit the attached idea(s) to Youth Specialties for publication in **Ideas** and guarantee that, to my knowledge, the publication of these ideas by Youth Specialties does not violate any copyright belonging to another party. I understand that, if accepted for publication in **Ideas**, the idea(s) becomes property of Youth Specialties. I understand that I will receive payment for these ideas, the exact amount to be determined by Youth Specialties, payable upon acceptance.

Signature _____

Write or type your idea(s) (one idea per sheet) and attach it to this form or to a copy of this form. Include your name and address with each idea you send. Mail to Ideas, 1224 Greenfield Drive, El Cajon, CA 92021. Ideas submitted to Youth Specialties cannot be returned.

CHAPTER ONE

CAMPING

Affirmation Booklets

Before your next retreat, assemble the following materials: colored paper, pens, pencils, markers, crayons, magazines, scissors, staplers and staples, glue, tape, and yarn. Then write the names of all the retreat participants (including the advisors) on slips of paper. On the first day of the event, have each person draw a name. The name you draw becomes your secret friend for the weekend.

Using the materials you've assembled, each person makes an "Affirmation Booklet" during the retreat, filling it with pictures, drawings, poems, Bible verses, and comments that will tell the secret friend what you have learned about him or her. This can include what you like or admire about the person, what talents you recognize, what you think the person contributes to the group, what you miss most about him or her when he or she is not around—anything that will affirm your secret friend. One goal is to keep your secret friend a secret, trying to get to know that person without getting caught (so you must get to know several other people as well in the process).

At the end of the retreat, gather everyone together for a prayer service, with time set aside to share the booklets. Present them one at a time so that all can enjoy watching the recipients reading their booklets. When you receive your booklet, it's your turn next to present the one you made. Close the prayer service with a group hug and a familiar song. (Contributed by Mary Kay Fitzpatrick, St. Louis, MO)

Basic Training

Try a military theme for your next retreat by calling it "Boot Camp" and using military jargon throughout the weekend. Begin the event with "In-Processing," where the kids are registered and given matching T-shirts which they must wear at all times.

(You can create a special logo for the shirts with your group's name and the words "Basic Training"). When each one is "dismissed," he or she must report to the "barracks" (cabin or meeting room) to learn the basic training motto: "Highly motivated, truly dedicated, rough, tough, can't get enough, praise God!" The first meal served that evening is C-rations.

Divide the "trainees" into "squads," each with a squad leader from the staff and an enthusiastic assistant squad leader from the group. Have each squad choose a name, mascot, color, motto, and Bible verse. Squad times can be used for devotions, discussions, reviews, or skit preparation. Design training exercises such as "Bible Marksmanship" (locating verses), and have the squads compete. Call the large group meetings for teaching and worship "mission briefings."

If you can locate a trumpet and player, rouse the troops in the morning with a genuine reveille, and start the day with "PT"—stretching and light exercise followed by a short jog. Create your own cadence for the group to chant as they run.

End the weekend with a "USO Show" of skits planned and performed by squads, individual youth, and staff. Be sure to take lots of pictures throughout the weekend so you can follow-up later with a slide show of the kids' first "Boot Camp."

(Contributed by Joan Nusbaum, Greeley, CO)

The Board of Destiny

Every church camp in the world has had a rule for at least a hundred years that if a camper gets a package or three letters at mail call, he or she must tell a joke or sing a song to get the mail. This idea could be used in similar circumstances.

The "Board of Destiny" is a poster board with about fifty little doors cut into it (like an Advent calendar). Behind each door is a message that can be either good news or bad news for the one who opens it. Messages might include:

- **The camp dean buys you a can of soda at the canteen.**
- **Go to the front of the line for your next meal.**
- **The faculty member of your choice serves you a meal.**
- **You are exempted from cabin cleanup tomorrow.**

However, some of the messages might say:
- **Do ten pushups.**
- **You must buy the camp dean a can of soda at the canteen.**
- **You are sentenced to ten**

seconds in front of the firing squad (squirt guns).
- **Eat your next meal without a chair.**

One section of the board can be called "Heaven on Earth," and these doors are opened only by people who deserve some special award. This section might include these messages:

- **You have priority on the diving board for one day.**
- **You can be the firing squad for the faculty member of your choice.**
- **You get a free ice cream sundae at the canteen.**

The board can also feature "Death Row," which is for kids who deserve something more negative. This could be used as a creative way to handle discipline problems. Messages in this section might include:

- **Wipe off all the tables.**
- **Sweep the dining hall.**
- **You're last in line at the next meal.**
- **Carry all the dishes from all the tables.**
- **You must be a staff "go-fer" for the rest of the day.**

You can use all these messages, or others of your choosing. This idea will add a little excitement at mail call and other fun times. Use it creatively. It's great fun and has a variety of applications. (Contributed by Rod Nielsen, LaPorte, IN)

Conversation Sheets

Here's a great way for kids to engage in dialogue with each other at a camp or retreat in a non-threatening way. Get a roll of butcher paper about four feet wide, and roll it out on a couple of tables or hang it on the wall. Provide pencils and markers and then encourage your kids to write down their feelings and comments as the week goes by. Don't limit what they write about (although they usually will want to write about things that are happening on the retreat). Tell them they can sign their names if they want, but they don't have to.

Then encourage the kids to read the comments and respond to them if they want to. You'll be amazed at how much the kids will help each other. Here is an actual sample from a "conversation sheet" used at one camp:

I'm really confused and don't really know what to do with my life. I know one thing though, and that's that I've drawn away from God and it hurts! I want to begin to grow again...
Signed, "Confused"

This is exactly the way I feel! Sometimes I think I can't have any fun being a Christian. I know deep down inside that I should be a Christian — a good one, I mean — yet it's so hard, especially at school. Signed, "Trying my best"

KEEP TALKING, PLEASE, WE ALL NEED IT SO BADLY! — ENCOURAGED

Kids can write things that are just for fun as well. Either way, it provides an outlet for some creativity and serious thinking. By reading these conversation sheets, your leaders can also get a good feel for what's happening in your group. Make sure it's located in a prominent place where kids will see it often. (Contributed by Jim Roberts, Plymouth, MI)

Friendship Candle

Lighting a "Friendship Candle" is a good way to begin a retreat or camp. Get a candle that will last the length of the event. When your group is first assembled, have one person light it and place it where it will be seen frequently by everyone. Then explain that the candle is to be a reminder of the many warm friendships you're making while you're together.

On the last night of the event, have the group form a circle with small candles of their own. From the flame of the friendship candle light one of the smaller candles and then pass on the light. Close with remarks such as these: "The warmth and light of the friendships that were made here will remain with us no matter how many miles come between us. So we no longer need the flame of our friendship candle, because the flame is now within our hearts."

Then blow out the friendship candle and end with prayer or a song. (Contributed by Jan Schaible, Wichita, KS)

Mountaintop Insurance

Young people are often disappointed when they come home from camp because their families or parents are not prepared for them. Kids who have been away for a week of camp usually have "mountaintop experiences" which are very meaningful and important for them—but when they return home, no one seems to notice. This often leaves them frustrated and wondering whether or not anything significant really happened at all.

The situation can be avoided by sending a letter to the parents of each young person before the camp begins to alert them to the problem. Such a letter can help parents be more sensitive to the emotional needs of their son or daughter when he or she returns home from camp. Here is a suggested format:

Dear Parents,

　　We in the youth department of (church) believe that youth ministry involves not only the students themselves, but their families as well. So we would like to take this opportunity to share with you a little bit about the camp your son or daughter is attending this week. We are hoping this week will be one of real growth, and that your child will experience God's love in a new and exciting way.

　　What will we be doing at camp? Well, there will be many activities, but the most important of all will be our evening campfires. We have invited a guest speaker, (name), who will be sharing with the kids each night. At these meetings, and in cabin groups throughout the week, we will be encouraging each young person to think seriously about his or her relationship to Christ, and to make or renew a commitment to Him.

　　There is a good chance that your son or daughter will have what we sometimes call a "mountaintop experience" while away at camp. So it's important that our youth return to an environment that is warm and supportive. Although your life may not have changed at all during the week, he or she will have probably been questioning, searching, and making some big decisions. Your teenager will be emotionally high, and may want to share some thoughts and feelings with you. He or she will be different, even if only for a few days or weeks. When the emotions of being close to friends and God wear off, you can support your child by listening and encouraging him or her to apply what has been learned.

　　We love our youth very much, and hope to have a continuing, positive relationship with both them and you.

Sincerely in Christ,

Gail Harris

Of course, you will want to tailor your letter to your own situation, and to the details of your camp or retreat. Letters can be written individually, or you can just print up a form letter for larger groups. Such an approach will help make that transition from the mountaintop to the real world a little easier for your kids. (Contributed by Gail Harris, Danville, CA)

Ready for the Long Bus Ride

For fun, pass out the following list of "Bus Ride Preparation Exercises" to your kids a few days before the long journey to camp. Guaranteed to keep away the faint-hearted!

BUS RIDE PREPARATION EXERCISES

To be in top shape for the grueling, marathon bus trip ahead, you should practice one or more of the following conditioning exercises before we leave:

THE GREASE BOMB

Go for several days without washing your hair, and see how slick-headed you can be.

THE RACK SLEEP

For those who are tough enough to sleep up in the luggage rack of the bus: Try sleeping on the top shelf of your closet for a night.

THE BROWN CLOUD COMBUSTION BREATH

Eat some cheese-flavored nacho chips, a bowl of French onion soup, a slab of garlic bread, and a burrito supreme. Then breathe into a Ph-balanced baggie to form a brown cloud.

THE OXY 10

Don't wash your face for three days, and watch the glick build up.

THE WRINKLE TEST

Walk around in un-ironed clothes for three days. (Works best with 100 percent cotton. This exercise will show what you look like after grappling with a bus seat for several hours.)

THE FLOOR BOARD SNOOZE

This will help you condition for sleeping on the bus floor. You simply sleep under your bed for a couple of nights.

JUNK FOOD JAUNDICE

Stay up all night and eat junk food to condition your stomach.

THE FAST FOOD SHAMPOO

Go to a local burger joint and wash your hair in the sink in 40 seconds or less.

(Contributed by Richard A. Cooper, Memphis, TN)

The Retreat Beatitudes

As your group leaves to go on its next retreat, have copies of the following "Retreat Beautitudes" ready to distribute to all youth and advisors. Post a copy as well in each cabin for the weekend.
(Contributed by Dave Carver, Pittsburgh, PA)

The Retreat Beatitudes

Blessed is the boy who remaineth in the boy's cabin, and also the boy who goeth not into the private rooms of the girl's cabin, for he shall live long and prosper. He shall also be allowed to remain here all weekend. But a curse is on those who find themselves in the wrong cabin; yea, both male and female shall remain in their appointed places.

𝕭𝖑𝖊𝖘𝖘𝖊𝖉 are the young who are on time for meals, for they shall not be called washers of dishes.

𝕭𝖑𝖊𝖘𝖘𝖊𝖉 are they who are called lovers of quiet, for they shall make many friends in the land. But a curse is on those who disturb others with thy radio or thy jam-box; and verily, I say unto thee, thy batteries may be taken if thou dost not heed a single warning to lower thy volume or stop thy tunes.

𝕭𝖑𝖊𝖘𝖘𝖊𝖉 are they who pick up any trash they see, for the advisors shall smile upon them. But woe to those who go about leaving candy wrappers on the ground, and trash among the shrubs, for surely the cat-o-ninetails shall be applied to their hind end. And yea, this is no vain threat, but rather a *promise* of exceeding great surety.

𝕭𝖑𝖊𝖘𝖘𝖊𝖉 are they who are known as "high and dry" this weekend, who avoid the creek; for they shall live to see their next birthday. But how terrible it will be for the one who falls into the cold, swirling waters of the deep, with no one to save. It is better if that person had never been born.

𝕭𝖑𝖊𝖘𝖘𝖊𝖉 are they who join with a whole heart in the games, songs, lessons, meals, and all that pertaineth to the retreat; for surely they shall be called "those who know how to have fun." Their fame shall spread throughout the land. But a curse of boredom will rest on those who playeth not our silly games.

Retreat Folders

Keep your youth in suspense on a retreat by revealing the weekend's agenda only one item at a time. Issue folders at the beginning, to which are added instructions, schedules, and other information page by page throughout the weekend. The kids can decorate the materials however they like. If you use folders with page clamps, they can be kept as a permanent keepsake of the retreat. (Contributed by David Johnson, Ottawa, Ontario, Canada)

The Scuz Retreat

Occasionally, kids like a really "scuzzy" event. Try to find a dilapidated camp facility, and have the kids bring their rattiest clothes. Then plan muddy, rough-and-tumble games like mud football and mud pie contests, as well as some of the messier, grosser food games like "Iron gut" (**Ideas #25**), pie fights, and pie-eating contests. The retreat speaker could even discuss some of the seedier Bible characters such as Nebuchadnezzar (who lived like a wild animal for seven years) or John the Baptist (who ate grasshoppers). (Contributed by Keith King and Steve Fortosis, La Marida, CA)

Shopping Spree

Here is an idea that saves you lots of time and is a fun way to begin a weekend retreat. Instead of buying all the food for the retreat in advance and transporting it in bulky bags and leaking ice chests to the retreat site, buy the food at a supermarket near the retreat site after you arrive. The entire youth group can get into the act if you all go together. Give everyone a shopping list with two or three items to bring to designated shopping carts located near the checkout stand. Award a prize to the fastest shopper and the one who brings back the best bargain! (Contributed by Stephen Williams, Claremont, CA)

Staff Auction

Here's a good camp activity the kids will enjoy. Ahead of time, ask everyone on the camp staff to "donate" a talent or service that can be auctioned off. Make certain that all staff members are agreeable with whatever ideas you have. Also make sure that everyone is prepared to make good on offers of a talent or service.

Here is a sample list:

1. Paula and Jenny will give backrubs to an entire cabin for two nights.
2. Sarah, dressed in a costume fit for a queen, will paddle you around the lake for an hour.
3. Missy and Sue will take a cabin on a formal sunrise trail ride. (We are a horseback riding camp.)
4. Mary will pop popcorn and serve it to a cabin around an evening campfire.
5. John will take a cabin out of camp for an ice cream cone.
6. Karen and Jill and Kim will dress a cabin up as punk rock entertainers and sing with them at Sunday dinner.

7. Cathy is willing to serve breakfast in bed for whichever cabin can pay the price.
8. Julie and Kelly will serve a candlelight dinner to a cabin, complete with formal dress and flowers on the table.
9. Cindy, Erica, and Jane will serenade a cabin with selected songs from our songbook, then tuck the cabin members in bed at night.

10. Joe and Linda, our lifeguards, will provide a nighttime splash party for a cabin.
11. Muriel will read bedtime stories from a book mutually acceptable to cabin and staff member.
12. Joseph will plan a campout, complete with ghost stories.

At the "auction," have the kids bid in cabin groups. Counselors can sit with their groups to help supervise the bidding. Appoint an auctioneer to handle the actual bidding. You will also need a bookkeeper to keep track of the money spent and purchases made.

Each cabin should be given an equal amount of "camp dollars" or play money to bid with. If you're raising funds for a project, use real money.

If you make sure that all the items on the list appeal to the campers, this will be a howling success! (Contributed by Eileen Thompson, Java Center, NY)

CHAPTER TWO

CREATIVE COMMUNICATION

All in the Point of View

For a parent's night discussion starter, present the following series of vignettes. Each scene is enacted twice, once as seen from the teen's point of view, and once from the parent's point of view. Have an announcer give each topic beforehand. You can adapt these to fit your group, or create your own. In either case, encourage actors to ad lib.

Teen Point of View	DATING	Parent Point of View

Daughter: *I'm leaving now, Dad.*
Father: *Just where do you think you're going? What time will you be home? Who is this guy you're going with? Does he have a car? What kind? Does he have new tires on it? Did you ask your mother? What kind of job does he have? Did you brush your teeth?*
Daughter: *He doesn't trust me!*

Daughter: *I'm leaving now, Dad.*
Father: *What time will you be home?*
Daughter: *What's that supposed to mean? What is this, Twenty Questions? Why do you keep hounding me? Can't I get any privacy? Do you have to drill me?*
Father: *It's only because I'm concerned.*

Teen Point of View	MUSIC	Parent Point of View

Mother: *TURN DOWN THAT MUSIC!* (Son turns it down.)
Mother: *TURN DOWN THE MUSIC!* (Son turns it down.)
Mother: *TURN IT DOWN!*
Son: *It's off now, Mom.*

Mother: *Please turn down the music a little.*
Son: *WHAT?!*
Mother: *Turn it down, dear.*
Son: *WHAT?!*
Mother: *Never mind, dear.*
Son: *WHAT?!*

Son: *Mom, may I please borrow the car keys now?*
Mother: *No way, Charlie! Not when you sit around in front of that boob tube all day and don't lift one finger to help around here.*
Son: *Yes, I know Mom, I do sometimes shirk my jobs, but I'm learning. Won't you just be understanding? I promise I'll mow the lawn tomorrow.*
Mother: *Stop that smart talk and get out there right this minute!*

Son: *Give me the keys now.*
Mother: *I'm sorry, Son. You didn't mow the lawn like we agreed.*
Son: *Oh c'mon! You're not going to hold me to that, are you? (Gives a long, ridiculous excuse.)*
Mother: *I'd like you to be able to use the car, but you must learn to be responsible. When you keep up your end of the bargain, I'll be happy to give you the keys.*

(Daughter approaches busily working father, starts to say something, decides against it, and walks away.)

(Father approaches busily working daughter, starts to say something, decides against it, then walks away.)

Father: *You go on to church now.*
Daughter: *Why don't you come with us, Dad?*
Father: *You know this is the only day I have to sleep in.*
Daughter: *But Dad, I think this is really important.*
Father: *Well, maybe I'll watch a religious show on TV. You go on.*

Daughter: *Do I have to go to church today?*
Dad: *It would be nice to go as a family.*
Daughter: *You know this is the only day I have to sleep in.*
Father: *Honey, I think this is really important.*
Daughter: *Well, maybe I'll watch a religious show on TV. You go ahead.*

(Contributed by Carolyn Roddy, Santa Barbara, CA)

B.A.D. Bible Study

Here's a Bible study outline that's really B.A.D.! The initials stand for "Being and Doing," and it's a perfect way to generate interest in a study in the book of James. If presented at a retreat, the theme can be carried a little further by dividing into teams with the names of "BAD" people like "The Dalton Gang" or "The Al Capone Mob."

A sample outline to follow for the study: (All scripture references are in James unless otherwise noted.)

I. Dealing with B.A.D. attitudes
   A. Anger (1:19–21)
   B. Hypocrisy (1:22–27)
   C. Prejudice (2:1–12)
   D. Pride (4:13–17)

II. B.A.D. Words
   A. Faith (2:14–26)
   B. Wisdom (3:13–18)
   C. Obedience (4:1–12)
   D. Patience (5:7–12)
   E. Prayer (5:13–20)

III. B.A.D. People
   A. Abraham and Isaac (2:21–24; Gen. 12, 15, 21–22)
   B. Rahab (2:25; Josh. 2)
   C. Job (5:11; Job 1–2)
   D. Elijah (5:17; I Ki. 17–18)

(Contributed by Tommy Baker, Florence, KY)

The Balloon Tribe

Sometimes the best way to approach a topic is to come in through the back door. The following allegory opens up a good discussion of drinking and substance abuse in a non-threatening way.

"The Balloon Tribe"

There is a tribe in a primitive country across the ocean with a unique social activity. This is the story of how that activity originated and the effect it had on the tribe. It seems that a short while back, one of the tribe members discovered a stretchy substance which came from a local tree. With limited experimentation at first, the tribe didn't think this discovery was very important. However, from that substance one tribe member was able to invent what we know as a "balloon." The tribe thought it a clever but seemingly useless invention.

One day, however, that same tribe member discovered something interesting about the balloons. After blowing up several of them, he became light-headed and out of breath, experiencing a euphoric, dizzy feeling. When he told of this to the rest of the tribe, everyone immediately wanted to try it. Eventually, as this activity increased, the tribe became divided into four groups: The "Dizzy Balloon Blowers," the "Occasional Balloon Blowers," the "Balloon Blowers for Career or Craft," and the "Anti-Balloon Blowers."

The Dizzy Balloon Blowers developed a tolerance to blow up several very large balloons in just a short time—usually in just one evening. This group would get together every week and blow up numerous balloons for many different reasons: Some would do it to get dizzier than the time before; some as just a reason to get together with their friends; some because it was a way to relax after a hard day in the jungle; some to celebrate; and others just because they weren't getting along with other tribe members. Each tribe member felt that his or her reason for blowing up balloons was worth it, even though they often felt sick and nauseated in the morning, promising never to blow up another balloon.

Now the Occasional Balloon Blowers enjoyed a balloon every once in a while. In fact, when they did join the "Dizzy" group, they would take up a whole evening blowing up just one balloon (which was usually not too large). These tribe members blew up balloons for all the same reasons as the "Dizzy" group, but were careful to avoid having to go through what the "Dizzys" went through the morning after.

The Balloon Blowers for Career or Craft turned balloon blowing into an art. They only blew up the best balloons, not just any old cheap balloon. In fact, many of this group made their own balloons. And fine balloons they were! It was not long after balloons were discovered that this group started contests and competitions to find the "best." They examined balloon shape, size, color, and how well it expanded. Many in this group got very good at making balloons and did so full-time.

On the other side of the jungle were the Anti-Balloon Blowers. They had seen the damage done from blowing up too many balloons and getting dizzy. They loudly protested that absolutely NO ONE should blow up balloons! Some members of this group had in the past been "Dizzys." Balloon blowing had caused tribe families to break up and hate one another, they said. Many tribe members had given up their tribal responsibilities so they could blow up balloons all day and get dizzy. Some Dizzys got too dizzy even to paddle their canoes home, and so they drowned trying to do so.

With the many groups of balloon blowers—and the Anti-Balloon Blowers—it was difficult to assess the overall benefit or detriment to the tribe as a direct result of the balloons. Some members would not touch balloons while some seemingly could not face life without them. In some way every tribe member had to make up his or her own mind.

After the group has read or heard the story of the Balloon Tribe, divide up into three groups according to the position each student takes toward the story:

Group One:
Blowing up balloons is fine, and it's okay to run out of breath and get dizzy if you feel like it.

Group Two:
Occasional balloon blowing is okay, but it's morally wrong to get dizzy.

Group Three:
Blowing up balloons is wrong at all times.

Have the groups defend their positions and allow switches if desired. (Contributed by Larry A. Dunn, Visalia, CA)

Bible Broadway

Most kids don't read or study their Bibles. There are probably many reasons why not, but one of the chief ones is that they erroneously believe the Scriptures to be dull and unworthy of their limited time.

Since most kids are incredibly creative, however, they should be encouraged to rework the biblical stories in novel ways so that the truth of God's Word can take root in their hearts and lives. Any number of approaches may be used—poetry, songs, skits, drawings, cartoons, paintings, monologs, home movies, mime—but the genius of such an approach is that the kids really dig into the Word so that it gradually changes their lives.

Assign your kids passages for interpretation in some medium. Videotape their efforts and show them at the next youth group meeting. Besides all the fun and laughter, you'll have some great discussions. And most importantly,

kids will begin to see God's Word as the most exciting book on earth. Here is a creative Broadway musical version of Acts 3 that may stimulate your thinking.

Characters:	Peter (loud, obviously a strong leader, impatient, antsy)
	John (very easy-going and laid-back, thoughtful)
	Beggar #1 (the one who gets healed—a real con artist)
	Beggar #2 (his friend)
	Townspeople
The Scene:	The temple gate, called "Beautiful," at 3:00 in the afternoon. A few grimy beggars sit on either side of the gate, looking for handouts.
	(Enter Peter, by himself. He surveys the scene, takes a few deep breaths, and then begins to sing to the tune of "Oh, What a Beautiful Morning.")
Peter:	There's a bright golden haze o'er the temple,
	There's a bright, golden haze o'er the temple,
	I feel so excited,
	I can't wait to pray—
	Oh, it looks like we're in for one heck of a day …
Chorus:	Oh, what a marvelous feeling,
	Oh, what a beautiful gate,
	I'm in the mood for a healing …
	(He pauses, realizing his sidekick John is nowhere to be seen.)
Peter:	*(angrily)* If John doesn't come we'll be late! John … JOHN! *(aside to the audience)* You'd think the guy was off in Patmos or something! *(Exasperated, he huffs and goes back out the gate, out of view. Then he speaks from backstage.)* Ah-ha! *(Re-enters and announces sarcastically)* Heeeerrrreeee'ssss Johnny!
	(John enters slowly, eating a camel burger as he trudges through the gate.)
Peter:	Egads, man! We're gonna be late for prayer … *(Exasperated)* Anyway WHY must you ALWAYS be eating? That's why you always have those weird dreams … You eat that spicy food this late in the day. Now c'mon!
John:	*(slowly)* Peter, Peter, Peter, or uh, what was that the Master called you … Rocky?
	(From the background, the theme from the movie "Rocky" blares out. The actors look surprised, then it dies out.) Pete *(putting his arm around Peter's broad shoulders in a fatherly manner)*, you're always in too much of a hurry … Yup, you need to learn to take life slowly … *(spying a flowerbox)* You need to take time to smell … *(breathing deeply, then scowling and looking with disdain at the beggars)* the beggars! *(He holds his nose in mock revulsion at the beggars by the gate, on either side.)*
Beggar #2:	*(nudging #1—in a whisper)* He said his name's Peter.
Beggar #1:	Yeah, yeah, I heard. *(He crawls over to Peter and tugs on his robe.)*
Peter:	May I help you?
Beggar #1:	*(singing to the tune of "Hello, Dolly"—music in background)*
	Well hello, Peter,
	Howdy Doo, Peter,
	Give me money, give me silver, give me gold.
(really ham it up)	How 'bout some cash, Pete?
	Hate to ask, Pete,

But my stomach is so empty,
That I'm feeling bold.

Please share the wealth, Pete!
You've got your health, Pete,
But I'm lame and I can't seem to get around ...

So—shell it out, Peter,
c'mon and help me out, Peter—
You know what I'm speaking of,
Give me a little o' that Christian love
I'll be the happiest beggar in this town!
(with a flourish, winking to his buddy, obviously proud of himself)

Peter: *(looking sorrowfully at John, then the beggar)* Sorry, pal.
Beggar #1: *(desperately)* Oh, pleeeeeezzze!
Peter: Read my lips. *(Slowly)* No habla munero, amigo! Comprende? *(The beggar nods slowly and starts to slink away as John nudges Peter and whispers in his ear.)* BUT, *(the beggar turns)* even though we're as broke as the 10 Commandments ... HA HA HA *(obviously amused at his feeble attempt at humor)* Well, hit it, John!

(John produces top hats and canes and they do a little soft shoe ... to the tune of "Getting to Know You.")
Jesus will heal you,
He's gonna make you all better ...
You'll soon be walking,
Thinking about where to roam.
You won't be begging,

Bothering us Christian leaders,
Because of all the beautiful and new
Things you'll be able to do
with ... the ... Lord." *(They bow eagerly, cockily)*
(Peter grabs Beggar #1, raises him up)
In the name of Jesus Christ the Nazarene—WALK!
(Beggar #1 stands, springs, bouncing a bit, testing his ankles. He reaches down in wonderment and grabs them. Then excitedly he jumps about shouting.)

Beggar #1: I can walk! My legs ... I'm healed, I really am! I CAN BEEEE SOMEBODY!
(Background music—"The Hallelujah Chorus" fills the temple majestically. The actors all look a bit confused. Then it dies out.)

Beggar #1: Lights please, and give me ...a C.
(To the tune of, "Sunrise, Sunset," with feeling.)
Are these the legs that I was born with?
How did they get to be so strong?
I never thought that I would walk,
But I was wrong ...

(Chorus) Walking, jumping,
Leaping, dancing
Laughing all the day,
(acting each of these out in turn, then thinking suddenly) Maybe I'll try out for the track team. *(He jogs in place, then pauses, sobered by the thought.)*
Or maybe I'll kneel right down and pray.
(He does so for a moment or two, as the rest look reverently on, then he jumps up and the others encircle him. They all hug and chatter excitedly.)

Peter: *(suddenly realizing the lateness of the hour, excitedly)* WHOA! The prayer time! John, c'mon before we miss THE WHOLE THING!
(They all turn and begin to try to file into the temple door over to one side of the set, but Beggar #2 blocks the way. He has felt very neglected during this whole episode and now wants to garner some of their attention and get in on all the action.)

Beggar #2: Wait, wait! *(He grabs the first beggar and, obviously proud of himself, begins to sing to him, a bit off-key to the tune of "On the Street Where You Live.")*
I have often walked down this street before
Yet I've never seen you standing on your feet before
Now I want to know
How this thing is so ...
(Peter, totally frustrated at the lateness of the hour, now has pushed through the little crowd at the temple door. He physically picks up Beggar #2 and carries him out of sight into the temple as the rest quickly follow. Three or four seconds later Beggar #2 reappears in the doorway to sing his last line.)
But I think that's the end of this show.
(A pair of hands pulls him out of view as the curtain falls.)

THE END

(Contributed by Len Woods, Dallas, TX)

Broken Banana

If you've been looking for the perfect wrap-up for a "Banana Night," try this. After the games and activities, move on to a lesson on vulnerability. The point of the lesson is that, in order for people to really know us, we must "peel off" our outer skin.

To make the point, get three bananas. Ahead of time, take one and bruise it badly so that the insides are brown, but the outside doesn't show it. Take another banana and slice it in several places without peeling it. Here's how to do it:

Take the needle and thread and "sew" the banana as shown in the diagram. Then grab both ends of the thread and pull. This will slice the banana inside without damaging the skin. Do this in several places.

Now ask the kids to describe the three bananas: How do they look the same, and how do they look different? Take the banana which has not been tampered with and peel it. Describe how good it looks, how pure, fresh and wholesome it is. Now take the smashed up, rotten banana. Peel it and the kids will describe it for you. The inside will be mushy, dark and rotten. Take the third banana and peel it. As you peel it, the sliced

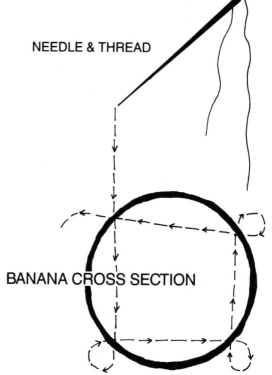

NEEDLE & THREAD

BANANA CROSS SECTION

sections will fall off. The kids will be amazed at how you were able to slice it without slicing the skin.

Some questions for discussion:
1. How were the bananas like people?
2. How can we really get to know people?
3. What must you do for people to know the real you?
4. How can you help a person who is hurting inside?
5. How is being vulnerable important for good relationships?

(Contributed by Matt Boyers, W. Lafayette, IN)

Building An Image

Here's a learning experience for your youth group which involves role playing and observation. It focuses on character traits and peer approval.

Divide into small groups of 8 to 10 kids. Each group is to function independently. Hand out the following list of character traits to each person, who is to go quickly through the list and assign a number value to each trait on a scale of 1 (low) to 10 (high): 1 = an absolutely worthless or negative character trait

5 = neither good nor bad

10 = essential to being someone you respect and like

CHARACTER TRAITS

____ Critical, fault finding
____ Inquisitive
____ Gullible
____ Spineless
____ Analytical
____ Picky, fussy, over-concerned about details
____ Daydreaming
____ Selfish
____ Competitive
____ Vain, conceited
____ Scheming, conniving, devious
____ Caring
____ Confident
____ Cooperative
____ Compromising
____ Courteous
____ Flattering
____ Decisive
____ Inflexible, one-track mind
____ Funny, joking
____ Serious
____ Impatient

____ Aggressive
____ Energetic
____ Melodramatic
____ Verbose, wordy, talkative
____ Indecisive
____ Patient
____ Big shot
____ Accusing, blaming
____ Frank, outspoken, blunt
____ Insensitive, unloving
____ Grateful
____ Friendly, cordial
____ Apathetic, indifferent
____ Stubborn, inflexible, intolerant
____ Self-critical, self-abasing
____ Pushy
____ Loud
____ Respectful
____ Mocking
____ Cool
____ Sensitive, touchy, easily offended

Next, put a batch of role plays in a hat. They can be of any type: crisis resolution, humorous situation, everyday experience, or whatever. Also put everyone's name on paper slips in a different hat. Select one name. That individual is to pick a role play. Then select more names out of the hat to fit whatever other roles are needed for the play.

All the people involved in the role play are to look over their list of character traits and select three which they will use during the role play.

Now, perform the role play. The leader should allow about 3 minutes per situation. As the kids role play, the rest of the group members must attempt to discern (privately) which traits each of the role-players is dramatizing.

After time is called, the group confers to decide which traits were being acted out, and awards each member the cumulative points for their 3 traits. The points come from each group member's list.

On the next round, a name is again chosen from the hat, and another role play is performed. This time the kids try to pick the character traits which will win them the most points. The object is not so much to accumulate the most points as it is to figure out what personality types are most acceptable to their peers, and to act that way.

You'll know you're nearing the end of the game when every kid acts just like every other kid. Sound familiar?

Follow up with a discussion. Here are some good questions:

1. Which are the most desirable character or personality traits? Why?
2. Why are these traits so important to your friends?
3. Which coincide with biblical values? Which contradict biblical values?
4. What happens to the kids who try to go against the flow of their peers' opinions?

(Contributed by Jim Walton, Rochester, NY)

Cleaning Up Your Act

For a lively discussion on a variety of topics, have your group decide whether they agree or disagree with the twelve statements below. Print them up on a sheet of paper and have the kids mark their position on an agree/disagree continuum something like this:

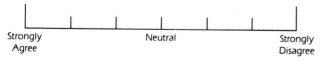

Strongly Agree   Neutral   Strongly Disagree

When they have finished, discuss each question individually and have the kids defend their positions. It would probably be wise for you as leader to research and think through your own position on each one ahead of time. In addition, it would be a good idea to choose a few scripture passages to help shed some light on the issues under discussion.

1. Pigging out is as wrong as smoking or drinking.
2. While you were walking home one night a thief jumped from the shadows and demanded all your money. You gave your wallet to the man. He looked in the wallet and asked, "Is this all the money you have on you?" You said, "Yes," and the thief left with bitter threats. You had lied to the man; you had a twenty tucked away in your shirt pocket. Was that wrong?

3. To goof off on your job is as wrong as stealing money from your boss.

4. There are degrees of sin with God, so He doesn't really sweat the little sins we commit.

5. As Christians we are to obey all people who are in a position of authority over us, including policemen, parents, and teachers.

6. You're late for church, so instead of driving at the 40-mile-per-hour speed limit, your dad drives at 55. Because you are rushing to a worship service, this is not wrong.

7. Going into your history final, you're just squeezing by with a C. Passing or failing this test could mean the difference between passing or failing the course. During the test you get a few answers from a friend's paper. As you walk out after the test you know you have failed the test. In this case it is not necessary to confess cheating to the teacher.

8. God made man and woman for each other. God has also created some very attractive bodies. It's okay to lust after someone you see because actually you're just admiring God's creation.

9. A girl is very much in love with her boyfriend, and he has said he loves her so much he would like to marry her eventually. Because she's in love and expects to marry this boy, her body belongs to him for the asking.

10. There is a guy at school who really gets on your nerves. Everytime you see him you could punch his lights out. In fact, sometimes you wish he didn't exist. The bitterness you have for this guy is as sinful as if you actually killed him.

11. God doesn't exactly expect you to live as much like Jesus at home as outside the home. After all, we are supposed to be witnesses to all the world, not to our own family.

12. Jesus whipped the money-changers in the temple and chased them out. So it's okay to be obnoxious or cruel if the other person deserves it.

(Contributed by Steve Fortosis, La Mirada, CA)

C.M. Magazine

"Christian Missionary Magazine" is a good way to give kids a better understanding of the missions program of your church or denomination. It's patterned after television "magazine" shows like **60 Minutes** and **P.M. Magazine.**

Put together a list of the missionaries your church or mission board supports. Present the list to the youth group and have the kids select a few of these missionaries for the "show."

Next, divide into groups, and give each group one of the missionaries to do a story on. They must create an interesting presentation which can include such things as a taped interview (done on the telephone or in person); slides (which can usually be obtained by request); photos; articles from publications; interviews with people who know the missionary or who have been to the foreign country they're serving in; and so on.

Obviously, this is a project which will take some time. Allow four to six months for the kids to gather all their

information and develop their presentations. Then the program "C.M. Magazine" can be presented to the entire church. (Contributed by Larry Stoffel, Danbury, CT)

Courtroom Drama

Try this courtroom drama for some stimulating role play to get your kids thinking about issues like justice and

peace making on a personal scale. Begin by reading to the group the news article reproduced here,

Vandals Attack Metropolitan School
600 lockers opened, contents strewn in hallways

by Allison Williams
Herald Staff Writer

Vandals struck the Metropolitan Intermediate School early Friday, breaking into 600 to 700 lockers and strewing books, binders and clothing throughout the hallways.

County sheriff's deputies spent several hours at the school looking for clues to the identity of the culprit or culprits, sheriff's officials said. Late Friday afternoon, however, sheriff's deputies said they had no suspects in the case.

The students weren't allowed to see the damage at first, seventh-grader Lani Johnson said. But when they did see it, they got angry, she said.

"Every hallway had piles of books on the ground. It looked like there had been a riot here," she said.

"The teachers are trying to keep everybody calm. But most of the kids are so mad ... There was an awful lot of cussing going on here today."

There was a dance at the school the previous

night, principal Roy Stapleton said. There were no signs of vandalism or suspicious activity when the custodian left the school grounds at 11:30 p.m. Thursday, Stapleton said.

When the morning custodian came on duty at 6:30 a.m. Friday, it was a different matter, he said.

Locks had been knocked off of somewhere between 600 and 700 lockers, he said. The contents of hundreds of lockers were thrown to the ground. Other lockers were jammed shut by repeated blows in an apparent attempt to break off their locks.

Although district officials still are investigating the extent of the damage, Stapleton said nothing of value appeared to be missing.

"It was vandalism. It wasn't burglary," he said.

When the seventh and eighth-graders returned to the campus Friday morning, they were told to go to their first-period classes and were kept there, he said.

First-period teachers extended their usual one-

hour lesson to two and a half hours, said one student teacher who asked not to be identified. "It went pretty smoothly," she said. "We improvised a lot."

Meanwhile, school officials, custodians and parent-volunteers cleaned up the mess, Stapleton said. The clothes were put in plastic garbage bags in the nurse's office. The books were stacked in the school library. Binders were piled in another room.

Surveying piles of bags on the floor, Stapleton said his staff and district officials would be sorting through the items over the weekend looking for clothing name tags and any names written inside books or binders so that they can be returned to their proper owner.

The Metropolitan school district, which normally charges a student for a lost or damaged book, would probably make exceptions for some of the students, he said.

By Friday afternoon, the school had returned to a normal routine, he said.

"Vandals Attack Metropolitan School." Then announce that your group will be enacting the legal case "Roger and Rip Locker vs. Mother District," based on the article. Read aloud the following role descriptions and appoint someone to take each role.

ROGER & RIP LOCKER:
*Two brothers attending the school who are vandal **suspects** in the case. They are being sued for half a million dollars.*

DR. LOCKER:
Roger and Rip's father. He wants to clear his name and medical practice by clearing his boys. He has $10,000 to work with.

DEFENSE ATTORNEY:
Hired by Dr. Locker to defend Roger and Rip.

OLIVER DO ISMYJOB:
Custodian on the late night shift. Dr. Locker is his physician and friend of 20 years. Oliver saw Roger and Rip at the dance.

LANI JOHNSON:
A student who was vandalized. She's angry, and afraid that she and her friends will have to pay for their lost and damaged books.

MRS. JOHNSON:
*Lani's mother, a parent volunteer who helped clean up the mess. She is protective of her daughter and has a close friend on the **Herald** newspaper staff—Allison Williams.*

ALLISON WILLIAMS:
She is an honest writer, but will do anything for the "right" story. What she writes in the papers can easily affect the lives of others.

PROSECUTING ATTORNEY:
He/she wants to sue Roger and Rip Locker and their parents for half a million dollars to pay for all new lockers (600 were broken) and for damaged and lost books.

ROY STAPLETON:
School principal. He wants this kind of thing never to happen again. He is upset with the custodial staff and wonders why they couldn't have prevented the crime. He will charge students for the lost and damaged books if the district doesn't win the case. He knows Lani Johnson as a spoiled child who always gets what she wants.

BOB WEGSTEEN:
Math teacher who likes both Roger and Rip. They were the first ones to join his math club this year.

JANICE AMES:
The student teacher quoted in the article, who had a run-in with Roger when she saw him cheat on a history test. She chaperoned at the dance Thursday night, and noticed Roger wandering the halls several times during the evening.

BONNIE BELL:
Rip's ex-girlfriend; she broke up with him at the dance. Her locker was never touched.

SCHOOL SUPERINTENDENT:
He/she hired the prosecuting lawyer to prosecute Roger and Rip, and wants these boys to be examples to all other vandals.

JUDGE:
Listens and decides case outcome and verdict.

JURY MEMBERS:
Must decide the case. Choose as many as you want, according to the size of your group.

Next, give everyone half an hour to prepare for the trial. The defense attorney should get with the defendants and witnesses to build their case. The school superintendent and prosecuting attorney should also interview witnesses to construct their case. The characters should not be allowed to talk to the judge or jurors while they make their "deals" prior to the trial.

As the characters are wheeling and dealing, set up the room to resemble a courtroom. When it's time for the trial to begin, have the characters take their places and follow this procedure:

1. The prosecution presents its case.
2. The defense presents its case.
3. The prosecutor calls on witnesses. These are first examined by the prosecution, then cross-examined by the defense, then examined again by the prosecution if desired.
4. The defense calls on witnesses. These are examined by the defense, cross-examined by the prosecution, and examined again by the defense if desired.
5. The prosecution makes its closing statement (no one else should talk).
6. The defense makes its closing statement (again, no one else should talk).
7. The judge and jurors are given up to ten minutes to decide the case.

After the trial, you can launch into a discussion of any one of a number of topics. One possibility is **peacemaking**. You would read Mt. 5:9 together and then ask the following questions:

1. What difference might it have made in the trial if each character had been a peacemaker? (Consider each character individually.)
2. What difference might it have made **before** the trial if those involved in the situation (principal, students, parents, teachers) had been peacemakers?

(Contributed by Cindy Fairchild, Sacramento, CA)

Create A Daily Devotional

This idea will work best with high school groups—the larger the better. Give everyone a small stack of 3″ x 5″ index cards. The number will be determined by how many kids you have. If you have 30 kids or so, then everyone will need about a dozen cards each.

Instruct the kids to spend some time in the Bible, and to write down a favorite meaningful verse or passage of scripture on each of the cards. If they want, they can also add a few words of commentary with the scripture like: "This verse gives me real hope for the future!"

When everyone has finished, collect the cards and organize them into a daily devotional guide for an entire year (365 days). If you prefer, you could shorten this time by making it a devotional guide for only nine months of the school year. You will need to remove any duplicates, add any others that you choose, and then assign each card a date, beginning with the first day of the first month.

Now the cards can be duplicated and distributed to each young person. You might want to have a meeting in which the kids create their own "card files" out of balsa wood (or whatever) to keep the cards in.

Instruct the kids to pull out the card for each day and to meditate on it before heading off to school, before going to bed, or whenever they choose. The fact that all the kids in the group are studying the same scripture passages each day can add considerably to a spirit of unity. This idea can also be used as a fund-raiser by making these devotional cards available for sale to others, or as a gift-making idea at Christmas. (Contributed by David Washburn, Brockport, NY)

Crisis Response

This is a good activity to help your kids develop their ability to deal with difficult situations quickly and decisively. It stimulates thinking and it encourages kids to realize that they really can come up with answers to tough issues on their own.

Divide into small groups of 3 or 4. Select a panel of judges (adult sponsors or a group of kids).

Next, present a problem, crisis, or ministry situation to the entire group. Here's an example:

"You are at school one day, getting something out of your locker, and you accidentally slam your finger in the locker door. Under your breath, you let out a choice swear word. A friend overhears this, and says to you, 'Hey, I thought Christians didn't say things like that.' Now what do you say?" (For a good selection of situations like this one, see **Tension Getters** or **Tension Getters Two,** by David Lynn and Mike Yaconelli (Zondervan/Youth Specialties, 1981 and 1985).

Give the groups exactly one minute to come up with a response to the situation. At the end of the minute, call time. Each group must have one person (a different person each time) present their group's response.

After this, the panel of judges chooses the best response and tells why they chose that particular one. It's a good idea for the judges to affirm as well the groups that lose.

This approach adds the elements of fun and competition to learning in a very effective way. (Contributed by Alan Hamilton, Long Beach, CA)

Debate Teams

At school kids often participate in structured debates. Why not try one in your youth group? Form debate teams and give each team a subject and a syllabus for study on the topic. Allow the kids a couple of weeks to do their research and to develop their arguments. Have one team argue for a specific proposition ("Abortion is ethical") and the other against it for a specified amount of time. If you want, you can use standard debate procedures. You might even want to invite the high school debate teacher to judge.

Choose topics which will stir up plenty of controversy. Here are some examples:

Abortion	**Eternal security**	**Divorce**
Drinking	**(of the believer)**	**The second coming**
Biblical inerrancy	**Church attendance**	**of Christ**
Rock Music	**R-rated movies**	**Faith vs. good works**
		Sex before marriage

(Contributed by Stan Lindstadt, Burlington, IA)

The Disease of Diotrephes

Does your youth group have "Diotrephes Disease?" Is there a dictator or boss in the bunch who insists on having his or her own way? That type of personality can be disastrous in a youth group. Here's a Bible study that allows kids to evaluate their lives and attitudes to avoid this ancient form of "illness," described by the Apostle John:

"I wrote to the church, but Diotrephes, who loves to be first, will have nothing to do with us. So if I come, I will call attention to what he is doing, gossiping maliciously about us. Not satisfied with that, he refuses to welcome the brothers. He also stops those who want to do so and puts them out of the church" (3 Jn. 9–10).

After reading together these words about Diotrephes, have the group consider the following six characteristics that can cause problems in the Christian community:

1. **He "loves to be first" (v. 9).** How does this desire usually show itself? Why do you think people want to be first? Is it possible for Christians to have this attitude? What did Jesus say to the disciples who had this problem? (Mk. 9:33–35) Instead of wanting to be first, what attitude should we have? (Phil. 2:3,4) How can we develop this attitude?

2. **He would "have nothing to do with us" (v. 9).** The "us" refers to John and his companions. Who was John? Why do you think Diotrephes would want to reject one of Jesus' apostles? Do we ever reject leaders in the church today? If so, how? What should our attitude be toward leaders in God's church? (Heb. 13:7,17) How can we be more supportive of our leaders?

3. **He is "gossiping maliciously" (v. 10).** How would you define gossip? What happens in a group when gossip is a habit? What does God have to say about gossip? (Ja. 3:1–12; Eph. 4:25,29) How can we stop gossip in our group and begin practicing useful,

26

helpful, encouraging speech?

4. **He "refuses to welcome the brothers" (v. 10).** Does this ever happen today? If so, how and why? Is there ever a time when we should separate ourselves from fellowship with certain believers? (Rom. 16:17–18; Tit. 3:9–11) Why is fellowship with other believers so important? What can we do to improve our fellowship? What can we do to make new believers welcome?

5. **He "stops those who want to do so" (v. 10).** There were those who wanted to welcome John and the others, which obviously is the right thing to do. Do Christians ever keep fellow Christians from doing the right thing? If so, how? What keeps us from doing what we know is right? What does God say about knowing the right thing and not doing it? (Ja. 4:17) How can we develop a willingness to do what is right every time? How can we encourage one another to do what is right?

6. **He "puts them out of the church" (v. 10).** Read I Corinthians 5:1–5 and Matthew 18:15–17 to discover when and why church discipline should be practiced by the local church. If it's practiced correctly, how does it help a church? Can church discipline ever harm a church? If so, how? What can we do to insure that correction of erring members is done in the right way for the right reason to accomplish the right results? How can our youth group practice this right kind of discipline?

With these insights in mind, every youth group member should ask him or herself, "Am I ever a Diotrephes?" Is there another Diotrephes in our group I could help in some way?" Then consider together whether your youth group as a whole suffers from the Diotrephes disease. If so, how can you be cured? How do visitors or new members see your youth group? What can be done to make your youth group more attractive and encouraging? (Contributed by Doug Newhouse, Florence, KY)

Divorce Panel

Here's a program that can help your kids develop a more realistic picture of the effects of divorce than they usually get from TV or the movies. It can also help them know how to help a friend whose parents are divorced or divorcing. Finally, it can be used to support kids whose parents are already divorced.

First, ask several kids whose parents are divorced to serve on your "panel of experts." Give them a list of potential questions in advance to help them decide whether or not they can handle the experience, and allow them to decline if they'd rather not be on the panel.

The adult who moderates the panel should be carefully chosen— someone who is sensitive to the pain which most of these kids experience. The moderator should do some pertinent reading ahead of time on the effects of divorce on children. A number of articles have appeared on the subject in both Christian and secular publications.

Here are some sample questions for the panel:

1. *How did you find out about your parents' decision to divorce? Did the way in which you were told help or hinder your acceptance of the divorce?*
2. *What kinds of feelings did you (or do you) have about the divorce?*
3. *Did your role in the family change after the divorce? How?*
4. *What kinds of things did friends do or say in response to the divorce? What do you wish they had done or said?*

This can be a powerful and instructive program for both the audience and the panel. (Contributed by David Wright and Al Arcuni, Vienna, VA)

Egg In A Bottle

Here's an object lesson that would be good around Easter, or as a good way to wrap up an "Egg Night."

Start with several games using eggs. Use your creativity or consult the **Ideas** library for a variety of egg games (egg toss, egg roll relay, and so on). After the games, describe how an egg is a lot like God. An egg can be compared to the Holy Trinity in that each has three parts. The shell is the part we see or Christ. The Holy Spirit is the white and God the father is the center or the yolk.

Hard-boil an egg and cut it to show the kids the three distinct parts. Describe how when you take any one of the three parts away, you don't have a complete egg.

In order for a hard-boiled egg to enter a milk bottle (the milk bottle is a person), the shell or the part we see must be broken. This symbolizes the breaking of Christ's body. Take a match or two. Light them and throw them in the bottle and immediately put the shelled egg on top of the bottle. The matches will burn up the oxygen in the bottle and the egg will be sucked into the bottle intact. Draw the analogy that in order for God to come into our lives, the shell must be sacrificed and there must be a tiny spark or opening of our will to allow him to come in.

Discussion questions:
1. How is the bottle like people who need to let God in?
2. What did it take for the egg to be drawn in?
3. Can the egg come back out?
4. What kind of fire within a person does it take to let God in?

(Contributed by Matt Boyers, W. Lafayette, IN)

Elderly Interview

Here's an idea that will help your youth bridge the generation gap and learn more about your church at the same time. Find a group of senior citizens in the church who meet together regularly—a Sunday school class or fellowship group. Ask if your youth can come "interview" them about the history of the church. You will want to think up a few sample questions to give the older folks ahead of time so that they can be thinking about their answers. Then on the scheduled day, take the youth to the class or meeting and hold an interview. Be sure your youth have pencils and paper or a tape recorder to get all the important facts about the church's past. Some of the questions you may want to raise are:

1. When did you join (_____)?
   <small>your church</small>
2. What was your most moving experience at (_____)?
   <small>your church</small>
3. Who were the church's great leaders during times of change?
4. What do you think have been the three greatest events in the history of this church?
5. What is the funniest thing that ever happened at (_____)?
   <small>your church</small>
6. When you were our age (youth), what was your Sunday school or fellowship group like?

At the end of the interview you may ask that the older folks exchange names with the youth so that they can keep in touch through the year. Then in about a month, encourage your youth to write a note or card to the person whose name they received. Both the interview and the correspondence will brighten the lives of the older people. (Contributed by Cheryl Smith, Nashville, TN)

Facts About Suicide

To introduce a discussion about teenage suicide, give a true/false quiz similar to the one that follows to your group. Have each person write "T" or "F" on a numbered sheet of paper (1–7) after you read each statement aloud. When you read aloud the right answers afterward, ask for a show of hands of those who responded correctly. (Note: Statistics change with the passing of time, so you might want to check the accuracy of those given here, or add other true-false statements as you have information.)

1. **People who repeatedly talk about killing themselves probably will never actually do it.**
   FALSE—Most people who commit suicide give clear warnings through their words or actions.
2. **Anyone who tries to kill him or herself is basically crazy.**
   FALSE—Most teens who try to kill themselves are very unhappy or depressed, but only 15 to 30 percent are mentally ill.
3. **If a person is suicidal, he or she will always be suicidal**

throughout life.
FALSE—If the causes of the person's unhappiness can be dealt with, he or she can probably lead a normal and full life.

4. **It is best to talk openly with someone who is suicidal about suicide rather than avoiding the subject.**
TRUE—This lets the person know you really care about him or her. Talking with people about suicide doesn't "give them ideas."

5. **More American teens commit suicide today than they did 20 years ago.**
TRUE—In the last two decades, the suicide rate among American adolescents has skyrocketed to a 300 percent increase.

6. **Most teenage suicides occur away from home.**
FALSE—An average of 70 percent of adolescent suicides take place at home, between the hours of 3:00 p.m. and midnight.

7. **Nothing can stop a suicidal person once the decision has been made.**
FALSE—Most people contemplating suicide feel a deep conflict between their desire to die and a desire to live. Intervention **can** change their minds.

Follow up the quiz by exploring these aspects of the subject:

1. Ask if anyone in the group has ever known anyone who was thinking about suicide. (They don't have to mention names.) What did they say or do to help the person? What was the person feeling? What were they themselves feeling?

2. Ask for suggestions about why someone would consider killing him or herself. Is the cause more likely to be external circumstances or an internal problem?

3. If a friend talks about suicide, what do your youth think they should do? Find an adult to talk to about it?

With the current rate of adolescent suicide attempts so high, this is a critical topic for your kids to consider. You may even discover later that young people who have themselves thought about taking their own lives will come to talk about it with you once you've brought up the subject.

Before you conduct a program such as this, be sure to acquaint yourself with the topic by reading available resources or discussing the subject with knowledgeable counselors. If you yourself are not experienced in the area of adolescent counseling, be sure you know of someone to whom you could refer young people who may be contemplating suicide. (Contributed by David Wright, Vienna, VA)

Family Matters

Here is a Bible study that can help you build personal relationships within your youth group by focusing upon the "family" responsibilities that are called for in the church. Begin by brainstorming this question: What are some ways a church is like a family?

Allow several responses. Affirm each. Then announce that you're going to examine the concept that a church should have intimacy like a family, and this intimacy should carry over into your youth group. Have them turn to Matthew 18.

Divide students into groups. Assign each group one of the following passages and topics:

Matthew 18:1–4
               "Family Attitudes"
Matthew 18:5–14
               "Family Concern"
Matthew 18:15–20
               "Family Discipline"
Matthew 18:21–35
               "Family Forgiveness"

Instruct the groups to read the passage assigned to them and write down how the church, and specifically their youth group, is to fulfill these responsibilities. They should also make note of how this illustrates the intimacy of a family. Encourage them to pay special attention to key words, concepts or statements.

After several minutes of study, allow each group to share their findings. These questions may be used to stimulate further discussion.

Family Attitudes
1. What is the key attitude described here? Why is it so essential? If it is present, what will it do?
2. Define the "children" in the kingdom.

Family Concern
1. According to verse five, what is the first concern?
2. Who are the "little ones" in the kingdom?
3. Why is leading others to sin such a serious thing? Do you think most Christians today recognize this? Why or why not?
4. What does verse 10 tell you about angels?
5. How faithfully should a church pursue "lost ones?" Do we do this? Why or why not?

Family Discipline
1. What is the purpose of this passage?
2. What is the role of the witnesses?
3. How would you explain verses 18–20?
4. Do you think this should be practiced today? Why or why not?
5. If this were practiced regularly, what do you think would happen?

Family Forgiveness
1. How does Peter's question in verse 21 relate to Jesus' teaching about discipline?
2. What prevented one servant from giving forgiveness? Does this happen today in the church? Why?
3. How easily do Christians forgive each other? What hinders forgiveness in the church?

Close your study by suggesting that all these responsibilities are given to individual Christians. If you must fulfill them, an intimacy will be created and developed within your youth group that will be like the intimacy of a family. Then ask, "What are some ways we can begin to do these things?" Allow the kids to brainstorm some answers, and

close the meeting with prayer. (Contributed by Doug Newhouse, Florence, KY)

Feeding at the Master's Table

Here is a Bible study you can use to celebrate communion. Have the group sit in a circle in preparation for the meal. Before taking part in it together, share the following insights from John 6.

1. **Who Prepared the Meal?** (6:32–35, 50–51)
   - Every meal has to be prepared by someone. Jesus said that God had prepared a kind of bread even better than the manna He gave the Israelites in the desert.
   - If God prepares a feast, you know that He'll serve the very best.
   - God Himself has made the preparations and provisions for the Lord's Supper.

2. **What is the Food Being Served?** (6:48,51,55)
   - Jesus said that the food found at the Master's table is his own flesh and blood (the sacrifice of these on the cross).
   - Jesus Himself is the bread God sent down from heaven.
   - Jesus described His sacrifice as true food and drink (v.55). This means that it was food and drink in the highest sense—an eternal food and drink that would satisfy the soul forever.
   - God offers us an opportunity to "eat" this food at the Master's

table—the Lord's Supper.

3. **How Do We "Eat" the Food?** (6:53,54–56)
   - The best way to understand what Jesus meant by eating the food is to remember what the food is: Christ's work of salvation on the cross. To "eat" His sacrifice is to receive it through **faith**, by trusting that what He did on the cross He did for you.
   - The utensils we eat with are our hearts and minds.

4. **What is the Nutritional Value of the Food?** (6:53–58)
   - Jesus explained these benefits of eating His meal:
     1. Eternal life.
     2. Hope of the resurrection in the last day.
     3. Unity with Christ—you are what you eat!
     4. His help to live every day.
   - The spiritual "nutrients" found in this meal can't be found in any other food.

5. **Who Can Take Part in This Meal?** (6:51,54,56)
   - Jesus said that this bread was given to the whole world.
   - The table is open to anyone who willingly comes to feed by faith at the Master's table.
   - We should confess our sins and cleanse our hearts as we

approach the meal (I Cor. 11:28).

6. **Three Things to Remember About This Meal:**
   1. We cannot have eternal life without eating and drinking this meal.
   2. Feeding by faith on this meal unites us with Christ and provides us with its benefits.
   3. Feeding is a personal act. No one can make you eat, or eat in your place. Only you can eat for yourself.

(Contributed by Brian Fullerton, Wenatchee, WA)

Four Pictures of Unity

Every youth group struggles to maintain relationships characterized by harmony and mutual concern. It's all too easy for young people to pick at petty differences, and without warning those small problems can become devastating schisms within the group.

This Bible Study is intended to help young people identify the aspects of living in God's family that are shared by all. By recognizing the kind of unity God desires for His people, they can take steps to restore that harmony and heal any breaks that may have occurred.

These four pictures identified by the Apostle Peter in I Peter 1:22–2:10 are outlined by Warren W. Wiersbe in his book **Be Hopeful** (Victor, 1982). Use the following questions to talk with your group about the need for unity:

I. **Children of the Same Family** (1:22–2:3)
   1. How did we become children in the same family?
   2. What brought about our new birth?
   3. How is the Word described? What do you think this means? How important is the Word to God's family?
   4. According to Peter, how should "brothers" treat each other?
   5. Can we disagree with each other and still have "sincere love" for each other?
   6. How was the Word "preached" to you?
   7. Describe how children in God's family are like "newborn babies." Do we ever leave this stage? How? Do some remain spiritual "babies?" Why? What's the result when babies won't grow up?

II. **Stone in the Same Building** (2:4–8)
   1. What is Jesus called in this passage?
   2. What are we called? What's the difference between Jesus and us in this building?
   3. How was Jesus treated? What's the result? What does that say to us, who are part of the same building?
   4. What are some characteristics of a stone? How do these apply to the Christian?
   5. Why is it valuable to have different kinds of stone when you're building? How does this principle apply to our group?

III. **Priests in the Same Temple** (2:9)
   1. What are the privileges of priests?
   2. What are the responsibilities of priests?
   3. How do other people view priests? Is this good or bad?
   4. How should priests live in relation to other priests?
   5. How should priests live in relation to other people?

IV. **Citizens of the Same Nation** (2:9–10)
   1. How are these citizens described?

2. What does "a people belonging to God" mean?

3. How does the ownership of something increase its value? Give some examples. Now apply that truth to the Christian who is "owned" by God.

4. Where should Christians find their source of self-worth? Where do we usually try to find it?

5. What "nation" are we a part of? Where is this nation located?

6. Read Philippians 3:20. What insight does this verse add to the words of Peter?

7. What is our responsibility to each other as citizens of God's nation? What happens when citizens fight each other?

8. What is our responsibility to other people?

Conclude your Bible study by reviewing the reasons Peter outlines for maintaining harmony and unity in your group. If time permits or need demands, briefly discuss any problems that have been dividing the group. Ask group members to resolve that they will make an effort to heal wounds and promote harmony. Ask for specific ways they can accomplish these goals. If group members can verbalize their decisions, encourage them to do so. Close your study with prayer. (Contributed by Doug Newhouse, Florence, KY)

Friendship Discussion

Friendships are of primary importance to most young people. Here are some good questions for an effective discussion of friendship. For best results, print them up for distribution and have the kids answer each question on their own before discussing them with the entire group.

1. **What is friendship? How do you define it?**
2. **Why do we need friends?**
3. **Describe a perfect friendship.**
4. **Describe a lousy friendship.**
5. **Name some of the qualities of a successful friendship you can learn from the following verses:**

1 Sam. 18:1;   Prov. 27:5–6
   19:1–7; 23:16–18   Jn. 11:33–36
Mk. 2:1–4   Job 2:11–13
Prov. 17:17   Ecc. 4:9–11

6. **In what ways is God a very special friend? (See the following verses for ideas:)**

Heb. 13:5–8   Rom. 8:38–39
I Pet. 5:7   Jn. 15:13

7. Fill out this card for your three closest friends:

Friend's name	Why he or she is my friend	What my friend contributes	What I contribute	How our friendship could improve
1.				
2.				
3.				

(Contributed by Bill Curry, Telford, PA)

Future World

The purpose of this exercise is to help youth see how their future is related to the preparation they make now, and how the church can help them prepare for the future. It will also encourage them to evaluate their preparation for the future.

First, divide the youth into small groups of three to four. Give each group three large sheets of paper and some markers. Then read the questions below one at a time, and let them brainstorm about answers. Each group should record its ideas on large sheets of paper, then report back to the large group. Have a

separate reporting time for each question.

Questions:
1. List some characteristics of the world as you think it will be in ten years.
2. List some characteristics of a person who will best be able to deal with the world as it will exist ten years from now.
3. List five goals the church should adopt in order to prepare youth for handling the world of the future.

After all the answers have been presented and discussed, ask the youth what they are doing now to prepare themselves spiritually for the future. In responding to this last question, many youth will realize that the church is already attempting to prepare young people for the future, but they aren't taking advantage of all the opportunities offered. Youth workers may also discover some needs of their youth presently being overlooked. (Contributed by Del McKinney, Cape Girardeau, MO)

The Game of Life

To stimulate some thinking about priorities and values, have your kids play Milton-Bradley's "Game of Life." You'll have about ten players and one banker (an advisor) for every board, so figure the number of games you need according to the size of your group. Have the kids choose partners—preferably someone they don't know well.

Before the game, display the prizes to go to the winning team. These will appear to be top record albums, but will actually be only empty album jackets. Then explain the game, noting that it claims to be "true to life." Point out that to win you must end up either as a millionaire tycoon or else as a resident of Millionaire Acres. Each team should start out with only one person in their little car, because in "The Game of Life," everyone has to get married.

If they move quickly, they should be able to play the game in just over half an hour. If you must, stop play after a certain time limit, and call everyone together to award the prizes.

Make a big deal over who won and who had the most money in each group. Then hand out the prizes in front of everyone. Most of the winners will protest immediately that the prizes weren't what they appeared to be. So make pious declarations about how you never promised that they would get albums; they got exactly what you showed them, and if they assumed that the jackets had albums inside, that's their problem.

Before they have much time to fume, discuss these questions:

1. What did you think of the prizes? Were they what you expected them to be?
2. What was the object of the game? Does having the most money make you a winner in real life?

36

3. Was this game "true to life" as it claims to be?
4. The prizes were hollow. Do you think that at the end of life, people who have gone after money will feel that their "prize" is hollow?

Finally, discuss briefly any one of the following passages in which Jesus talks about money and priorities:

1. Mark 1:16-20
2. Matthew 6:19-20; 7:24-29
3. Luke 18:18-30

Ask if they think anyone lives according to Christ's words today. Does His view of success agree with our society's view of success? (Contributed by Dave Carver and Carrie Wolukis, Pittsburgh, PA)

Graven Images

The second commandment, forbidding worship of "graven images" (Ex. 20:4), can apply to any false concept of God that takes the place of our true Creator. To help your kids identify some of the "idols" common today which are distortions of God's real character, have them write down one thing they would change about God if they could. Then give them the following list of "gods," and ask them to identify the ones they struggle with.

1. **Heirloom God**
   This is a secondhand god, one you inherited from your parents. You never really discovered this god for yourself; you just believed in him because of what others told you.

2. **Cultural God**
   This god represents the dominant values of the society. He wants us to be beautiful, rich, and successful.

3. **Killjoy God**
   This god is in your conscience, always reminding you not to have too much fun. He has no sense of humor and is always saying "no."

4. **Enforcer God**
   This god is always punishing you for your sins even though they're forgiven. You can never relax because you know he's looking over your shoulder, waiting to nail you.

5. **Jellyfish God**
   This god is helpless in the face of injustice. He allows sin in the world because he's not strong enough to do anything about it. This god promises to answer your prayers, but never comes through.

6. **Traditional God**
   This god is carefully defined by your particular church or denomination, who have him all figured out. You can never challenge their view from Scripture, because there's nothing new to learn about him—he's utterly comfortable and predictable.

7. **Absentee God**
   This god may have created the world and might be returning some day, but nobody can really know him today.

8. **Cosmic Bellhop God**
   This one is also called the Santa Claus god. You call him up on the hot line and give him your list of requests. He exists just to serve you, and can be ignored whenever you don't need anything.

Now that you've considered these "graven images," take a look at how the Bible describes the **true** nature of God:

1. **Unchanging**—Ps. 93:2; Ex. 3:14.
2. **Majestic**—Ps. 145:5; 2 Pet. 1:16.
3. **Wise**—Ps. 119:99–100; Job 12:13.

4. **Loving**—Tit. 3:6.
5. **Gracious**—Rom. 9:16; 2 Thes. 2:12–14.
6. **Just**—Heb. 12:23; Ps. 75:7.
7. **Wrathful**—Nahum 1:2–8;

Lk. 21:22–24; Rom. 11:22.
8. **Jealous**—James 4:5; Ex. 20.5

(Contributed by Tom Westing, Albuquerque, NM)

Group Story

This idea can help kids appreciate the fact that although the Bible took 40 authors and over 1,500 years to write, it has an amazing unity. This in itself is one evidence of God's hand in the work.

Prepare some index cards, as many as there are people in the group.

Number them consecutively, and on card number one, write "Once upon a time …" On the last card, write "And then …" at the top, and "The End" at the bottom. On all the other cards, write "And then…" on the top. Then distribute the cards randomly, so that each person has one.

Next tell the kids to write a portion of a story on their card. They should use their imagination and write anything they want that would make up part of a good story. When they are finished, the cards are collected, and put in order, and the story is read. The result will be a very funny but very disjointed story. Talk about how the Bible had many authors, yet it tells a single story of salvation. (Contributed by David Farnum, Coudersport, PA)

Handicapped All-Nighter

To help your group gain a better understanding of the challenges faced by people who are physically handicapped, try an all-nighter like this. First, have a discussion about handicapped persons and their problems. Then give each youth a disability for the rest of the evening. Design the handicaps so that they are of maximum significance to each person: Star athletes, for example, can be confined to wheelchairs, given walkers, or restricted to crutches. This should include splinting legs or taping them together. Anyone in a wheelchair is not allowed to use the bathroom without two others to help him or her. Your "motor mouth" can be given a stroke, simulated by a right leg splint, the right arm taped to the side, and mouth taped shut. Other active youth can be blindfolded, or fitted with cardboard glasses that have off-center holes so only side vision is possible. Some can be made to see through several layers of sandwich wrap to give clouded vision. Use your imagination.

Once everyone has a handicap, the evening proceeds like any other all-nighter, with dumb games, relays, skill activities, and mixers. Try making and eating pizza, with the youth doing all the work so that they must help one another to succeed.

Finally, have a Bible study focusing on several stories about Jesus healing. At midnight, hold a communion service. As each youth is given the bread and wine, each person can be "healed" of his or her handicap.

Follow with a discussion of what happened, what was easiest and most difficult about the experience, and what they learned. The rest of the night can be spent in the usual youth night activities. (Contributed by Jon Erickson, Lake Lillian, MN)

Hidden Treasures

Here's a creative way to allow your group to understand the value of God's wisdom. Before they arrive for Bible study, hide money somewhere in the room. Open the Bible study with prayer. Then tell them that there is money hidden in the room and whoever finds it can keep it. Of course, the higher the denomination, the harder the teens will look. When the money is found, take your Bibles and turn to Proverbs 2. It will cause you all to think about how diligently we search the Scriptures as compared to how diligently we're willing to look for "hidden treasures." (Contributed by Dave Stevens, Cherry Hill, NJ)

Homemade Communion

Here's a meaningful way to involve your young people in communion. It's especially effective with junior highers. After a time of prayer and a few songs, move the group into the kitchen and allow them to make their own unleavened bread. Give each person a job to do, from cracking the eggs to taking turns rolling the dough out paper-thin. Here's the recipe:

Cream together:
  ¼ c. sugar
  ¾ c. shortening
Mix in:
  1 t. salt
  1½ c. buttermilk (milk soured
       with 1 T. vinegar may
       be substituted)
  ½ t. soda
Add:
  4–5 c. flour
Divide the dough into four balls.
Roll out on floured surface until wafer-thin. Place on greased cookie sheet.

Fork the dough to prevent shrinkage.

Bake at 450 degrees until light brown, approximately 15–20 minutes.

While the bread is baking, have the kids make the "wine" (grape juice). Provide a large quantity of whole, seedless grapes and let the kids crush them in a bowl using a crushing stick. This last act can symbolize the fact that because we've sinned, we all had a part in the crucifixion of Christ. When the grapes are all crushed, pour the juice into glasses.

Now, serve communion as you normally would, using these homemade elements. It will add a great deal to this important sacrament of the church. (Contributed by Jon Adams, Crosby, MN)

How To Raise Your Parents

Here are some good questions for a discussion about parents. For best results, print them up and pass them out to each person. Give the kids time to answer all the questions individually, then discuss them one at a time with the entire group.

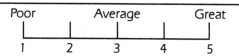

1. How would your rate your relationship with your parent(s)?

2. What are some of the problems in your relationship with your parent(s)?

3. What are some of the good points of your relationship with your parent(s)?

4. What would help improve the relationship?

5. What do the following verses teach about relationships with parents?
   Col. 3:20
   Prov. 3:1–4
   Ex. 20:3

6. Rate yourself in the following areas:

	Almost Never				Almost Always
a. I obey my parents in all things.	1	2	3	4	5
b. I am patient with my parent's weaknesses.	1	2	3	4	5
c. I apologize to my parents when I hurt them.	1	2	3	4	5
d. I trust God to change my parents if they are wrong.	1	2	3	4	5
e. I do more than my parents ask of me.	1	2	3	4	5
f. I try to see life from my parent's point of view.	1	2	3	4	5
g. I ask my parents for their advice.	1	2	3	4	5
h. I thank my parents for all they do for me.	1	2	3	4	5
i. I pray for my parents.	1	2	3	4	5
j. I show my parents I love them.	1	2	3	4	5
k. I tell my parents I love them.	1	2	3	4	5
l. I live the kind of life my parents can be proud of.	1	2	3	4	5

7. The area which I most need to improve is _____
   _____

– –

8. Check any of the following ideas you'd like to commit yourself to do in the next 48 hours:

_____ Buy my mother flowers	_____ Take my parents out to eat
_____ Tell my parents I love them	_____ Do some chores without being told
_____ Ask my parents to pray with me	_____ Ask my parents for some advice
_____ Write a note of appreciation to my parents	_____ Wash the car
	_____ Give my parents a hug or kiss

(Contributed by Bill Curry, Telford, PA)

Influence Survey

Make photocopies of the survey on the next page to get kids thinking about influences on their lives. It serves as a great discussion starter for a talk about peer pressure. (Contributed by Joe Harvey, Ft. Myers, FL)

INFLUENCE SURVEY

Rate each of the following according to the degree of influence they have on your thinking and behavior. Place an "X" in the category that applies.

+ , −, or 0	INFLUENCE	NONE	A LITTLE	A LOT	AN AWFUL LOT
	MOM				
	DAD				
	FRIENDS AT SCHOOL				
	FRIENDS AT CHURCH				
	TELEVISION SHOWS				
	COMMERCIALS				
	MOVIES				
	RADIO				
	RELATIVES				
	BOOKS				
	MAGAZINES				
	TEACHERS				
	NEIGHBORS				
	BILLBOARDS				
	WEATHER				
	BROTHER(S)				
	SISTER(S)				
	MINISTER				

Now go back and put a " + " or "−" to the left of each influence listed to indicate whether the influence is mostly positive (+) or negative (−). If you think the influence is neither positive or negative, put a "0" by the word.

Interview Teams

Here's a good way to encourage interaction between the youth of your church and the adults. Ask adult members of your church to allow a team of interviewers from the youth group to interview them on a variety of subjects. Supply the interview teams with some sample questions, both non-threatening questions and a few that are more personal. Subjects can include the church, the family, American culture, values, faith, goals, life-style choices, the future, and anything else the kids might find interesting.

You will discover that this activity produces overwhelmingly positive results. If the interviews take place in interviewees' homes, the young people enjoy the hospitality as well as the opportunity to engage in some serious conversation with adults.

After each team has completed its interviews, have a meeting (or meetings) to present their findings. (Contributed by David Johnson, Ottawa, Ontario, Canada)

Jesus Had Feelings, Too

The purpose of this activity is to help kids realize the humanness of Jesus Christ. The focus of the program is on emotions.

For this activity you need pencils, paper, felt tip markers, one large sheet of poster board, one die or coin, and a table against a wall. During the activity a game board is constructed and used. If time does not permit, the game board can be created in advance by one of the group leaders.

First, introduce the subject of emotions, noting that we all have them, and that they are normal and part of being human. Emphasize that it's how we respond to and express our emotions that determines whether they lead to growth or problems. Next, ask the youth to think of their family, school, and friends. As they remember different emotions they've experienced because of these people, they should write the emotions down.

Now ask them to think of Jesus Christ and His life as we know it through the Bible, writing down a separate list of emotions they believe He experienced.

Once the lists are complete, have the youth read their two lists aloud to the other members of the group while someone compiles two lists from their suggestions. (Each emotion should appear only once in each list.) If the list of feelings or emotions is shorter for Jesus than for the rest of the group, use the opportunity to talk more about Christ's humanness.

Now transfer the complete list of emotions to the poster board as in the diagram.

Forgiveness		
Love		Fear
Compassion		
Anger		Sadness
Joy		
Amusement		Grief
Loneliness		

To use the board, place it on a table against a wall. Each person takes a turn throwing the die/coin at the board from a reasonable distance. Whatever emotion the die/coin lands on, the player must think of one situation from the Bible where Jesus could conceivably have felt that emotion. He or she must also describe how Jesus expressed it.

To personalize this game even more, you can ask players to describe an occasion when they themselves experienced that particular emotion, and how they expressed it. They should also say how they think it **should** have been expressed.

After everyone has had a turn, conclude the activity with a prayer asking Christ's help in expressing emotions in ways that help rather than hurt. (Contributed by Sean Mahar, Hampden, ME)

Letter Of Resignation

The following "letter of resignation" from a pastor of a church can be used effectively to open up discussion on a variety of topics, such as faith, God, doubt, and suffering. Simply read it to the group and ask the kids to share their reactions. What would they say to this pastor who seems to have lost his faith? How would you respond to his questions about God and faith? Have you ever felt like that? How is it possible for people who are in the ministry to lose their faith?

For the sake of a good discussion, try to imply to the group that the letter is real. Afterwards, you can inform them that you really don't

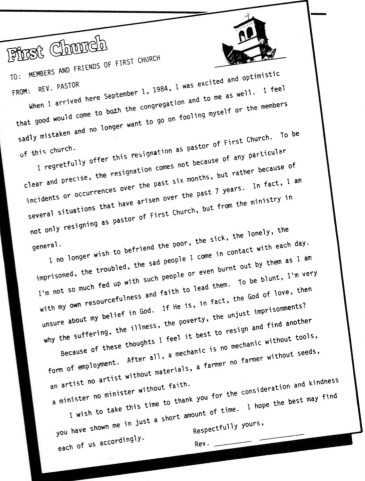

First Church

TO: MEMBERS AND FRIENDS OF FIRST CHURCH

FROM: REV. PASTOR

When I arrived here September 1, 1984, I was excited and optimistic that good would come to both the congregation and to me as well. I feel sadly mistaken and no longer want to go on fooling myself or the members of this church.

I regretfully offer this resignation as pastor of First Church. To be clear and precise, the resignation comes not because of any particular incidents or occurrences over the past six months, but rather because of several situations that have arisen over the past 7 years. In fact, I am not only resigning as pastor of First Church, but from the ministry in general.

I no longer wish to befriend the poor, the sick, the lonely, the imprisoned, the troubled, the sad people I come in contact with each day. I'm not so much fed up with such people or even burnt out by them as I am with my own resourcefulness and faith to lead them. To be blunt, I'm very unsure about my belief in God. If He is, in fact, the God of love, then why the suffering, the illness, the poverty, the unjust imprisonments?

Because of these thoughts I feel it best to resign and find another form of employment. After all, a mechanic is no mechanic without tools, an artist no artist without materials, a farmer no farmer without seeds, a minister no minister without faith.

I wish to take this time to thank you for the consideration and kindness you have shown me in just a short amount of time. I hope the best may find each of us accordingly.

Respectfully yours,

Rev. _____

44

know for sure if it's real or not (you don't). If you have an extra dose of courage, you might want to make it a letter from yourself to your own church. But if you do, you need to be prepared for the emotions and questions that will inevitably come up. (Contributed by Chuck Behrens, Washington, PA)

Levels of Communication

The following four skits can be used to demonstrate four levels of communication people commonly use to relate to one another: 1. superficial; 2. gossip; 3. opinion; 4. feeling; to introduce a discussion about the "games" people play in their communication with others.

1. SUPERFICIAL LEVEL

(characters a and b)

a: Hi.
b: Hi.
a: How's it going?
b: Okay; how are you?
a: Fine ... ah ... nice day, huh?
b: Yeah ... real nice.
a: Seems like a great day for the beach.
b: Really—I was just about to say the same thing.
a: Say, did the Cubs **(add your own team)** win yesterday?
b: Yeah ... 5 to 3 in the ninth inning. Didn't you see the game?
a: No—my T.V.'s broken.
a: Well ... I guess I'll see ya' later.
b: Okay. See ya. **(Walk away.)**

2. GOSSIP LEVEL

(characters c, d, and e)

c: Hi, D.
d: Hi, C. How's it going?
c: Oh, okay. How are you?
d: Fine ... Say, did you hear about George?
c: George ... you mean George E.?
d: Yeah, **that** George.
c: No ... what happened?
d: Well ... I don't know ... and I wouldn't repeat this, because I promised not to say anything to anyone but ...
c: **But what?**
d: Well, you gotta promise you won't tell anyone first.
c: Okay. I promise and I cross my heart **(crosses heart)**.

d: Okay. Well, Barb ... you know Barb ... she told me that George is not going back to school this fall.
c: How come?
d: Well, I heard he flunked out last semester.
c: Well, that's not so bad; I can think of worse things that can happen.
d: No, wait—there's more. He dropped out because he got a girl pregnant.
c: Oh, I see.
d: And the reason he got her pregnant was that they were out partying and he drank too much, I mean he really got blitzed and he couldn't control himself, and one thing led to another and **bang** ... she's expecting.
c: You're kidding!
d: No! And I guess the girl is a real **dog**! She's so ugly they call her E.T.
c: Gee ... what a bummer!
d: Well, hey, I gotta go ... but now, remember, don't tell anybody else about this, okay?
d: Oh, no, I won't ... I promise.
c: Okay. See ya later. **(Exits.)**
(Enter e.)
c: Hi E. How's it going?
e: Okay, Hey, what's up?
c: Not much ... Hey, did you hear about George?
e: No ... what happened?
c: Well, you're not gonna believe this ... but you gotta promise you won't tell anybody ... **(Both exit.)**

3. OPINION LEVEL

(characters 1, 2, and 3)

1: I know I'm a little overweight; I should go on a diet.
2: Well ... I know how you feel; I put on ten pounds after my sister's wedding and I feel lousy.
3: Well ... I know all about fitness. I run every day, and I know it's the best thing for me. I know I'm really healthy.
1: I wish there were some way I could get into better shape. Maybe I do need some exercise.
3: Hey, try jogging—it's excellent aerobic exercise. I run every day and I feel terrific. In fact I've read

both of Jim Fixx's books on running and he's an authority, you know.

2: Well maybe what "1" needs right now is just a little self-confidence to boost her ego.

3: **Confidence**— well I know **all** about that. Yes sir. Why I've run two marathons and about 25 road races over the past two years. It takes a lot of confidence to complete a 26.2-mile marathon, you know. And I even did it under four hours. It was a **terrific** feeling.

1: Gee. I could never run 26 miles. I probably couldn't even finish one lap around the track. I'm really out of shape.

3: Hey. I know about being in shape! I went to a week-long running camp once. It was great. I got up at 6:30 every morning for our morning workout. Then we had talks on running, nutrition, physiology, injuries, stretching, and workouts. It was fantastic.

2: Well, "1," maybe you should start out small—like an aerobics class at the YMCA. They offer all kinds of fitness programs for beginners. They even have a swimming pool.

3: Swimming? Great sport! I remember last year when I was in the triathlon. We had to swim a quarter mile for the first part. Then we had a ten-mile bike ride and a four-mile run. What a challenge! But I finished in an hour and six minutes.

1: Gee, I can't swim, either. I just guess I can't do anything. Now I'm depressed—what a bummer. This is the pits—let's go get a pizza.

2: I'll go with you. You seem like you need a little company, and some cheering up. Are you coming, "3?"

3: Oh no. I'm on a special training diet, getting in shape for a 10-K run next week, and I want to set a new record. I'm staying away from junk food. You are what you eat, ya know.

1 & 2: Okay. See ya.

3: Bye. Hey, don't forget to pray for me next week during my race ... **(as he exits)**.

4. FEELING LEVEL
(characters 1, 2, and 3)

1: Well we've been on retreat quite a while already. How do you think it's going?

2: Well ... to be honest, I was really scared at first.

3: Why's that?

2: Well ... I thought everyone else would know all the others, and I felt like I was the only one who came by myself.

1: Oh really?

2: Yeah. I was almost ready to turn around and go home last night—I just felt so out of it.

3: Hmmmm ... I think I understand how you feel. I know my first retreat was the same way. I was a sophomore in high school. I didn't know how I got there, and I didn't know anybody. It took me a while to warm up to people.

1: Yeah. Give yourself some more time. I think talking about how you feel helps, too. I know if I don't let people know how I'm feeling at times, they never know. I think I expect them to know—but they can't read my mind.

3: That's right—me, too. I think I'm a lot more honest with myself if I can let people know how I'm feeling. Lots of times it's hard because I never know how the other person is going to react—whether he's going to be open and really listen to me.

2: You mean you're afraid they might reject you and think you're weird or something?

3: That's it.

1: I know what you mean. Why do we do that to one another? I'm sure I've turned people off before, when I should have taken time to listen to them. **(Pause.)**

(To the audience)

2: Do you feel like we're really listening to **you**? And trying to be understanding? How do you really feel about the retreat so far?

If you're really on a retreat when you do these skits, have #2 tell his or her real feelings about the weekend; then let #1 and #3 respond in kind. Otherwise, change #2's words to ask how the audience feels about the group, the church, or whatever. Follow up with a discussion stressing the importance of honesty and openness in communication in order to grow healthy friendships. (Contributed by Frank Zolvinski, La Porte, IN)

Life Goals

Here's a good discussion starter about setting goals in life. Pass out the following list of "goals" (add any others that you want) and have the kids rate them as "Got to have it," "Would be nice," or "Not necessarily for me."

When they've finished, have the kids look up the following scripture passages and determine what they have to say about setting goals:

Ps. 27:4   Ex. 33:18–23
1 Ki. 3:5–13   Phil. 3:7–10

Next, have the kids list their top three goals, along with a few good ways to achieve them. (Contributed by Steve Fortosis, La Mirada, CA)

	Got to have it.	Would be nice.	Not necessarily for me.
1. A great family life without any hassles.			
2. All the money I want.			
3. Never to be sick or seriously injured.			
4. To find a good-looking and fulfilling mate.			
5. To do what I want when I want.			
6. All the power the President has.			
7. To be the best-looking person.			
8. A great hunger for the Bible and prayer.			
9. To be able to understand all things.			
10. To eliminate all hunger and disease in the world.			
11. To be always super-close to God.			
12. Never to feel lonely or put-down.			
13. To know the future.			
14. To be able to learn quickly and excel in all things.			
15. To be filled with God's presence in the most dynamic way.			
16. To know always that I'm in God's will.			
17. To be the greatest athlete in the world.			
18. To become a famous movie star.			
19. To have always a lot of close friends who never let me down.			

Make a Melody

Make photocopies of the musical note pattern on page 49 and distribute them to your group (one per person) with crayons or colored felt tip markers. Have them personalize the notes with their names and any other writing or drawn design they like. The final product should reflect their own uniqueness in some way.

Now collect the notes, and have the group choose together a hymn or other song which would serve as a good theme song for them. Later, find a simple arrangement of the theme they've chosen. Draw a large musical staff on a long sheet of butcher paper, hang it in a prominent place, and arrange the notes so that they form the melody of the group theme song. At your next get-together, talk about how just as every note is important to the song, every person is important to the group. (Contributed by Brad Hirsch, Seattle, WA)

Make Way For The Queen

Here's a role-playing simulation that helps open up meaningful discussions about relationships, cooperation, and community. It's also a lot of fun.

Divide into teams of five to six kids each. Each team consists of a Queen, a Grand Duke, a Priest, a Cripple, a Rebel, and a Slave. If there are only five on the team, there is no slave.

Each person on the team should receive a card, like those pictured below, which identifies his or her role and gives instructions on how to carry it out. The rules are:

1. You can't change roles.
2. You must do what your role requires, carefully obeying what is written on your instruction card.
3. You can only hold one leg of the chair.

Each Queen is seated in a chair along a starting line, with the Queens from the other teams. The subjects gather around their Queen and wait for the signal to start. The object is to lift the Queen by cooperatively lifting the legs of the chair, and then to carry her to a designated spot. For best results the distance should be far enough to make the task fairly difficult (perhaps a hundred yards). The first team to complete the task has their Queen crowned as the Ruling Monarch.

The roles of the Rebel and the

You are the **QUEEN.** (Congratulations!)
You must sit in the chair while your subjects carry you across the room. When you touch the wall, they are to bring you back and let you down.

You are the **SLAVE.**
DO *NOT* TELL ANYONE WHAT YOUR ROLE IS!
Your job is simply to do whatever the Queen or the Grand Duke or the Priest tells you to do.

MAKE A MELODY

Instructions: Color, design, or decorate
your note any way you want. Be creative!
You may want to use this note as a pattern
for a construction paper note; collage a
note; draw your face on it; etc. ... Make it
YOUR note, personal and unique, just as
your life is personal and unique.

Your life is a note and a song to Jesus:
Sing and make melody in your heart to
the Lord!

Cripple complicate the task and can cause some real trouble if the Duke and Priest don't do their jobs. But because of those roles, there is good potential for discussion after the game. Here are some questions:

1. What problems or obstacles did your team face?
2. How were they handled?
3. How did you feel about the others on your team?

You are the **REBEL**.

DO *NOT* TELL ANYONE WHAT YOUR ROLE IS!

You are to be as uncooperative as you can. Say things like, "This is stupid. She's not a queen. I'm not carrying her."

You can give in and carry her, but try to let someone else be Ruling Monarch by making your team lose.

The only thing you can *NOT* do is drop the Queen when you are carrying her.

You are the **PRIEST**.

You are to see that your Queen wins, and you are to make sure that your team plays by the rules.

If you have any uncooperative members or people aren't getting along, you are to act as a peacemaker and try to get everyone to cooperate so your Queen can be crowned.

You are the **GRAND DUKE**.

You function as the team captain, and your job is to get your queen to the finish line so she can be crowned.

You are a Duke for life, which means you are not allowed to give up. If you do, the rival Queen will make sure you're not Duke much longer. (Get the hint?)

You are the **CRIPPLE**.

DO *NOT* TELL ANYONE WHAT YOUR ROLE IS!

The only thing you can tell them is that you have a broken arm and you cannot carry the chair.

Your job is to walk in front of the chair and shout "Make way for the Queen!"

(Contributed by David Farnum, Coudersport, PA)

Mall Mania

This activity makes an excellent discussion about accepting other people as they are. Divide your group into small groups of four to five each. Write out instructions to be given them to help in observing people at a mall. For example, they could be instructed to count how many people they see who are fat, or how many are skinny, short, tall, ugly, beautiful, clean, dirty, well-dressed, or slobs. Also have them describe the two people they liked the most and the two they liked the least.

After a few hours of observation, meet in a central location at the mall or back at your church for a discussion of God's acceptance of all people. Have the kids share results from their views of the people at the mall. Tie it together by asking questions about God's acceptance. James 2:1–3 can be used as scripture for this discussion. (Contributed by Matt Boyers, W. Lafayette, IN)

Measuring Up

Here's an exciting way to get your group to think about the almost-taboo subject of obedience to God and His will for them individually. Have a "Measuring Up Party" to which they must bring a ruler, yardstick, tape measure, or some other measuring instrument as their admission. Meet at the local high school football stadium. Divide them into three groups, and have them mark off the measurements of the ark inside the stadium (450 feet long × 75 feet wide × 45 feet high). When they finish, have them meet in the bleachers and point out to the others the area they measured (for example, show how high up the side of the bleachers equals 45 feet). Next, lead them in a discussion of how difficult this task must have been for Noah to accomplish. Relate Noah's difficulty to their own responsibility for following God, but be sure to point out that Noah was chosen on the basis of his attitude (Genesis 6:9) rather than his ability to build big boats, of which there is no previous record. You may want to refer them as well to Noah's open sin in Genesis 9:20 to help them realize that he was not perfect, and that all of us can "measure up" to God's calling if we are only willing to be obedient. (You can also read the related passage of Heb. 11:7.)

Note: Measuring height is easier if they measure a single brick or block in the wall, divide 45 feet by that distance, and then count that many bricks or blocks up. For example, if the bricks are six inches (half a foot) high, divide 45 by .05, which equals 90. Count 90 bricks up for the correct height. (Contributed by William A. Gunter, Kingsport, TN)

Microcosm

The following skit is a good way to dramatize the need for world missions. The youth can present a program like this to the entire congregation with effective results.

The setting: At a small table on the platform, four speakers sit with microphones. They carry on a conversation similar to the one below. (You should adapt it to present an accurate picture of your own church's mission program.)

Script:

Person #1: You all have a copy of next year's budget and projections. What do you think?

Person #2: This is the same as last year's! All of our costs have gone up! And we need to send out more people! How can we keep the same figures as last year?

Person #3: He's right. Transportation, printing, equipment, are all way up from last year. And food costs have sky-rocketed in the Philippines and Irian Jaya because of the droughts. How can we expect our missionaries to get by on this? Let alone expand their ministries!

Person #1: You all know that we've had trouble making our budget these last few years. If the money doesn't come in, we can't spend it. It's been a step of faith even to come up with this budget, yet we're confident that God will supply. But it will mean sacrifice.

Person #4: The people in our churches give to missions and God has blessed our work so far. But some still don't see missions as being very important.

Person #2: Don't they see the need? Don't they understand the number of lost souls out there?

Person #4: Well, probably not. We try our best to educate the churches, but remember—most of them haven't had the kind of exposure to overseas missions we have. Most don't realize how many are lost.

Person #1: On top of that, some are hesitant to give to missions because they don't think they can afford it.

Person #4: Or else they feel that we have enough missionaries now.

Person #3: Enough missionaries! (Pause) Enough missionaries. Jesus said, "The harvest is plentiful but the workers are few." That's still true today.

Person #2: In Bogota we have eight missionary families in a city of almost three million! We have only two in Bombay, and 18 in the entire country of Upper Volta! Even with the national pastors and evangelists, it's a huge task. There are so many people...

Person #3: And so many forces are working against us. There are all the false religions. And the cults work overseas, too.

Person #1: God has called us to a difficult task; there's no doubt about that. But he's also promised to equip us for that task.

52

Nothing is impossible when we're in God's will.

Person #3: That's right.

Person #2: I wish people would stop seeing missions as an extra—or as something for somebody else to do. Jesus told us to go. If we can't go ourselves, we can at least support those who go.

Person #4: Well, Jesus also told us to pray that God would send laborers into his harvest. Let's pray that the Holy Spirit will work in the churches. He can convince people of the needs much better than we can. If he does, and people listen, we will be able to expand the work.

While this dialog is going on up front, other young people are circulating throughout the congregation trying to get "converts." These young people play the following roles:

1 Christian
2 Hindus
3 Moslems
1 Confucian
1 Buddhist
1 Communist (or atheist)
2 Worship the Spirit of the River
2 Worship the Sun
2 Worship the spirits of their ancestors

These young people can wear appropriate costumes, but that is not really necessary. They should move quietly throughout the congregation distributing "literature" for their religion, asking people if they would like to "follow Buddha" or "worship the spirit of the river," and so on.

When the speakers on the platform have finished, the "missionaries" who have been circulating in the congregation come to the front and introduce themselves:

Ancestor, Sun, and River Worshippers: "We are animists. We worship many different spirits in nature."

Communist: "I am a communist. I do not believe in any God."

Buddhist: "I follow the teachings of Confucius."

Moslems: "We are Moslems. Our god is Allah."

Hindus: "We are Hindus. We worship many gods."

Christian: "I am a Christian. I follow Jesus Christ. God does not want anyone to perish, but many in the world are lost because they do not know Jesus. Please, help me to tell them."

It can then be explained to the congregation that the people in the line are proportioned by religion in approximately the ratio as the world population. Christians are outnumbered 14 to one. (Contributed by David Farnum, Coudersport, PA)

Missions Impossible

If your church is in a large, ethnically-diverse metro area, you have a microcosm of the world's mission fields at your door. To focus on some of the challenges missionaries face in ministering to people of a different culture, send your kids out as teams to encounter people of other religious faiths.

Use a "spy motif," preparing a "Missions Impossible" packet for each team of six to eight young people. Packets should include instructions for the event on cassette tape (with a background of music from a James Bond or other spy movie); a written copy of the instructions; a blank tape; $2.00 in cash; a pen; a list of points to be earned; a map of the area with the route to their destination marked; a small paper bag; and some evangelistic tracts.

When the kids are assembled for their "spy" mission, give each group a packet, cassette player, and Polaroid camera. Make sure every group has a leader who is an adult or a mature young person.

The instructions should inform each group that they are being sent to a local temple of another faith to find out what the people who worship there believe. They will earn a designated number of points for accomplishing certain tasks which you have chosen as meaningful ways to become acquainted with peoples of other cultures. Suggestions:

- ☆ 100 points for finding someone on the street who will say, "Hi, how are you?" in a language other than English so that the group can record it.
- ☆ 100 points for a photo of a priest or other religious professional from the temple they visit.
- ☆ 500 points for a map of another country.
- ☆ 100 points for every item they can buy with the $2.00 which comes from another country and culture.
- ☆ 1000 points for a taped or written statement from someone in the temple they visit, describing that person's concept of God.
- ☆ 1000 points for their own taped or written statement telling how the person's concept of God differs from the biblical one, supported by specific scriptural texts.

Add as many other point-earning tasks as you like. The team earning the most points wins. Caution the teams to be respectful of the people they visit. They will be seen as representatives of Christianity. Make sure you have personally spoken with the person in charge of each temple you send a group to visit, asking for permission for the kids to find out more about their faith.

Tracts should only be given out on the street—not in a temple—and should not be forced on anyone.

Have a debriefing session when the teams return at the designated time. Talk about the team's strategies; how they felt as they approached people; how the people responded; what they thought of the temples; and any other significant aspects of the experience. They'll never forget it! (Contributed by Dave Miller, Flushing, NY)

Money Management Game

Try this game to help your young people learn a little more about money management. It allows players to decide how they will spend their "salary" on certain items which are worth points. The object is to accumulate the most points by making wise purchases.

Divide into pairs, with one player in each pair designated player "A" and one as "B". Give each pair a photocopy of the playing board shown on page 56. Every pair should also have a die and a pencil.

To begin, player A rolls the die. The number on the die represents A's "salary" for that turn, which is recorded in the first **middle** block labeled "Dollar Credits." Then player B rolls the die and records the salary for his or her turn in the first dollar credit box of the B section on the playing board.

When it's A's turn again, he or she can choose to buy any item shown at the bottom of the board for which he or she has sufficient dollar credits. For example, if A's dollar credit total is 6, a camera can be bought for 5 dollar credits, leaving 1 credit. For this purchase a "–5" would be recorded in the second of the **upper** boxes labeled "Item Cost." This will help players maintain a record of purchases.

According to the "Cost-Point Schedule" at the bottom of the board, the camera is worth 20 points, so A now writes "20" in the second of the **lower** boxes (labeled "Points") where the cumulative point total is kept. Then the die is rolled again, and the new dollar credit total is figured by adding the new salary to the

credits remaining after the purchase was made. For example, if the new salary shown on the die is 4, then the new cumulative dollar credit total will be: 6 (salary from turn 1) minus 5 (cost of the camera) plus 4 (new salary), which equals 5. So "5" will be recorded in the second dollar credit **(middle)** box. Then it's B's turn.

If at the beginning of his or her turn A had insufficient dollar credits to make a purchase, or had chosen not to do so, A would simply have rolled the die for a new salary and recorded the new total of dollar credits in the second dollar credit box. Then B would take a turn.

B follows the same procedure for his or her turns, and the game continues this way. On turn 3, players graduate from high school; after that turn, their salary is doubled. Players will receive twice the amount shown on the die for the turn.

On turn 7 players have a choice to go to "college" or to continue in their present "career." Players who choose college must lose 1 turn. After that turn, however, salary will be figured by throwing the die twice and adding the total of the 2 throws (then doubling, as for all plays after finishing high school). Players who choose to continue in their present career lose no turns but continue on their current salary schedule.

Play continues until one of the players reaches box 24. At that point play stops immediately—no other plays can be made. Total dollar credits for each player are transferred into points according to the "Transfer Schedule" at the bottom of the playing board. Then add the total of these points plus the cumulative total

A

Item Cost												
Dollar Credit												
Points	1	2	3	4	5	6	7	8	9	10	11	12

Item Cost												
Dollar Credit												
Points	13	14	15	16	17	18	19	20	21	22	23	24

B

Item Cost												
Dollar Credit												
Points	1	2	3	4	5	6	7	8	9	10	11	12

Item Cost												
Dollar Credit												
Points	13	14	15	16	17	18	19	20	21	22	23	24

COST-POINT SCHEDULE:

	Cost	Points		Cost	Points		Cost	Points
	5	20		40	300		50	500
	10	30		15	40		30	150
	30	100		30	60		25	120

TRANSFER SCHEDULE:

Credits		Points
0–9	=	0
10–49	=	8
50–99	=	15
100–149	=	30
150 and up	=	40

from the "Points" box. Player with the highest number of points in each pair wins. You may also want to have playoffs between winners and losers of different pairs.

Be sure to combine this game with some discussion of biblical principles of financial management. Some appropriate verses to read together would be Colossians 3:23-24; Ephesians 4:28; and Mark 12:41-44. (Contributed by Phil Blackwell, Charleston Heights, SC)

Movie Reviews

As cable television increases in both popularity and accessibility, young people will be watching more and more movies. In some communities, there are as many as a dozen movie channels to choose from. In addition, more and more movies are being targeted directly at the adolescent audience.

In light of this trend, it's a good idea to teach kids how to watch a movie in a discerning manner. The worksheet below can be used by students to evaluate the movies they

---

HOW TO **WATCH** A **MOVIE**

Please view the movie with the rest of the group. While you are watching it, though, keep the following questions in mind—we will talk about them briefly after the flick. Remember, a movie is not made just for entertainment; there's a "point" to it. Let's see if we can discover it together:

1. **Who do you think is the HERO of this movie? Why?**

2. **Who is the VILLAIN, or "bad guy?" Why?**

3. **Is there an "evil" in this movie? That is, what is the bad thing that could or does happen (for example, the hero dies or the universe is destroyed)? How is that evil dealt with—what happens to it?**

4. **Summarize the basic story of the movie in one or two sentences.**

5. **What do you think the producer and director are trying to teach us with this movie?**

6. **Do you agree with what they're saying?**

Thanks for answering these questions. I hope that you'll keep them in mind when you watch any movie, because you have to be careful about the stuff people are trying to teach you. I dare you to take a copy of this to the next movie you go see, or to fill one out after the next movie you watch on TV. Try it: It'll be good for you, and once you get the hang of it, you'll enjoy the movies a whole lot more!

see in light of the Christian faith.

To introduce the idea of learning to watch movies discerningly, rent a popular film (on VHS) and get your group together to watch it. Let the kids know that in today's films, moviemakers don't use camera angles, lighting, background music, and so on haphazardly. Nothing is done without a purpose. So it can be very helpful to the viewer to understand the intent and purpose of a film.

After viewing the movies, have the kids fill out the worksheets and discuss their answers. Other questions that would be good for discussion might include:

1. Is it dangerous to view a movie without thinking about what the film is really saying about the world?
2. Will this movie help me in my relationships (to God, my family, my friends)?
3. What does this movie have to say about biblical norms for living?

(Contributed by David Carver, Pittsburgh, PA)

Music in the Bible

The next time you run a series on rock music, get your young people involved in a study of music in the Bible. Buy some old Bibles at a local thrift store, and give them to your kids with scissors, rubber cement, and a couple of concordances, Topical Bibles, or Bible Dictionaries. Have them look up and cut out every reference to music they can find that they consider significant, and glue the verses to a large sheet of paper. Using the finished product as a basis for discussion, consider these questions:

MUSICAL STYLE/TASTE

1. What kinds of musical instruments were used in ancient times? (A Bible dictionary would be helpful here.)
2. How do you think the music of the Bible sounded? Would you have enjoyed it? Does it matter whether or not you would have enjoyed it?

MUSICAL FUNCTION

1. Why did people make music in ancient times? Name the various functions of music in the Bible (e.g., praise, exorcism, battle signals, idol worship).
2. Is music always used rightly today?

USING MUSIC RIGHTLY

1. Does the Bible have anything to say about how music should be played, or the place of music in the life of the believer?
2. What are the implications of these commands for our use of music today?

(Contributed by Steve Perisho, Boise, ID)

The Music of the Gospel

This idea makes good use of music as a teaching tool. Distribute to the kids a list of popular song titles that most of them will recognize. These can be songs from the current pop or rock charts, or old standards. Then ask the kids to choose from the list one song that best describes their walk with Christ right now. Allow the kids to share their choices with each other and to explain their choices.

Next, ask the kids to read Mark 10:13-16, Mark 11:1-11, and John 17:20-26 (or any others that you choose), and to pick a song from any that they know that would fit the story in the Scripture. If kids are in small groups, have the groups decide on the song, and then sing a verse of it after reading their assigned scripture.

Next, in small groups, have the kids select a well-known song or hymn and then find Scripture that speaks to the message of the song in some way. Allow each group to share their song (either sing it or read the lyrics) and then read the passage of Scripture, explaining how the passage relates to the song. This exercise could be done instead of or in addition to the previous one.

Lastly, have the kids sing together a favorite song and close with prayer. (Contributed by Brad Hirsch, Seattle, WA)

Music Messages

Try this game as a hook into a program on contemporary music messages. First think of as many tunes to current commercial jingles as possible. Have someone prepared either to hum the **tune** (not the words) or to pick out the tune on a musical instrument.

Divide the group into two teams. Have the "music person" begin to play or sing the tune. The object of the game is to be the first to name the **product** which is being advertised by the tune.

Score is ten points a song. (You can choose whether or not to count off for wrong answers.) Team with the highest score at the end of a given time wins.

After the game, you can point out how it demonstrates the power to communicate a message when a catchy tune is put together with lyrics. Even when we don't consciously pay attention to the lyrics of commercials, the message still gets through. Suggest that perhaps the same thing happens with the other music we listen to. You can then move into a discussion of the lyrics of several contemporary songs. (Contributed by David Wright, Vienna, VA)

My World

Here's a good discussion starter about social values, friendships, and the world's view of success.

Tell the kids that they have the rare opportunity to wield ultimate authority. Have them work alone or in small groups and create their own versions of society. They should list all the people they want to have in their private society, and tell why they want them. This list may include people from the past, but preferably people who are living. Give them approximately 15 minutes to do this, and then ask them to report to the rest of the group what their perfect society looks like. You may want to use questions such as these:

1. Which person did you choose to be in charge of your society? Why?
2. Give reasons why you chose each of the people in your society.
3. What values are represented in the individuals you selected?
4. What was your main concern when you began forming this community?
5. What concerned you the least?
6. If another Christian looked at your society, would he or she consider it worldly or godly? (Contributed by Dan Vaughn, Cheyenne, WY)

Object Lesson Generator

To generate new ideas for lessons which are illustrated by common household objects, ask the kids to bring to the next meeting five such items from home. Tell them that you're looking for objects that will illustrate biblical truths. When the items are collected, tag each one with a piece of masking tape that has the name of the person who brought it. Then place them all in a box.

Now let the kids take turns pulling an object out of the box. Allow them five minutes to come up with a biblical principle or insight somehow associated with the object. Then turn on a tape recorder and give each person a turn to talk. When everyone's finished, open the floor for further discussion. Find out which lessons were most meaningful, and ask for additional lessons which may have come to someone's mind as others were talking.

One variation of this exercise is to have everyone write down and place in a hat three scripture verses he or she would like to hear something about, and then prepare a short two- to three-minute message based on the verse drawn out. (Contributed by David S. Parke, Renville, MN)

Open House

Distribute paper, felt tip markers, crayons, and rulers to the group with the instructions that they are to design a floor plan for a home. What makes this home unique, however, is that it should reflect their own lives, with each room representing a specific area of their experience. One room, for example, might be a "hope room," where they write or draw a picture of some of their hopes for the future. Another might be a "love room," showing the things they love most. Suggest a fear room, thanksgiving room, question room, progress room, or whatever, and encourage them to think of some of their own.

Now divide into small groups and let each person volunteer to talk about one of the rooms in his or her floor plan. (Contributed by Brad Hirsch, Seattle, WA)

Parable of the Sower

Here's a good way to help your junior highers understand the parable of the sower a little better. Using a plant starter box, fill each tray with one of the four types of soils mentioned in the parable: hard, dry soil; soil with rocks in it; soil with weeds in it (grass seed can be used)

and good soil. Discuss the parable with the group, and speculate about how the various kinds of soils might affect the growth of a plant.

Next, plant some seeds in the four different soils. Corn seed will work fine. Make sure someone is in charge of watering the plantings as required over the next few weeks, and let the plants grow. As the weeks go by, you can chart the progress of the plants and draw comparisons to the principles taught by Jesus in the parable. It takes approximately 80 days for corn to grow, so you might want to take some pictures at weekly intervals just to keep track of how they're doing. The pictures would make a nice poster at the conclusion of the experiment.

You can transplant the good corn into a garden when it's ready, and maybe even eat the corn with the group. They'll never forget the parable. (Contributed by Terry Dawson, Newberg, OR)

Parent Swap Night

Here's a good way to get parents involved in the youth program of the church. On a prearranged date, have parents "swap" places with their teenage son or daughter at a youth group meeting. In other words, they (the parents) come to the meeting instead of the kids. If a student cannot get his or her parent to show up, then that student must come anyway. Most kids will badger their folks to death to come and take their places.

Once parents are there, conduct your regular youth meeting as you normally would, giving them a firsthand taste of your youth program. Most parents are grateful that you invited them, and will come away impressed with what you're doing. It also gives you a good chance to meet and interact with parents if you haven't already had the opportunity. (Contributed by Frank Zolvinski, La Porte, IN)

Parent/Teen Eye-Opener

Here's an idea that helps young people to see that the struggle they may be having with their parents isn't all their parents' fault. It can be a real eye-opener for the kids, and can prove to be a good "peacemaker" in the midst of family strife.

Pass out a 3x5 card to all the young people. Then have them draw a line down the middle of the card and write "Mom" above one column and "Dad" above the other. Tell the kids that they will be asked ten questions, and they are to answer them separately for their mothers and fathers. They must grade their parents on a scale of 1 to 10, with "1" being the lowest or worst possible grade and "10" the highest or best. Here are the questions:

1. Do your parents show you affection?
2. Do your parents listen to you?
3. Do your parents talk with you about schoolwork? your interests? your boy/girlfriend?
4. Do your parents trust you?
5. Do your parents respect you?
6. Do your parents initiate leisure activities that involve you (shopping, camping, tennis, walks)?
7. Do your parents treat your friends the way you want them to be treated?
8. Do your parents always have a settled opinion about things? (a "1" indicates they do, a "10" means they don't)
9. Do your parents respect your privacy?
10. Do your parents treat you the way you want to be treated?

After both parents have been graded on these points, you will want to discuss the kids' answers on a few random questions. What usually follows is a discussion of all the things parents do wrong. But the real key to this exercise is the next step. After the discussion, have the kids turn their cards over, and again make two columns with the headings "Mom" and "Dad." But this time they are to grade **themselves**, using the same questions turned around. (For example: Do you show your mom affection? Your dad?) In this way they can think about their relationship to both their mothers and fathers. The young people will likely see that, in many cases, their attitudes toward their parents are very similar to their parents' attitudes towards them. Close the discussion by having the kids think of ways they can improve the relationship they have with their parents. (Contributed by Chris and Liz Rhodes, Santa Rosa, CA)

Parent Pressures

To help kids empathize with the pressures their parents face, talk about the following factors which can contribute to stress in their parents' lives: aging grandparents; marriage problems; finances; physical changes and health problems; midlife crisis; the "empty nest"; job pressures; retirement. Then divide into groups and allow 15 minutes for each group to create a skit which illustrates two or thee of these factors. Afterward, discuss what happened in the skits and why.

Be sure to emphasize the responsibilities of parenthood, and the way pressure can cause both parents and teens to overreact in family conflicts. (Contributed by Joe Harvey, Ft. Myers, FL)

Passing Out Compliments

Have the group sit in a circle and give out a sheet of paper and a pencil to each person. Instruct everyone to write his or her name at the top, and then pass it to the person on the right. Now have everyone write down one thing he or she appreciates about the person whose name appears at the top. Then pass the sheets to the right again and repeat the procedure. Sheets should go around the circle in this way until they reach their owners again.

Now go around the circle and ask each person three questions: 1. Which was the funniest comment on your sheet? 2. Which was the most heart-warming? 3. Which surprised you the most?

Next, have people voluntarily tell something they wrote on another person's paper, speaking directly to that person. When everyone who wants to has had a chance to give a compliment directly, talk about how they feel when they're openly praised this way (good, awkward, proud, embarrassed). Ask how long it's been since group members received a compliment face-to-face, and if it's been a while, talk about what keeps us from praising one another. End by reading 1 Thessalonians 5:8-15 together. (Contributed by Phil Nelson, Seattle, WA)

Patience Role Play

This program would work well for the topic of either "Patience" or "Self-Control." Prepare several scenarios from daily family life that would test any kid's (or parent's) patience. Here are suggestions for some scenarios:

1. Your grandmother asks you to come over to help her set up the Christmas decorations. She ends up telling you exactly where to put every single light and strand of tinsel.
2. **Parent:** You have just come home from a long day at the office and your son is glued to the television. You see that the dishwasher is not unloaded, which was something you asked him to do this morning. **Child:** You have made your bed for the first time this summer, but you forgot to unload the dishwasher, which your mother asked you to do this morning.
3. Your aunt comes to visit for three weeks and stays in your room. One day you find her going through your drawers because she says she's interested in "finding out more about young people today."

4. You are the coach of an all-state team. The captain approaches you and says she can't come to pre-season practice because she's going to church camp.
5. Your son has gone to the prom and has promised to be home by 2:00 a.m. Suddenly you wake up at 3:30 and he isn't home yet. He finally comes in at 4:00.
6. You're nice to the class geek for a day, and he thinks you're in love with him.
7. You've got a great idea about the theme of the novel you're reading in English class, but the teacher says you're wrong.

After all the situations have been acted out and reacted to by the rest of the group, divide into small groups for a discussion of patience, and how God works in us to bring about this specific fruit of the Holy Spirit.

Suggested questions for discussion:

1. *What makes us feel frustrated? (feelings of helplessness, vulnerability, whatever)*
2. *How should Christians handle impatience?*
3. *Do you think God tests us? Why or why not?*
4. *When and why do you get impatient with God?*
5. *How can we become more patient?*
6. *How does the Holy Spirit change us in this and other areas?*

Seeing family life scenes from the parents' as well as the kids' perspective helps make this exercise an effective reminder of the need to cultivate patience in daily life. (Contributed by Laura D. Russell, Bryn Mawr, PA)

Phone Devotional

Here's a good way to help kids with their devotions, and to do some creative outreach ministry as well. Set up a daily youth devotional phone line with its own private number. The phone company can arrange one for you at reasonable rates. Give the phone number a clever name, like "T.N.T. (Totally Necessary Telephone) LINE" or whatever. The phone company might help you find a number that is easy for kids to remember. You will also need a telephone answering device.

The idea is for kids to call the number every day for a short devotional message. This means, of course, that you (or someone else) will have to change the message every day. It can include a short passage of Scripture and a thought for the day. If you wish, you can also include some information about the youth group.

To use this idea for outreach, have your youth group members distribute attractive business cards that display the phone number and a phrase like "Call for a dynamite life every day." Many "outside" kids who might not come to church or the youth group will call and be exposed to the Gospel. On weekends, you might change the theme and have one or two of your kids share their testimonies on the tape. Kids love to use the phone, so here's a good way to take advantage of it! (Contributed by Steve French, Wheaton, IL)

Prayer Candles

This idea will help your youth group pray together more effectively, and pray for each other. Have the entire group sit in a circle (in a darkened room or outdoors at night) with everyone holding a candle. One candle is lit, then the person holding that candle silently or aloud prays for one other member of the group in the circle (preferably someone across the circle). After completing the prayer, that person goes over to the person he or she just prayed for and lights that person's candle, then returns to his or her seat with the lighted candle. The one whose candle was just lit then prays for another in the circle and does the same thing. This continues until all the candles are lit and the leader closes in prayer. All the candles can then be blown out simultaneously. The symbolism involved can be very meaningful. (Contributed by Rod Rummel, Hayward, CA)

Prayers In The Wind

Here's a meeting idea that takes the expression "go fly a kite" literally.

Begin by discussing the Greek word **PNEUMA**, which means "wind" or "spirit." Using John 3:8 as a text, discuss how God's Spirit is a lot like the wind—you can't limit God in how He works and reveals Himself to us any more than you can control the wind.

Next, have the group write down prayers on small, thin pieces of cloth, about eight inches long and two inches wide. Then connect them all together to make the tail of a kite. Have the group assemble a kite and "launch" their prayers into the wind (**pneuma**), symbolizing the spirit. Run the kite out as far as it will go to the end of the string. When the end of the line is reached, let go, and the prayers will be "taken up" to God. Watch it disappear. Remind the kids that in a similar way, the ancient Israelites burned their offerings and incense so the smoke would rise to heaven with their prayers.

In Old Testament times, many believed that if God didn't answer prayers, it was because He didn't hear them—which, of course, is not true. If the kite doesn't go up (for lack of wind, or whatever), let the kids know that it's not because God didn't hear their prayers. Rather, it's because He chose to return their gift (kite) back to them. God always hears their prayers.

Use your own judgment in how you use this. Do it on a windy day. Make sure it will be okay to release the kite. (Don't violate any existing "litter" laws—the kite will eventually come down somewhere.) If you prefer, you could use this same idea with a large helium balloon. (Contributed by Dave Washburn, Brockport, NY)

Priority Slips

To get your kids thinking about their priorities as Christians, give each one an envelope containing 12 slips of paper. Each slip should have one of the following phrases written on it: supportive of mission projects; faithful in church attendance; studying the Bible to learn more about God; active in community affairs; sharing his or her faith; looking for opportunities to help others; constantly seeking God's assistance in daily life; truthful and dependable; more concerned about others than about him or herself; modeling his or her life after Jesus' example; angry at what's wrong in the world; kind and friendly to strangers.

Tell the group that these phrases complete the statement, "A Christian should be . . ." They must study the slips, decide which four are **least** important, and put those four back in the envelope. From the remaining eight they must now choose the four **most** important. Those four must then be prioritized and numbered 1 through 4 (1 = most important). Talk about the results when they finish. This simple exercise will help kids recognize their priorities as Christians and give you a good idea of what kinds of programming are needed for your group. (Contributed by Joe Harvey, Ft. Myers, FL)

Prodigal Problems

Next time you're doing a study or talk on the parable of the Prodigal Son, use this little "pop quiz" to get everyone's attention. It's fun and educational, too!

1. According to the parable of the Prodigal Son found in Mark 15:11–31, how many sons were there?
   a) 1   b) 2   c) 3   d) multitudes   e) none

2. Which son is considered the "prodigal"?
   a) oldest   b) youngest   c) middle
   d) the one with the earring

3. When did the oldest son get his inheritance?
   a) when Pop died   b) at the same time as the other   c) when the sun stood still

4. What job did the prodigal son take once his wealth ran out?
   a) youth pastor   b) farming
   c) pig slopper   d) carnival barker

5. (Fill in the blank.) "But while he was a long way off, his father saw him and was filled with _____ for him . . ."
   a) disgust   b) totalitarianism
   c) compassion   d) punishments

6. What items did the father give his returned son?
   a) robe, gold chain, and sandals   b) ring, sandals, and Walkman   c) ring, robe, and 'rithmetic   d) sandals, ring, and robe

7. Where was the older son when the younger son returned home?
   a) BMX racing   b) tending the cattle
   c) in the field   d) out somewhere

8. The older son knew something was up when he heard . . .
   a) the doorbell   b) music   c) music and dancing   d) a still, small voice

9. What did the older son say his father never gave him so he could celebrate with his friends?
   a) fattened calf   b) party hats
   c) goat   d) lamb

10. What didn't the younger son feel worthy
    to be called any longer?
    a) chicken-lips   b) Jewish   c) son
    d) prodigal   e) Buford

11. Who was unhappy at the homecoming?
    a) the fattened calf   b) the homecoming
    queen   c) older son   d) a and c

12. According to verse 19, who did the
    younger son want to be like?
    a) Big Brother   b) Dad   c) hired
    servants   d) Pastor Dave   e) Buford

13. Where did the older brother refuse to go?
    a) Africa   b) in the house   c) to the
    party   d) Bismarck High   e) Mott, ND

14. According to verse 18, what was the
    mother's name?
    a) Mildred   b) Rachel   c) Hildegaard
    d) heaven   e) uncertain

15. What did the older son say the younger
    son spent his money on?
    a) video games   b) friends   c) women of
    the evening   d) wine, women and song

Answers:

#1—e. The story is in **Luke** 15, not **Mark** 15.
#2—b. Verse 12.
#3—b. Verse 12 says he divided his property "between them."
#4—c. Verse 15.
#5—c. Verse 20.
#6—d. Verse 22.
#7—c. Verse 25.
#8—c. Verse 25.
#9—c. Verse 29.
#10—c. Verse 19.

#11—d. The calf wished he'd never come home, too!
#12—c.
#13—b. Verse 28.
#14—d. Verse 18 says, "Father, I have sinned against **heaven** and against you. Besides, have you ever known someone named "uncertain"? "Heaven" must have been his mother's name, right?
#15—c. Verse 30.

(Contributed by David P. Mann, Bismarck, ND)

Quaker Worship Service

The Quaker Worship Service (or you may call it "Spontaneous Worship") may be used in any setting. It works well on retreats as climax of the weekend. The service eliminates the anxiety of one individual making or breaking the service, and allows total participation from the group. It places the responsibility for worship where it should be: on the worshippers rather than on the one "up front." Here are some guidelines for leading such a service.

Assemble together. A small chapel or a room with chairs in rows or in a horseshoe works well. Stand before the group and give them an introduction something like this:

"Today we're going to share in an old-fashioned Quaker Service. We could have planned an order of service as we have on other occasions. But instead we want the Spirit to lead each of us today. The early Quakers believed in sitting quietly until someone was moved by the Holy Spirit to sing or speak or testify, and then they would do it.

Worship must be more than someone performing to our satisfaction. In fact, in worship *we* are the performers and *God* is the audience. So let's take our directions for worship from the Bible."

(Read Ephesians 5:19; Colossians 3:16; Hebrews 10:24–25)

Today no one will tell you what to do or when to do it. Each one is responsible to respond to the leading of God's Spirit. You may want to read a Scripture for us all to hear; you may think of a song to sing; you may want to provoke or encourage us in some way with an exhortation, or give a testimony of God's work in your life. It's up to you. If you think of a song, either start it, or say, 'Let's sing so and so' or 'Someone start so and so.' The only rule is that the same person should not share twice in a row. After someone else has had a chance, then you may share again.

There will be times during the service when we are all silent. Let the silence happen. Use it to worship God individually rather than being uncomfortable with it. After we have shared, when it seems appropriate I will lead into our communion service."

Allow as much time as necessary, but count on at least 45 minutes to an hour. When you see a good place to lead into communion, do so either with Scripture or a song. Have the elements already prepared on a table at the front of your worship room. Encourage them to partake individually when they are ready.

When all are finished, stand before the group for the closing. Share your own thoughts, or use the following:

"When Jesus and His disciples finished the Passover meal, the Bible says they sang a hymn and went out to the Mount of Olives. Let's stand and sing..."
(Contributed by Gary Black, Indianapolis, IN)

Real Men, Real Women

To start discussion about what it means to be truly masculine or truly feminine, distribute copies of the following list of personalities. Ask each young person to rank the women from 1 to 7 according to their femininity (1 is the most feminine, 7 is the least). Then have them do the same for the list of men, ranking them according to masculinity.

You can vary the names to make them more appropriate for your particular group. For example, Scott Studwell is well-known in Minnesota as a linebacker for the Vikings, but in Texas you might use the name of a popular Dallas Cowboy. Keep in mind as well the age range of your group.

When your kids have finished, make a tally of each personality's rankings to determine who was most rated #1 and who most often came in last. Talk about which qualities were considered in the ranking.

Women:
Mary Lou Retton
Mother Teresa
Joan Collins
The current Miss America
Madonna
Sally Field
Nancy Lopez

Men:
Ronald Reagan
Tom Selleck
Bill Cosby
Bruce Springsteen
Scott Studwell
Prince
Billy Graham

Next, choose a few of the following questions to continue the discussion:

1. How would you define masculinity/maleness? What does it mean to be a man?
2. How would you define femininity/femaleness? What does it mean to be a woman?
3. Who has the right to define masculinity and femininity?
4. Is it unmasculine to express emotions openly and cry in front of people?
5. Is a boy who doesn't like sports unmasculine?
6. Is it masculine to be macho?
7. Is a girl athlete unfeminine?
8. Is an aged woman unfeminine?
9. Is it feminine to be a female "sex symbol?" Is it masculine to be a male "sex symbol?"
10. Does physical attractiveness make a person more masculine or feminine?
11. To what extent are our concepts of masculinity and femininity influenced by God? Our parents? Our peers? The media?

Conclude the discussion with some biblical references on the subject: Psalm 8; Genesis 1:27, 31; 2:18-25; Galatians 3:26-29. (Contributed by Jim Olia, Eagle Bend, MN)

Rent-A-Christian

The following skit can be used effectively to open up a good discussion about "What does a real Christian look like?" Feel free to adapt the script or add other "model" Christians as you see fit.

The dialogue is carried on by two people, the shopper and the salesman. You will also need a narrator, and people to pose as each of the Christian "models" available for rent. Dress them appropriately.

Narrator: "Choose"—to select, prefer, decide; making those selections and decisions that have to be made, like what are you gonna do with your life? *Lots* of choices! Perhaps this skit can help you see the choices ahead.

Salesman: Welcome to our "Rent-A-Christian" showroom. We have a wide selection to choose from, all at reasonable rates! If you'll come right this way ... Let's begin with Model #6052, what we fondly call our "C.E." model—Christmas and Easter. This model lasts for years, because you only use it twice a year. On these important occasions when you need to be in church, send the "C.E." model in your place. It comes in all ages, styles, and colors.

Shopper: Hmmm. Very nice, but I was thinking of something I could use a little more often.

Salesman: Of course. Then, let's look at Model #0411, our "Looking Good" model. Made of inexpensive materials, this model is designed especially for Sundays—it has the durability to make it through Sunday school, church, and evening worship without a hitch. It doesn't function well during the week, but our customers have been very pleased with its Sunday performance.

Shopper: Do you have anything a little more ... uh, convenient? I mean, I'm not sure I want to be tied down *every* Sunday.

Salesman: I know just the thing! Right this way ... this is #1553, a very popular model. We call it our "Hit and Miss" model. This model can say and do the right thing on most any occasion; it grew up in the church so it has a good background, but it's not always predictable. It may or may not show up each week, but in general it gives a good impression and is well liked by all. It also comes with a special feature. It can create the perfect excuse for anything in under 30 seconds—a very popular item!

Shopper: Yes, that would be nice ... But what is that one over there in the corner?

Salesman: Oh ... well, *that* one. You probably wouldn't be interested in that one. #0012 is rather a rare breed. Some have dubbed it "The Real Thing." It's deeply involved in church life, but even more involved in living out its convictions on a daily basis. It doesn't always mix well with others, because it tends to stand out for its peculiarities, but it can always be counted on for its consistency and dedication. This one is harder to find—we have to special-order it, and it does cost more than the others.

Shopper: I see. You have quite a selection here.

Salesman: I should tell you that due to the nature of our products, we regret that we cannot offer a warranty, because we do not know when their "number will come up," so to speak. Have you chosen the model you would like?

Shopper: Oh dear, I can't decide. It's such a hard choice ... (they walk off together).

(Contributed by Esther Hetrick, Terre Haute, IN)

Rewriting Rock

Instead of just condemning the immoral lyrics of so many popular rock songs, try having your group rewrite them with Christian themes. For example, Starship's "We Built This City on Rock-n-Roll" could be "We Built This Youth Group on Jesus Christ." It's fun and thought-provoking, and you may find that when the song comes on the radio again your kids will start singing along with the alternative lyrics. (Contributed by Steve Gladen, N. Hollywood, CA)

Robin Hood

Here's a fun simulation game that can open up some good discussion on the subjects of giving, selfishness, anger, relationships, and more. Divide into 3 groups. One group is the "Givers" group; another is the "Takers"; and the third is the "Robin Hoods."

Give everyone in the room 5 clip-on clothespins and have them fasten them onto their clothes anywhere they want (as long as they're visible). When the signal is given to begin, each group moves about the room doing as its name implies. If you're a Giver, then you give the clothespins you have to others of your choice. If you're a Taker, then you take. If you're a Robin Hood, then you try to "right the wrongs" that are being done by stealing from the rich and giving to the poor.

After a few minutes of this, discuss what happened with the group. Ask questions like, "How did you like your particular role in the game? Did anything in the game seem unfair? Did you get angry? Did you ever want to change roles? How does this game compare with real life? Are there any real-life Robin Hoods around today?" (Contributed by E. Parke Brown, Sunbury, PA)

Rock Soup

Has your youth group ever eaten rock soup? Rock soup can generate some good discussion as well as a lot of curiosity. Here's how to do it.
Preparation:
1. The week before you plan this activity, give everyone an assignment to bring a certain ingredient to the meeting. It doesn't have to be cleaned or cut, as you will prepare the ingredients at the meeting. Make sure there will be onions, carrots, peas, celery, potatoes, and whatever else you need for a hearty soup.
2. Find a clean rock. (Use your own judgment.) Boil the rock for two or three hours until you think it's sanitary.

3. Prepare your favorite dumpling recipe so that all you have to do is spoon it out into the soup. This is what will turn your rock soup into a feast!

4. Have cutting boards, sharp knives, and potato peelers ready to use.

5. Have cooked chicken or ham ready to be diced. If a young person brings it, make sure it's thoroughly cooked. Some bread or crackers would also be nice.

6. Have enough water boiling and ready before you begin your meeting.

The Meeting:

1. Go to the kitchen where everything is ready to go.

2. Give everyone a job to do. Assign the kids to wash the different ingredients, peel potatoes and carrots, and cut or dice the onions, celery, and meat.

3. Have someone wash the rock. (You have already done this ahead of time, but make a big deal out of it anyway. Everyone should be watching.)

4. Now you can put the rock into the boiling water. Then have each person put his or her contribution into the pot. Don't forget the dumplings! Put the pot on the stove to cook for 20 to 30 minutes.

5. While this is boiling, go to a different room for your discussion. (The aroma of the soup is strong and distracts too much.) Read I Corinthians 12 and discuss the importance of a diversity of personalities in the church. Have each person give a

possible personality for the item he or she brought. Don't use real people and their names. Some possibilities:

Dumplings—happy; everyone likes them.

Celery—not real noticeable until you're in a crunch.

Carrots—someone who has lots of insight.

Onions—use your imagination —every church has one!

Meat—stable; keeps the church solid; a good teacher.

The Rock—tasteless; you could do without it just fine.

Discuss which of these you feel you are the most like. Ask "How would the church taste if all the ingredients were just like me? Would it still make a good soup? Which ingredient do I want to be like?" Stress how everyone is important—even the onion has a beneficial flavor.

6. Now go back to the kitchen. Give each person a bowl or cup and a spoon. You'll probably have to ask for volunteers to start the line moving. They'll be skeptical about that rock. Make sure everyone gets a dumpling and some meat in a cup. Most of the kids will love it once they work up enough courage to try it.

As for the rock ... save it as a starter for your next pot of rock soup. And if the kids want to know why it was in the soup, tell them it represents the Rock of Ages! (Contributed by Jon Adams, Crosby, MN)

Roman Melodrama

This "spontaneous melodrama" is a fun way to review the main concepts of Paul's letter to the Romans. First, review the key words and their appropriate responses (see below) with the audience. Add others if you like. Then pass out the numbered Bible verses from the text on 3 × 5 cards, to be read aloud by the audience when the appropriate number is called.

When you're ready to begin, the narrator stands in front of the audience to read the script, and the audience provides the appropriate response when they hear a key word or phrase. When the narrator gets to a numbered Bible verse, he or she calls out the number and allows the audience to read in unison the appropriate verse from their cards. Be ready for lots of laughs—it gets crazy!

Key Word:	Response:
Paul	Shout, "Paul, not Saul!"
Romans	Sing the march of the witch's henchmen from the Wizard of Oz (oh-ee-oh ...)
letter	Shout, "Dear so and so!"
salvation/ saved	Shout, "You bet your life saver!"
evil/sin/ sinful	Shout, "Boo, hiss!"
God	Shout, "Yea, God!"
death	Hum the first line of the funeral march.
Christ/Jesus	Sing the first two "hallelujahs" from the "Hallelujah Chorus."
love	Blow a kiss.
good	Shout, "Mmm, mmm good!"
Holy Spirit	Shout, "Who ya' gonna call? Ghost Busters!"
justify/ justification	Shout, "Just as if I'd never sinned!"
grace	Shout, "God's riches at Christ's expense!"
redemption	Shout, "Saved from the consequences of sin!"
Huh?	Shout, "Huh?!"

Example: "Well, the subject of this **letter** (Dear so and so!) to the **Romans** (oh-ee-oh) is the **Good** (mmm, mmm good) News, **God's** (Yay, God!) method for making **sinful** (boo, hiss!) people **good** (mmm, mmm good)."

Once upon a time, many years ago, there was a man named *Paul*. Paul wrote a *letter* to the *Romans*, which was so important that we still read it today. So, you may ask, why did *Paul* write this *letter* to the *Romans* and why is it so important? Well, the subject of this *letter* to the *Romans* is the *Good* News, *God's* method for making *sinful* people *good*. *Huh?*

Well, *Paul* says, *(#1)* "I have complete confidence in the gospel: *It* is *God's* power to *save* all who believe." Okay, but who needs to be *saved* and what do we have to believe? *Paul* says *(#2)* "For all have *sinned* and fall short of the glory of *God.*" We are all *sinners* and can never make ourselves *good* enough for *God.*

But how does *God save sinners?* Paul says, *(#3)* "*We* are *justified* freely by his *grace* through the *redemption* that comes by *Jesus Christ.*" *Huh?*

Well, let's review. What's "*justified?*" "Just as if I'd never *sinned.*" What's *grace?* "*God's* riches at *Christ's* expense." What's *redemption?* "*Saved* from the consequences of *sin.*" So let's try that last one again: We are *justified* freely by his *grace* through the *redemption* that came by *Christ Jesus.* Got it? *Paul* sums it up like this: *(#4)* "For the wages of *sin* is *death*, but the gift of *God* is eternal life in *Christ Jesus* our Lord." So those are the basics of the *Good* News.

But does *Paul* stop there? No, he continues to tell the *Romans* other important things about living this life after they believe the *Good* News. First of all, there are benefits from this *salvation* we have gained: 1. We have peace with *God.* 2. We stand in *God's grace.* 3. We rejoice in hope in the glory of *God.* 4. We can rejoice in problems and tough times. 5. We have *God's love* in our hearts. 6. We know *God loves* us. We are *saved* from the wrath of *God. Huh?*

Paul is telling the *Romans* that there is much more to being *saved* than just eternal life, because now *God* lives in us every single day. *Paul* tells the *Romans* that they are no longer slaves to *sin*, but now live by the *Holy Spirit*, Who helps us in our weaknesses and declares that we are children of *God.*

But this is not always an easy life. *Paul* gives the *Romans*, and us, three promises about how *God* will help us live the Christian life. *(#5)* "And we know that in all things *God* works for the *good* of those who *love* him, who have been called according to his purpose." *(#6)* "If *God* is for us, who can be against us?" *(#7)* "For I am convinced that neither *death* nor life, neither angels nor demons, neither height nor depth nor anything else in all creation, will be able to separate us from the *love* of God that is in *Christ Jesus* our Lord."

But Paul wasn't finished yet. This was some long *letter* he wrote to the *Romans. Paul* wanted to make sure he gave them some final instructions before he signed his *letter.* Let's look at some of the things *Paul* told the *Romans* about serving *God: (#8)* "Offer yourselves as a living sacrifice to *God*, dedicated to his service and pleasing to him. This is the true worship that you should offer. Do not conform outwardly to the standards of this world, but let *God* transform you inwardly by a complete change of your mind. Then you will be able to know the will of *God*—what is *good*, and is pleasing to him, and is perfect." *Huh?*

Well, this means that we give *God* our whole lives and let him be the boss; and that we follow *God's* way instead of the way of everyone around us. But we're not alone. *Paul* says we are all a part of one body. We are each a separate part, like a hand or an eye or a heart, but we all need each other and need to work together in order to make our body healthy.

Paul also tells the *Romans* how to respond to the government and authorities, and most importantly, *Paul* gives the *Romans* instructions about how to *love* each other. *(#9)* "So then, let us stop judging one another. Instead, this is what you should decide: not to do anything that would make your brother stumble, or fall into sin." *(#10)* "Accept one another, then, for the glory of *God*, as *Christ* has accepted you." *(#11)* "Rejoice with those who rejoice, weep with those who weep." *(#12)* "If someone does *evil* to you, do not pay him back with *evil.* Try to do what all men consider to be *good.*" With all these instructions *Paul* figured the *Romans* had enough to work on for awhile, so he finally ended his *letter.* But before *Paul* signed off, he told the *Romans* about having hope in *God* and the *Good* News, even when it was hard; and that's why all these years later, this *letter* is important to us as well. *Love* to all the *Roman* Christians—Signed, *Paul (#13)* For everything that was written in the past was written to teach us so that through endurance and the encouragement of the Scriptures written to teach us, we might have hope.

(Contributed by Lisa Andersen, Hollywood, CA)

Rug Discussion

Here's a great idea to use when you just don't have time to plan your usual terrific youth meeting. It's simple and works like a program that you've spent hours working on.

Pass out 3 × 5 cards to everyone

in the room. If you have a topic you were planning to discuss, ask each of the kids to write out a question relating to the theme about something that's been bothering them or that they're struggling with in their lives. If you aren't using a theme, then they can just write out questions they have of any kind. Cards should not be signed.

You'll get a great variety of questions. After kids finish writing them, pass a box or container around the room to collect them. Then have the leader read the questions, one at a time, and let the kids suggest some answers.

This is a useful approach to questions because kids can often do a great deal to help out their peers and because honest questions can be asked when they're anonymous. To make this a "rug" discussion, have all the finished 3 × 5 cards thrown on the rug in the center of a discussion circle, mixed up, and then read. Kids love it. (Contributed by Mark C. Christian, Santa Rosa, CA)

Sanctuary Study

For a stimulating discussion of the Sanctuary Movement in American churches, try this idea. Use the public library's index to the **New York Times** or a local paper to locate and photocopy articles on the subject. Begin looking with January 15, 1985.

When it's time for the discussion, ask the kids to complete this sentence: "Sanctuary is . . . " Then divide them up into small discussion groups and give each group one or more articles (no two articles should be alike). Their task is to read the articles, formulate questions to help them understand the Sanctuary Movement better, and then bring their questions back to the large group.

Try to arrange a guest speaker or panel for the meeting who would be competent to answer the questions raised in the small group, as well as further questions from the floor. This approach can be used effectively for almost any topic your group wants to discuss. (Contributed by Bob Stebe, Phoenix, AZ)

Sanctuary Campfire Service

Have a campfire service right inside your church sanctuary by constructing a mock camp setting. You can invite the whole congregation and let the kids lead the service.

Set up artificial trees and maybe even a pup tent in the front of the sanctuary, and build an artificial "fire" in the middle using the diagram provided. The kids can be seated on the floor around the fire, in front of the congregation.

Invite everyone to wear jeans, flannel shirts, or other outdoor attire, and to bring flashlights. Use food

How to Make an Artificial Campfire

1. Cut several clothes hangers here.

2. Bend them out.

3. Tape them together.

4. Tape them to a fan.

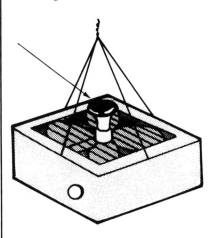

5. Fix a red or yellow floodlight here.

6. Tape orange and yellow crepe paper on alternate sides of the wire, cut in the shape of flames.

7. Place logs around in teepee fashion to complete the effect.

8. Turn on the fan and light, and get out the marshmallows!

gear made for camping to share communion, and pass around a "commitment log" for everyone to sign as a way to symbolize that they intend to give their lives to God. Sing camp songs accompanied by guitar, and make sure the lights are out so you have to do everything by flashlight. You may even want to give out marshmallows! (Contributed by Dave Seely, Raytown, MO)

Security First

Here's a plan for a youth meeting which deals effectively with the subject of "security."

Begin with a "Stuffed Animal Contest." Have each young person bring his or her favorite stuffed animal to the youth meeting and share it with the rest of the group. If they don't have a favorite now, have them bring one they had when they were younger. Most parents save them, so everyone should be able to bring one. Animals can be entered in a variety of categories: cutest, ugliest, most loved, most huggable, best bear, and best "other" animal. The winner can be judged by applause from the group.

Next, divide into small groups, and play a few "trust" games, like a "trust walk" (one partner is "blind," another is "dumb," and they guide each other through a maze); a "trust drop" (blindfolded, you drop backwards into your partner's arms); or "Wind in the Willows" (in a circle of six, one person stiffens his or her body and is passed around the circle).

These activities can then be followed by a discussion. Here are some sample questions:

1. How did you feel during the games?
2. How do you feel (physically and emotionally) when you are secure?
3. How do you behave when you feel secure? Rejected?
4. When do you feel most secure? Most rejected?
5. What are some ways you ensure security?
6. Does God make you feel secure or rejected? How do you know?
7. Did Christ feel accepted all the time? When did He feel rejected and why? What did He do when He felt rejected?
8. Christ teaches that to find our lives, we must lose them. Substitute the word "security" for "life." Is this a true saying? How does it apply to you?
9. Can we as Christians feel secure all the time? Or can we?
10. How does the church help us feel secure? How does our youth group help us feel secure?

The meeting can be closed with a community-building exercise of some kind, or a time of prayer, allowing each person the opportunity to give thanks for the security they have in Christ. They can also give thanks for one or two other people in the room or elsewhere who provide them with security. (Contributed by Beth Dubois, Basking Ridge, NJ)

Sex in the Movies

Teenagers need to take seriously the effects sexually explicit material in movies can have on their lives. To generate discussion, ask some of the kids to tell their favorite movie or scene from a movie and why. Then tackle the following questions in small group discussion:

1. *Do you think it's okay for actors and actresses to act in the nude or in sexually explicit scenes since they are "only acting?" Why or why not?*
2. *Why do you think movies today contain so much sexually explicit material? What is its purpose?*
3. *Do you believe that the movies present an accurate portrayal of sexual behavior or male/female relationships?*
4. *Do you think Christians should attend or view sexually explicit*

films? Why or why not? Would the age or maturity of the viewer be a factor in this regard?

5. *What kinds of effects might viewing sexually explicit scenes have on you? On your relationship to others? On your relationship to God?*

After the small groups come back together, have someone read aloud one or more of the following Scripture passages. Ask what light, if any, they shed on the subject under discussion.

Mt. 5:27–30
Eph. 5:1–12
I Thes. 4:1–8
Gen. 2:22–25; 3:1–12

In the large-group discussion that follows, point out or review some of the possible effects of viewing

sexually explicit material. These might include: immediate sexual arousal and lust at inappropriate times; guilt or shame; and a questioning of God's standards for sexual behavior. Encourage the kids to consider these and other possible effects when they're making decisions about film viewing. (Contributed by David Wright, Vienna, VA)

Situation Response

Here's a game to get your kids thinking about how they respond to compromising situations. First, create seven "response cards" by writing each of the following instructions on a separate index card:

1. *Respond by doing immediately what you know is wrong, then try to justify your behavior.*
2. *Respond with hesitation, debating with yourself about what you should do, then give in to what you know is wrong.*
3. *Respond by refusing to do wrong but acting judgmentally toward others involved.*
4. *Respond by refusing to do wrong, but refuse for the wrong reasons.*
5. *Respond by lying to avoid conflict or the consequences of your behavior.*
6. *Respond by refusing to do wrong and tactfully correcting others involved.*
7. *Respond by immediately doing wrong and then feeling sorry for what you did.*

Have the group sit in a circle, then tell them you're going to present some imaginary situations in which they might one day find themselves. Tell them that you want them to respond to the situations according to the instructions they'll be given on the response cards. Then read the cards aloud, mix them up, and distribute them.

After each situation is described, have the card holders role-play a response according to their instructions. Let the rest of the group guess which card each person was given. Then collect the cards, mix them up again, and distribute to a new set of role-players. Here are some sample situations to describe:

1. *A good friend asks you for an answer during a biology test.*
2. *You're standing around with the gang, everyone else is smoking, and someone offers you a cigarette.*
3. *You're invited to a keg party at the beach.*
4. *At the checkout counter in the neighborhood convenience store, a busy cashier hands you change for a $20, but you had only given her a $10.*
5. *You watched TV instead of doing your homework last night. This morning a friend offers to let you copy his or her paper.*
6. *A friend tells you that he or she found out someone's locker combination, and suggests that the two of you break into it when no one's around.*
7. *A conversation turns into gossip about one of your friends.*

Add your own situations, or have the kids make suggestions themselves. They may even want to describe real situations they've experienced firsthand (no names should be mentioned). After you've spent as much time in role-play as you wish, discuss with the kids which response was easiest, most difficult, most natural, or most likely, and why. (Contributed by Joe Harvey, Ft. Myers, FL)

So You Want To Cut An Album?

This activity will take 30 to 45 minutes. You'll need to divide into groups of 3 to 5 people. Bibles, paper, pencils and great imaginations are needed.

Each group will select a chapter from the Bible and then "produce" a record album that reflects the themes of that chapter. Each group reads the passage and selects 8 to 10 song titles to be put on the album. Encourage originality and creativity. Next, each group must design an album cover with proper credits. The album also needs to be entitled.

Here are a few sample passages of scripture that could be used:

Matthew 18	John 15	Mark 16
Acts 2	Luke 10	Acts 3
Luke 15	Acts 10	John 3
Acts 16	John 10	Romans 12

When the groups are finished, allow them to share their results with each other. For added fun, have them perform one of their songs. (Contributed by John Peters, Bedford, KY)

Spiritual Adventureland

Many of the games in the **Ideas** library can be used to teach spiritual truths. For example, you could plan a whole evening of game playing and learning using the games below.

1. Play the game "Line Pull," found in **Ideas #1–4**. Two teams line up on opposite sides of a line and try to pull members of the other team across the line. Once a person is pulled across the line, he or she becomes a member of the opposing team and tries to pull additional former teammates across. Play by these rules for a while, and then put everyone on one side of the line except for one strong guy, who becomes a team all by himself.

   Application: Have someone read John 6:40–48. Ask the question "What does Jesus mean when he says, 'No one can come to me unless the Father who sent me draws him'?" Ask the kids to compare the game they just played with that insight.

2. Play the game "Sardines," found in **Ideas #17–20**. This game is essentially hide-and-go-seek in reverse. One person is "It," and when players find "It" (who is hiding), the object is to hide with "It." Pretty soon more people are hiding than are looking. The object is to avoid being the last person to find the hidden group.

   Application: Ask someone to read Philippians 3:7–16. Divide the kids into groups of four and ask them to design a coat of arms that displays what Paul knew to be the purpose of life. This scripture centers on Paul's desire to be like Christ, and to share in his sufferings.

3. Play this variation of the game "Hares and Hounds," found in **Ideas #5–8**. Have everyone stay in one room for a few minutes while two members of the group go through the church (or wherever you are playing), leaving a trail to another point in the church. The trail can be marked with small pieces of paper, by adjusting the furniture, or whatever. It should be clear, yet only traceable by careful, deliberate observation. The object of the game is to successfully track the two volunteers when they have completed the trail. The challenge is not in doing it fast, since the whole group is to work together; or to catch the first pair, since they are to finish before the tracking begins; but simply to track them successfully.

   Application: Have someone read Mark 1:16–20. Ask the kids, "What did it mean to those people to follow Christ? How did the game simulate what you go through as you try to follow Christ?" At this point, you can enter into a discussion of the lordship of Christ, and allow the kids to reflect on how they attempt to follow Christ in their daily lives.

Many scriptural principles and applications can be found in the simplest and wildest of games if you look for them. Such an approach is especially good for junior highers and kids who don't enjoy sitting in one place for very long. (Contributed by Jim Walton, Rochester, NY)

Spread A Little Love Around

This idea can be used with large or small groups, and does wonders to teach about Christian unity and how God's love is shared.

You will need several slips of paper with the words "The Love of God" printed on them. The number of slips can vary, depending on the size of the group.

The group should be seated in a circle. The leader begins by taking a slip of paper and giving it to another person. This can be accompanied by a handshake, a pat on the back, a hug, or a warm word of encouragement—some demonstration of God's love. The receiver then waits for the giver to return to his or her seat, and does the same thing to another person, using a gesture of his or her own choosing.

While this continues, the leader puts another slip of paper into the action, so that 2 people "are passing God's love around," then 3, 4, and so on. Eventually, almost everyone is involved, all at the same time. Stop whenever you feel it is appropriate. (Contributed by John Peters, Bedford, KY)

Steal the Bacon Bible Game

Divide the group into two equal teams and have them count off. Then seat the teams in two parallel rows of chairs, facing each other with about six feet between the rows. Players should be seated in order of their numbers, with the two number 1 players seated at opposite ends of the rows. Place an upside-down garbage can at the midpoint of the rows and halfway between them, then set a chalk eraser on the can.

When the leader calls out a number, the player from each team with that number must race to get the eraser first. Whoever gets it has the chance to earn his or her team a point by correctly answering a Bible-knowledge question. You can make up your own questions, or use some from one of the popular Bible trivia games. Team with the most points after all the numbers have been called out twice wins. (Contributed by Laurie Christian, Santa Rosa, CA)

Stone An Atheist

This is a unique way to see how secure your kids are in the Christian walk. It will expose them to hidden attitudes they may have toward people who don't call themselves "Christian." It will also show them their need to understand how to witness, and the importance of having a working knowledge of Scripture.

To begin, you must recruit someone who is a Christian to role play an atheist. Whoever this person is, he or she must not be known by any of the kids. The person should be prepared to speak about 15 minutes on why he or she doesn't believe in God. Areas to be included in the speech could be:

1. The problem of evil in the world.
2. Hypocrisy in the Church.
3. How Church history is filled with brutality and war in the name of God.
4. Evolution and other theories of science that contradict Scripture.
5. The Church's seeming unconcern for the ills of society.
6. The existence of many different religions in a variety of cultures.

You may even tell the kids that you have invited an atheist to speak on the subject of "Why I don't believe in God." Following the speaker's 15-minute speech, instruct him or her to have a discussion period, with questions from the kids. Now sit back and watch the stones be thrown! Be sure to take notes on the kids' reaction to this "atheist." Don't talk or get involved yourself.

Stop the discussion after about 15 minutes and reveal the secret. Now you can lead a discussion with some of the following questions:

1. What was your attitude toward the atheist when you couldn't answer him/her during the speech?
2. Did you feel frustrated over not being able to give an adequate answer to all the problems he/she mentioned?
3. Was there any truth in some of his/her complaints? If so, how did you feel about it?
4. What should the Church be doing in society to minister to its ills?
5. What about the problem of hypocrisy in the Church?
6. How can we in love minister to those around us who don't believe in God?

(Contributed by Dennis Marquardt, Vergennes, VT)

There Is A Time

The following activity works well as a way to help your young people realize how they use their time. It also allows them an opportunity to compare their own life-styles to the life-style of Christ.

Have the kids choose a "typical" day of the week. It could be any day,

Monday through Saturday. Then give them a chart like the one below. Have them evaluate how much time they spend in the various activities that are listed for their typical day, making sure that the hours total 24. They should put this information in the column labeled "Yourself."

When they've finished doing this, have them label the column at the far right "Jesus." They should now imagine how much time they think Jesus would spend in the same activities if He were living as a human being today in our culture and community.

Next, they should compare the two columns and see if they can come to any conclusions about their own use of time. Do a quick study of Romans 8:28–30 and emphasize the point that they need to do their best to imitate Christ. This can either lead into a study of the life of Christ, or end with a discussion about how to be more like Jesus at school, home, work, and church. (Contributed by Joe Harvey, Ft. Myers, FL)

TIME ANALYSIS FOR AN AVERAGE DAY (24 HOURS)

ACTIVITIES	# OF HOURS	
	Yourself	Jesus
SCHOOL		
HOMEWORK		
CHURCH		
PRAYER		
BIBLE STUDY/READING		
SPORTS, PLAY		
WATCHING TELEVISION		
LISTENING TO MUSIC		
PLAYING GAMES		
DATING		
EXTRACURRICULAR SCHOOL ACTIVITIES		
SLEEPING		
HANGING OUT		
EATING		
DRIVING AROUND		
OTHER		
TOTAL		

This Bothers Me

Here's an idea that seeks to get kids to air their gripes or hang-ups about the Church or Christianity. It can be set up like a T.V. game show entitled "This Bothers Me" or "What's Buggin' You?" The kids are the players and the youth leader is the host. The rules are simple: A kid tells what bothers him or her most about the Church or about Christianity, and the group members vote for the complaints they agree with the most. Each kid in the group gets a chance to describe what really bugs him or her the most.

You can then use the answers the kids give as a springboard for discussion. Other topics can include "What Bothers Me About Parents ... Dating ... the Youth Group." It might be a good idea to start with a topic which is non-threatening and fun, like school or T.V. (Contributed by Phil Print, Denver, CO)

Thoughts About Dying

Read to your group the poignant true story in the newspaper article reproduced on this page. It can stimulate your youth to discuss some of the finer, often overlooked feelings concerning death, especially sudden death. Ask the group: "If you were in this man's place, what would you write and to whom?" Or instead of using it as a discussion starter, you can simply read it at the end of a meeting before everyone leaves, as a source of private reflection. It will plant the seeds for some serious thought. (Contributed by Chuck Behrens, Washington, PA)

'Goodbye ... Be good to each other'
JAL crash victim's diary

By Jack Burton
Special for USA TODAY

TOKYO—A Japanese executive scrawled his final thoughts across seven pages of a pocket calendar in the last terrifying minutes of life aboard the doomed Japan Air Lines jumbo jet.

"I'm very sad, but I'm sure I won't make it," scribbled Hirotsugu Kawaguchi, 52. The notes were shown Sunday on Japanese TV.

As others donned life jackets, Kawaguchi wrote to his wife and three children: "Be good to each other and work hard. Help your mother."

To his son, Tsuyoshi, he wrote, "I'm counting on you."

To his wife, Keiko: "Goodbye. Please take good care of the children. To think our dinner last night was the last.

"The plane is rolling around and descending rapidly."

His 17th and last sentence was: "I am grateful for the truly happy life I have enjoyed up to now."

Kawaguchi was among 520 killed when the jet hit a mountain, the worse single-plane disaster.

In his description, which investigators called valuable evidence, he wrote of "something like an explosion" that "triggered smoke."

Time Capsule

Have your group send a "mission" to their children or their children's children by putting together an authentic time capsule. The kids must first decide how large they want it to be, and when they want it opened (in their own lifetime or in a later generation). Then give them a week to consider what kinds of items they want to consider including in it, and why.

To make the capsule itself, buy a length of plastic PVC Pipe (2½ feet of 4-inch pipe is a good size) and two

MISSION TIME CAPSULE

PVC SOLVENT GLUE

TOP

BOTTOM

OPEN→

BLACK PERMANENT MAGIC MARKER

SILICONE GEL PACKET (CAN BE PURCHASED AT HOBBY-CRAFT STORES)

end caps. Attach one cap with PVC solvent glue. You'll need envelopes for the small items, a black permanent marker, and a small packet of silicone gel to remove unwanted humidity (silicone is available in hobby or craft stores).

A number of items could be selected for inclusion in the capsule to reflect your group's faith as well as common or significant aspects of their daily lives. The kids will have to narrow their choices, however, to items that will fit the size capsule you choose. Some suggestions:

* A video tape of the community, with views of the church, people, streets, stores, and surrounding countryside.
* An instant photo of the group that made the capsule, with a list of their names, ages, and addresses.
* A small, recent translation of the Bible (NIV, for example).
* A sermon of the current pastor.
* A history of the local church to date.
* A local newspaper.
* A current news magazine.
* A current local phone directory.
* A cheap digital watch.
* A current issue of *TV Guide*.
* A can of Coke.
* Any small, common items in daily use—a mechanical pencil, can opener, light bulb, or whatever.

* Brief thoughts written down by group members about the problems of the day, and how they predict these problems will be resolved in the future.

If you plan to bury the capsule somewhere, make sure it's well marked in permanent ink or paint, and that records of its existence and whereabouts are left in other places. Don't include liquids unless the capsule is so far underground (such as in the subbasement of the church building) that the ground temperature is a constant in the low 50s. Items that might leak (ink pens) should be placed in separate envelopes. Mark one end of the pipe outside as the bottom, and place lighter items on top of heavier ones.

After you've put all your items inside, seal the top cap with PVC solvent glue and mark on the outside where it should be cut to open. Label it clearly, along with the intended date for opening, and put it in its resting place while the group looks on. You may even want to pray for the people who will open it, asking God to bless your "mission" to the future. (Contributed by David S. Parke, Renville, MS)

Twenty Questions "Who Am I?"

Divide the group into two teams. One person from each team must

draw from a box containing slips of paper, each with the name of a Bible character written on it. Then the two players have 45 seconds to huddle with their teammates and find out as much as possible about the person whose name has been drawn. They should not let the opposing team know who it is.

At the end of that time, teams take turns asking each other a yes/no question about the identity of the opposing team's character, and are given one chance after each question to guess who it is. Questions can only be answered by the player who drew the name, and the only answers which can be given are "Yes," "No," or "I don't know." If the player doesn't know the answer, or if the answer given is wrong (you'll have to be the judge), the opposing team gets to ask another question. The team that guesses the correct character first wins a point for that round; highest score after ten rounds wins. Each round should involve a different pair of players.

Some useful questions might be: Is this character in the Old Testament? Is this character human (as opposed to God, angels, devils, or animals)? Is this character a woman? Is this character a political leader? You might want to have someone from each team record the answers—it's easy to forget in the excitement of the moment! (Contributed by Laurie Christian, Santa Rosa, CA)

Understanding the Handicapped

A number of simulation exercises can help your kids become more aware of the handicapped members of our society and the challenges they face daily. Try some of these:

1. Have half the kids walk around the buildings and grounds blindfolded while the other half act as their guides. After 15 minutes, switch roles. Then talk about how it felt and what problems they encountered.

2. Blindfold the kids and hang a number of small items on a clothesline. See how many items they can identify by touch.

3. Blindfold the kids and serve them a meal. Suggest that as they serve themselves, they can use a strategy employed by many blind people: They simply imagine their plates to be clock faces as a way of remembering where each food item is located (meat at 12:00; vegetables at 6:00; bread at 3:00; and so on). Or see if the kids can tell what they're eating simply by taste.

4. Have the kids "watch" TV blindfolded for half an hour, preferably a show they don't normally watch. Then have a discussion to find out how much they understood about what was going on. Watch another program with the sound turned all the way down, and see how well the kids can lip read or otherwise figure out what's happening without the benefit of sound.

5. Have the kids with lace-up shoes take them off. Then see how many of them can tie their shoes blindfolded and with one hand behind their backs.

6. Make a collection of small items such as safety pins, buttons, dimes, buttons, paper clips, and sequins. Let kids try to pick them up with rubber gloves on. This will simulate handicaps which restrict use of the hands.

7. Stand a mirror up on a tabletop. Then have the kids try one at a time to write their names on a sheet of paper in front of the mirror so that it reads correctly in the mirror. They cannot look directly at the paper—only at its reflection in the mirror. This exercise simulates the difficulties encountered by people with cerebral palsy or dyslexia.

8. Find a book at the local library that shows the deaf alphabet. Have your group learn it together, as well as a few common words in sign language. Then try breaking up into pairs and conversing for ten minutes without any spoken words. Whatever they can't say by word signs or improvised motions they must finger spell.

9. Go for a walk as a group down a street in a business section of town and take note of how accessible particular buildings and facilities are to handicapped people. Do they have ramps as well as stairs? Are doorways wide enough for wheelchairs to pass through? Are phone booths and drinking fountains low enough for wheelchairs? Do the bathrooms have facilities for the handicapped? Are there braille floor numbers on elevators?

After each of these experiences, be sure to focus on helping the kids put themselves in the place of a handicapped person, to understand what it would be like. What would be different? What would be the same? How would it feel to be ostracized or ridiculed because of a disability? (Contributed by Ruth Shuman, Chicago, IL)

Unwanted Guest

One problem most church youth groups confront is making new people feel welcome. The following project has been proved and tested several times.

Arrange for a kid from another youth group (far away enough so as not to be recognized) to come and spend a Sunday at your church. He should come to Sunday school and church, and maybe to a softball game that afternoon which you will have to set up in advance. Plan to have a get-together after church that night.

In the meantime, your guest should be dressed normally, but not at all stylishly. He or she should be asked to be friendly but quiet, and to speak only when spoken to. This will take a little bit of acting.

That night at the get-together, have your mystery guest report to the crowd how he or she was received and treated. If you want to get really heavy, have the person even share with the group how individuals went out of their way to accept or ignore him. Before the visitor begins, take the pressure off by introducing him or her to the group and letting them know that the person was a "plant." Some will want to crawl under the tables. Others will feel as if they have finally done something right. Either way it's a great learning experience for everyone. (Contributed by Marty Edwards, Oxnard, CA)

Uppers And Downers

For an excellent exercise in community building, have the kids in your group fill out a chart similar to the one below.

OTHERS		ME	
Upper	Downer	Upper	Downer

Ask the kids to think of a time when someone said something to them that was really a "downer"— something that made them feel bad. This could be a put-down, an angry comment, anything. Then have them think of a time when someone said an "upper" to them—something that made them feel good. If they can think of several entries for the first two columns, encourage them to write them in.

Next, have the kids do the same thing in the third and fourth columns, only this time they should think of times when they said an "upper" or "downer" to someone else.

Chances are your young people will be able to think of many more "downers" than uppers, if your group is typical. Discuss what this means. Talk about how easy it is to discourage or to put down others without a second thought—how damaging our tongue can be, and how the damage takes so long to repair.

Follow up with a look at Hebrews 10:23–25, which deals with encouragement, and then discuss practical ways to put it into practice. You might want to continue with another exercise such as "What Others Think of Me" (from **Ideas Numbers 9–12**) or "The Encouragement Game" (from **Ideas Numbers 13–16**).

You can also help kids identify the things they say to each other as an "upper" or a "downer." This will encourage them to be more careful about what they say. If you are on a weekend retreat, challenge them to confront each other during the retreat when they hear someone giving someone else a "downer." This can cut down on the negativism that often ruins youth group meetings and activities. (Contributed by Bill Williamson, Los Angeles, CA)

Vidiots Unite!

A "vidiot" is a person who sits for hours at a time watching Music Television (MTV) with his or her brain in neutral. Unfortunately, many church kids are vidiots.

Why not discuss the content and message of a few popular music videos with your youth group? Tape a few selected ones (on VHS) and play them back for the group to watch together. Then discuss them, using the worksheet below.

You can print up additional sheets for the kids to take home so they can fill them out for some of their favorite music videos. The purpose is to get the kids to begin thinking about what they are watching, in light of their faith. (Contributed by David Carver, Pittsburgh, PA)

ARE YOU A VIDIOT???

We all know what an idiot is. An idiot is a person who does things without thinking about them. When you call someone an idiot, it is generally accepted as an insult. A *vidiot* is almost the same thing. You are a vidiot if you continue to watch videos (MTV, etc.) for any period of time without stopping to think about what they are saying. A vidiot lets other people influence his or her mind without even asking questions about anything.

Today marks the first day of a campaign designed to make the vidiot an endangered species in our area. Please help us do this by watching some videos and then recording your thoughts about them on this paper. We can then discuss them together, eliminating the vidiot from this place. As you watch the video and then we discuss, please keep in mind these verses from Philippians 4:8 & 9: "Here is a last piece of advice. If you believe in goodness and if you value the approval of God, fix your minds on whatever is true and honorable and just and pure and lovely and praise-worthy. Model your conduct on what you have learned from me, on what I have told you and shown you, and you will find that the God of peace will be with you." (J.B. Phillips translation)

Name of song _____ Artist _____

Did you like this video? Why or why not?

Did the visuals have anything to do with the song?

What was the song about?

What did the person singing the song want to happen? Is that a good thing to have happen? Why or why not?

As a Christian, do you think that this is a "good" video for someone to watch or listen to? Why or why not?

Does it fit the qualifications that Paul wrote about in Philippians? How?

Whatever Happened To Sin?

Here's a creative discussion and object lesson on sin and forgiveness. Begin with a discussion of sin, using questions such as these:

1. What is sin?
2. Name several specific sins that come to your mind.
3. What sins are considered acceptable with the group?
4. Are some sins worse than others?
5. How do you deal with sin? In what ways do you succeed and in what ways do you fail?

After the discussion, ask the group: "Would you like to be sure of forgiveness for your sins? You can." Then pass out pieces of paper to everyone.

Ask the group to write down on the pieces of paper any sins in their

lives they still worry about. Tell the kids that what they write will only be seen by themselves and God, so they can be very specific and honest. After they have written down their sins, have them sign their names and write "Forgive me" under it. This will take some courage, so you need to reassure them all again that they will not be betrayed—no one will see the words except God.

Now ask them to fold up their pieces of paper and put them in an open coffee can which is up front. When all the sheets are collected in the can, talk about how Christ cleanses us from all our sins. You might want to read an appropriate scripture at this point.

Then, to illustrate how Christ forgives and forgets, take a match, light it, and drop it in the can. There will be a "flash" and poof! The can is empty. Not even ash will be left. After everyone sees the can, explain that it is just like that with God's forgiveness. "Go and sin no more."

How is it done? The sheets of paper passed out are magician's "flash paper" which can be bought at any novelty or magic supply store. When a flame is added, it literally vanishes. The can, by the way, should be placed on something that can take a little heat. (Contributed by David Parke, Renville, MN)

Whop That Work

Here's a fun skit that will help kids to understand better the concept of grace and faith in Christ. It should be set up like a television game show.

Characters: Announcer—Wanda Whiteheart
    Host—Wendy Wellwisher
    Contestant #1—Larry Liveright
    Contestant #2—Becky Begood

WANDA: Welcome to "Whop That Work," the game show in which contestants compete for the "winning work" that will win them a one-way ticket to paradise. And now, here's your host, Wendy Wellwisher.

WENDY: Thank you, ladies and gentlemen. Have we got a show for you today! Let me introduce our two contestants for today. Let's give a warm welcome to . . . Larry Liveright and Becky Begood. (Applause) Before we get started, there's Wanda Whiteheart to tell us about our first prize.

WANDA: Thank you, Wendy. The winner of "Whop That Work" this week will win a wonderful trip. First, our winner will fly the friendly skies of the Angelic Northern Airline till he or she reaches the Pearly Gates, then he or she will walk the Golden Streets and stay at the Hilton on the Hilltop, a mansion built for you! That's right, our winner

92

will receive a one-way trip to heaven! (This trip provided by "Heavenly Hosts, Inc." Have you visited the best-built in Heaven lately?) Back to you, Wendy.

WENDY: Thanks, Wendy. Larry, let's start with you. What fantastic work have you done that you can share with us?

(At this point, the contestants go back and forth, trying to top the other's great deed; Wendy can interject an occasional "That's great ..." and "Inspiring!" and the audience should be encouraged to get involved by clapping for their choice. The contestants can come up with their own list of "works" ahead, the more ridiculous the better. Here are a few suggestions:

—I picked up two hitchhikers on my way to work ... and they were none too clean! It made me five minutes late for work.

—I bought a Christian bumper sticker for my car. It says, "Honk 8 times if you know Jesus." It's a real witness wherever I go.

—I went with the youth group to McDonald's—we all wore our matching Christian T-shirts. Talk about large-scale evangelism.

—I memorized the steps of salvation. The next time someone comes up to me and says, "What must I do to be saved?" I'll be ready.

As the "show" progresses, the contestants should get increasingly rude to each other, until Wendy calls a halt.)

WENDY: I hate to stop—we're just getting warmed up, but we're almost out of time. We'll give the judges a moment to choose the winner, and while they're doing that, I'd like to take this opportunity to thank our contestants for being on the show, and wish them both the best ... Ah, the judges have reached a verdict. (Reach for an envelope) And the winner is ... Folks, this has never happened before—we had a tie! Let me read the scores—Larry Liveright ... zero; Becky Begood ... zero! (Everyone freezes.)

VOICE: "For it is by grace you have been saved, through faith—and this is not from yourselves; it is the gift of God—and not by works, so that no one can boast." (Eph. 2:8–9 NIV)

(Contributed by Esther Hetrick, Terra Haute, IN)

93

Will The Real Gospel Please Stand Up?

As an intro to the book of Galatians, particularly chapter 1:6–9, this adaptation of the old television game show "What's My Line?" works great. Have 6 people come to the front of the room, each representing the Christian gospel. They read their "affidavits" as printed below, and then the group discusses the pros and cons of each one. For best results, have each person know the role well enough to defend his or her position when questioned by group members. Finally, let the group vote on which one (or ones) they feel best represents the gospel.

The six "affidavits" (add to them or change them as you see fit):
(Contributed by Jack Schultz, Appleton, WI)

---

1. I am the Gospel of hope. Knowing that mankind is utterly sinful and lost, I claim that Jesus died on the cross and rose from the dead to give all people everywhere forgiveness of sin and eternal life. God does it all, mankind does nothing—therefore, all people everywhere will be saved.

2. My Gospel teaches that Jesus died and rose for the forgiveness of all mankind. Those who believe in Jesus will have this forgiveness and eternal life. I also expect you to follow Jesus' command, "Go and sin no more" (Jn. 8:11).

3. I am the Gospel of grace. Jesus suffered, died and rose that mankind might have forgiveness and life. If you believe, it doesn't matter what you do. You are under a blanket of forgiveness and grace. Enjoy yourself, don't worry how you're doing—Jesus did it all!

4. My Gospel teaches that Jesus died and rose for the sins of mankind. This Gospel creates a relationship with God in which a person repents and believes in Jesus. This believer's life is one of repentance and faith, expressing itself in love (Gal. 5:6).

5. My gospel is one of action. The same Jesus that suffered and died for the forgiveness of our sins, also said, "Let your light shine before men, that they may see your good deeds and praise your Father in heaven." I teach that unless your faith is active, it is no faith at all. Your faith must be visible.

6. I am the Gospel of faith. Jesus died and rose for the sins of all who believe. All that God requires of us comes freely through the death and resurrection of His Son. We need only to believe that. Romans 5:1, "Therefore, since we have been justified through faith, we have peace with God through our Lord Jesus Christ." And from John 6:28, "Then they asked him, 'What must we do to do the works God requires?' Jesus answered, 'The work of God is this: to believe in the one he has sent.'"

Youth Pew Protocol

If your kids are a bit unruly in Sunday morning worship services, try posting in the youth room the following list of "Appropriate and Inappropriate Behaviors" in church. You may also want to photocopy, distribute, and go over it at your next meeting. Feel free to substitute your own list for the one shown.
(Contributed by Kevin Slimp, Odessa, TX)

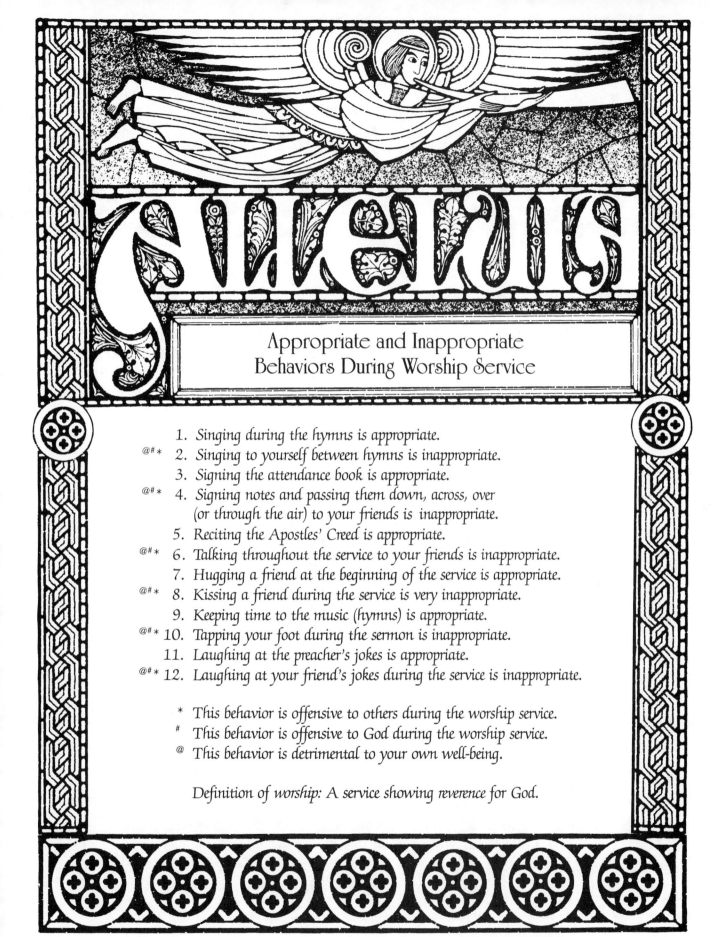

ALLELUIA

Appropriate and Inappropriate Behaviors During Worship Service

1. Singing during the hymns is appropriate.
@#* 2. Singing to yourself between hymns is inappropriate.
3. Signing the attendance book is appropriate.
@#* 4. Signing notes and passing them down, across, over (or through the air) to your friends is inappropriate.
5. Reciting the Apostles' Creed is appropriate.
@#* 6. Talking throughout the service to your friends is inappropriate.
7. Hugging a friend at the beginning of the service is appropriate.
@#* 8. Kissing a friend during the service is very inappropriate.
9. Keeping time to the music (hymns) is appropriate.
@#* 10. Tapping your foot during the sermon is inappropriate.
11. Laughing at the preacher's jokes is appropriate.
@#* 12. Laughing at your friend's jokes during the service is inappropriate.

* This behavior is offensive to others during the worship service.
# This behavior is offensive to God during the worship service.
@ This behavior is detrimental to your own well-being.

Definition of *worship:* A service showing reverence for God.

CHAPTER THREE

CROWD BREAKERS

For Your Eyes Only

One of the ongoing problems with a youth group meeting is the very beginning—how to keep the interest of the kids who have shown up on time or a bit early, until everyone else has arrived and you can get into the program proper. One way to overcome this is with the following "memo," which can be handed out to the kids one at a time as they arrive.

FOR YOUR EYES ONLY!
TOP SECRET!
URGENT!
CONFIDENTIAL!
And like that!

MISSION:
The FINAL and COMPLETE elimination of zits.

YOUR TASK:
Our government, in conjunction with other governments around the world, has declared TOTAL WAR on zits.

Our department's ongoing task in this vital effort is the total elimination of CHOCOLATE BARS from the face of the earth!

Our intelligence has been able to advise us that a CHOCOLATE BAR has found its way into our church building, and is hiding in open sight somewhere on the main level. We have been able to verify that it definitely is NOT in any of the offices or washrooms.

I want you, personally, to hunt down and DESTROY this fiendish CHOCOLATE BAR, in whatever manner you deem best. You have until exactly 7:43 to achieve this.

Our intelligence was able to determine that if not found by 7:43, the CHOCOLATE BAR would be turning itself in at the gym, to be DESTROYED by me; therefore, regardless of results, you are to report to the gym NO LATER THAN 7:43:30 for your next assignment.

Oh, one other thing—agent 003 was able to get some vital information to us: With his dying breath, he told us that ONE of the statements listed above is a lie, and is not to be believed. Unfortunately, however, he died before he could give us any further details.

Good luck, 007. Oh, and by the way—you should memorize and destroy this memo.

For added atmosphere, the "memo" can be sealed in an envelope marked CONFIDENTIAL, and you can have some James Bond movie themes playing in the background. This will keep the kids occupied and running around the church looking for the chocolate bar until it's time for the meeting to start.

Of course, you'll need to hide the chocolate bar well enough to keep them looking. One suggestion would be to have it in one of the sponsor's pockets, so that the outline of it is in plain view. The "lie" mentioned in the memo can be anything you want. Be creative. You can adapt this idea any way you like—it works! (Contributed by Gene Defries, Calgary, Alberta, Canada)

Good Riddance

While the group sits in a circle, have each person write his or her responses to the following questions, making sure that everyone has finished answering each one before going on to the next.
1. Name something you really want to get rid of.
2. Why do you want to get rid of it?
3. How much would you ask for it?

Next, have everyone scratch out the first answer and replace it with the name of the person sitting to his or her immediate right. Now have each person read off the answers, using the other person's name:
1. **Who** do you really want to get rid of?
2. Why do you want to get rid of that person?
3. How much would you ask for him or her?

The results will be good for some laughs! Make sure that it's all done in fun. (Contributed by Lavonne Gras, Zeeland, MI)

Mystery Buckets

This is a great crowd-breaker for one-time use, or it can be used as an opener on a semi-regular basis. Have five small buckets sitting on stools at the front of the room. Number the buckets one through five. Explain to the crowd that there could be anything in the buckets: water, honey, squashed snails—anything imaginable. Then tell them that one of the buckets has money in it, anywhere from $5 to $20 (usually $5 in change is enough). The chance to get some money will get you more volunteers than you need. You will need five more people (prearranged) to go and stand behind the stools. When your five volunteers are seated at the stools, start one by one, with GREAT suspense and drama, to pour the first bucket over the first kid. There will be sighs of relief, groans, cheers and laughter. Be sure somebody gets the money, and occasionally make it more than $5. (Contributed by Marty Edwards, Oxnard, CA)

98

The Wave

"The Wave" is a popular cheer seen at sports events in large stadiums across the country. Usually one section of the stadium begins the Wave by jumping up, throwing hands up in the air, and letting out a cheer. The next section follows suit, and this continues all around the stadium in a kind of "domino" effect. It really looks like a wave. (Trivia buffs will be interested to know that the Wave is said to have originated at the University of Washington.)

The Wave can also be done on a much smaller scale. If you have an auditorium full of people, divide the group into two sections, and try it by rows. The first row in each section begins by standing up, throwing hands up in the air, and letting out a cheer. The second row follows, then the third, and so on the the last row. After the Wave reaches the last row, it can move in reverse back up to the front again. See which side can complete the Wave first.

With even smaller groups, have the kids do the Wave one **person** at a time. Set it up to go down rows of chairs or around a circle. It really looks crazy when done around banquet tables.

"What's The Meaning?" Strikes Again

On the next page are 32 more word puzzles your kids will enjoy trying to solve. Each puzzle represents a common saying or phrase. You may, if you choose, photocopy the page and pass it out to your kids. (You have our permission.) Give a prize to the one who can solve the most within the time limit (ten minutes should be long enough). Give extra points to anyone who can solve the last one (8-D)—it's a toughie. The answers are below.

1-A spreading the gospel
1-B upper room
1-C a mess of pottage
1-D frankincense
2-A rightly dividing the word of truth
2-B mixed messages
2-C too much of a good thing
2-D not enough money to cover the check
3-A stretching the truth
3-B smokestack
3-C three-piece suit
3-D eggs over easy
4-A fly in the ointment
4-B sign on the dotted line
4-C sideshow
4-D pie in the sky
5-A feeling under the weather
5-B splitting the difference
5-C fancy footwork
5-D to be or not to be
6-A cornering the market
6-B bouncing baby boy
6-C slanting the news
6-D condensed books
7-A it's a small world
7-B skinnydipping
7-C a bird in the hand equals two in the bush
7-D scrambled eggs
8-A that's beside the point
8-B hanging in there
8-C flat tire
8-D the end of the game

(Contributed by Kay Lindskoog, Orange, CA)

	A	B	C	D
1.	g o s p e l	room	*pottage*	CENFRANKSE
2.	WO RD O F TR UTH	EMSEASSG MEGASSSE SAMEGESS GEMASSES MEASEGSS	a good thing a good thing	MONE ✓
3.	*truth*	smoke smoke smoke smoke smoke smoke smoke smoke smoke smoke smoke	S UI T	EGGS EASY
4.	OINTFLYMENT	. . . . SIGN	SHOW	SPIEKY
5.	THE WEATHER FEELING	diffe rence	*FOOT WORK*	BBORNOTBB
6.	MAR KET		NEWS	BOOKS
7.	WORLD	BABY BOY DIPPING	HABIRDND = BUTWOSH	GƎƧ⅁
8.	T H A T S, S ·	IN THERE	TIRE	e

CHAPTER FOUR

GAMES

A Day At School

The object of this game is to see who can go through a day of "school" the fastest by completing the assignment in every "class." Choose 11 locations around the church facility (Sunday school classrooms are best) and station a staff "teacher" in each one with the appropriate assignment from the list below. Then have the "students" meet with you in another room—their "homeroom"—where they are given a copy of the "report card" shown on the next page.

Students must go to every class, answer the question or complete the assignment to the teacher's satisfaction, and have the teacher grade and initial the report card. The first and last classes students "attend" must be the same as their first and last classes at school (if it's summer, they can use the previous year's schedule). Other classes may be attended in any order they wish. To make it a little more complicated, don't tell the students where each class meets; let them find out on their own. The first student to return to "homeroom" with all assignments completed (regardless of grade) and all classes initialed is the winner.

SAMPLE CLASS ASSIGNMENTS
(To be given to the "Teachers")

Math: Have them add the number of the apostles and the number of the Gospels.
English: Have them write "Jesus Loves Me" as a title for their next composition. (Check their spelling!)
Literature: Ask them what was the first book ever printed on a printing press. (Answer: the Bible)
Science: Ask them where they can read about the origin of the universe. (Genesis 1)
Physical Education: Calisthenics—Have them do five push-ups and five deep-knee bends.
Lunch: Have them give you directions (a map) to their favorite off-campus eatery.
Band/Choir: Have them sing "The B-I-B-L-E" all the way through.
Drama: Have them act out the Bible passage "And they were sore afraid!"
Vocational Education: Tell them to "charade" any occupation of their choice until you can guess what it is.
History: Ask them "Who was buried in Joseph of Arimathea's tomb?" If they say Joseph of Arimathea, give them an "F" in the class.
Foreign Language: Ask them to translate the Greek word **agape**. (Godly love)

REPORT CARD

CLASS	GRADE (PASS/FAIL)	TEACHER'S INITIALS
MATH	____	____
ENGLISH	____	____
LITERATURE	____	____
SCIENCE	____	____
P.E.	____	____
LUNCH	____	____
BAND/CHOIR	____	____
DRAMA	____	____
VOCATIONAL ED	____	____
HISTORY	____	____
FOREIGN LANGUAGE	____	____

(Contributed by Todd Capen, Lodi, CA)

Bail-O-Wack

This game is like volleyball, but it's played with a balloon and without a net. To set up, use masking tape to make a straight line across the middle of the playing area. The length of the line in feet should be twice the total number of players on both teams (e.g., ten players—a 20-foot line).

```
TEAM A    X   X   X   (X)   X   X   X
TEAM B    O   O   O   (O)   O   O   O
                       ↑
                  Team Center
```

Divide into two teams, and have each team stand facing the other across the line (as if it were the net) in a single row on each side. Players should stand four feet apart from teammates, and two feet back from the line. Players cannot move from this position during play, though one foot may leave the floor to kick the balloon if the other stays in place.

The object is to volley a balloon back and forth across the line without allowing it to touch the floor on your team's side. The balloon can be batted with hands or kicked. As with the ball in volleyball, contact with the balloon may alternate between players on the same team, but the balloon cannot be touched by the same player twice in a row. Unlike volleyball, however, teams are not limited to three contacts in order to get the balloon back over the line to the other team.

The middle player in each team's line is the "center." Each round begins with one of the centers serving by tapping the balloon across the line to the other team. The team that won the point in the previous round gets to serve. A team scores a point when the balloon touches the floor on the opposite team's side of the line. There is no out-of-bounds play, so if the balloon is batted over the heads of players and out of their reach, the opposite team scores a point. A team also scores a point when a player on the opposite team makes contact with the balloon twice in a row or moves out of position.

You'll need extra balloons in case one bursts, and a referee to make sure players stay in position. (Contributed by Phil Blackwell, Charleston, SC)

Balloon Mini-Golf

Here's another good variation of miniature golf that you can set up in your church.

Provide the kids with plastic "floor hockey" sticks. These are the golf clubs. The golf balls are small, round balloons (about 4" in diameter). The "holes" are boxes and containers of various sizes.

Just number all the boxes and containers, and lay out your golf course all over the church—in and out of rooms, down hallways, up stairs, over "water hazards" (the baptistry), and so on. You might even set up some adverse "weather" conditions, like placing a fan along one of the "fairways." Have someone pre-shoot the course to establish par for each hole. Since balloons are a bit tough to control, the game can become rather unpredictable, but that adds to the fun. (Contributed by Mark Boughan, Hamilton, Ontario, Canada)

Barn Swinging

Here's an "Ozark mountain country" idea. To pull it off, you'll need a heavy-duty rope, lots of hay, and a barn (a real one).

Stack the bales of hay so that you have a stack about 7' wide and as high as you want (20' works well). In the center of the barn, tie the rope to a strong beam and loop the rope so you can sit in it. Kids then jump off the stack of hay, swinging on the rope. The object is to get back up on the stack of hay. The rope should be just long enough to make that possible. (Contributed by Pete Franzone, Branson, MO)

103

Baseball Ping Pong

Here's a good indoor game for small groups. To set it up, you'll need a card table, a ping pong ball, and some masking tape (for lines).

On the card table, mark off lines according to the diagram pictured below. You need foul lines and lines which indicate a base hit, a double, and a triple.

To play, place the ping pong ball on home plate. The team "at bat" rotates one by one and attempts to "blow" the ball across the bases to a home run. The team "in the field" places three players on their knees on the opposite side of the table who attempt to "blow" the ball off the table before it's allowed to score a base hit.

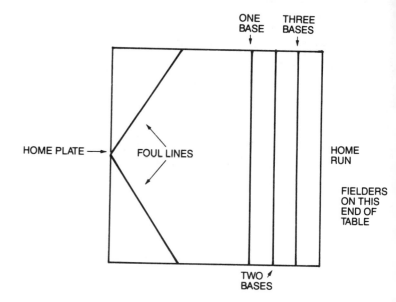

Here are some additional rules:
1. The batter may blow only once.
2. The fielders may not touch the table at any time.
3. If the ball crosses the foul lines, that player is allowed another blow, even if it was the fielding team that blew the ball back across the foul lines.
4. A ball's score is calculated at the point where it makes its farthest forward progress before being blown off the table toward the foul lines. (Example: If the batter blows the ball and it reaches the third base tape before being blown off the table, the batter is credited with a triple. The next batter may get a double, putting two people on base—one on second, and the previous batter on third. The next batter may hit a home run, which would score three runs.) Runs may only be forced in.
5. Outs are made by blowing the ball off the table before it reaches the first base line, so that it does not go back across the foul line.
6. Home runs are made by blowing the ball off the table on the opposite end from home plate, for whatever reason. Fielders need to be careful about where they're blowing the ball; they can unintentionally score for the opposing team.

(Contributed by Phil Blackwell, West Columbia, SC)

Bedlam Elimination

Just for fun, before you start, see if you can say the title of this game ten times real fast without making a mistake.

This game adds a new dimension to the game "Bedlam," described in an earlier volume of **Ideas**. Here's how to play: Divide your group into four equal teams. Each team gathers in different corners of the playing area. Lines are drawn on the floor to designate "safe" areas for each team.

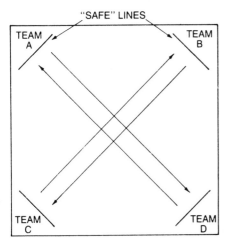

"SAFE" LINES

TEAM A   TEAM B

TEAM C   TEAM D

Each team member gets a flag like those used in flag football, which must hang free from his or her waist (in back). When a signal is given, the object of the game is to get to the opposite corner of the room without losing your flag. As you pass through the middle, you can grab one or more of the other three teams' flags, as long as you still have your own flag in your possession. Once your flag is gone, so are you. You're out of the game.

For best results, each team should have a different color flag. This will prevent players from replacing their own missing flag with a captured flag. Once all of the team's flags have been captured, the entire team is eliminated from the game. The game continues until only one team is left. Create your own variations of this game, with your own rules.

To add an extra dimension to the game, have the kids run across the playing area in a variety of different ways: on one foot, piggyback, on their hands and knees. In fact, such antics might be a good idea for slowing them down a bit to avoid injuries in the middle when everyone is moving in four different directions. (Contributions by Tom Beaumont, Portland, OR)

Birthday Shuffle

This game is similar to "Fruitbasket Upset." Have everyone sit in chairs in a big circle. There should be one extra person in the middle of the circle, without a chair. The leader calls out any three months of the year, and everyone in the circle whose birthday is in those months must get up and find a new chair. While they're scrambling to find a new seat, the extra person tries to sit in a vacant chair. This will leave a new person in the middle.

If most of the kids in the group are roughly the same age, the leader can call out a year, and all those who were born that year must switch chairs. If the leader calls out some other pre-designated word or phrase (like "Happy Birthday!"), then **everyone** must get up and change chairs. (Contributed by Randy Cooney, Scottsdale, AZ)

Blindman Bacon

This variation of "Steal the Bacon" works best when played in a circle. Two teams of equal size number off, so that there is a player on each team for each number. When a number is called, the corresponding player for each team puts on a blindfold. After hearing the whistle, both players proceed to the middle of the circle, and with the guidance of screams from teammates, they both try to locate a squirt gun lying in the middle of the circle. Once the squirt gun is found by a player, he or she then tries to squirt the other player before that player can escape out of the circle, behind his or her teammates. If the player with the squirt gun successfully shoots the other player, a point is awarded to his or her team. If the other player

escapes, his or her team is awarded the point.

The game is made more exciting if, after the blindfolds go on, the leader moves the squirt gun, making it more difficult to locate. (Contributed by David Rasmussen, Edmonds, WA)

Boundary Ball

Kids love dodge ball, but as the "kids" become young adults a game of dodge ball can become deadly. Thus, "Boundary Ball."

Divide into two teams. If your group combines junior and senior highers, make the competition fair by including kids of both age groups on

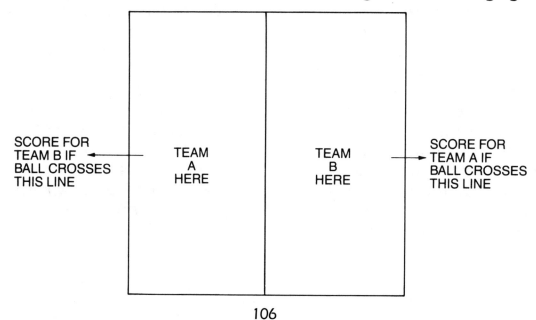

SCORE FOR TEAM B IF BALL CROSSES THIS LINE ←

TEAM A HERE

TEAM B HERE

→ SCORE FOR TEAM A IF BALL CROSSES THIS LINE

both teams.

For a playing field, choose an area with a square boundary. A gym, parking lot, or roped-off field all work well. Establish a center dividing line and have teams take their sides.

The game is played by rolling or bouncing the play ball back across the boundary behind the opposing team. The ball **must** be rolled or bounced. (This eliminates potential bodily injury inflicted by strong-armed throwers.) The game can be played up to 25 points (or whatever). A referee is helpful, and point judges can be a great help as well in determining whether a point is valid. Points are not valid unless the ball is rolled or bounced over the line. (Contributed by John Gilbert, Ravenna, OH)

Bunko

Here's a good party game that has been a favorite for many years. Twelve or more players (in multiples of four) are needed, plus lots of dice. Set up small card tables with four chairs at each, two apiece on opposite sides of the table. Tables should be numbered, with #1 designated as the head table.

Each player chooses a partner, who sits directly across the table from him or her. Players are given their own personal score cards which they take with them wherever they play. Each table is provided with three dice, a pencil, and a score card, which stay at that table.

The object of the game is to win more points in each round of play than the opposing team at your table, so that you and your partner can move toward the head table and attempt to stay there. Play begins when the head table rings the bell. Partners at the head table attempt to win 21 points in each round, while teams at all other tables win as many points as they can. When a team at the head table reaches 21 points, they ring the bell, and the round ends immediately at all tables.

To score: Players take turns throwing all three dice at once, with teams alternating turns. If the player rolls a 1 in the first round, his or her team earns a point, and the player rolls again. Every 1 rolled in that round earns a point; but if no 1's are rolled, a player on the other team takes a turn. Team scores are recorded on the table score cards.

When the head table rings the bell to end the first round, each team calculates its score for that round on the card. The first team at the head table to reach 21 wins the round at table #1; at all other tables, the team with the higher score wins. If there is a tie when the bell rings, teams roll again until someone wins ("sudden death").

The winning team at the head table remains there for the next round, while the losers go to the last table. Winners at each of the other tables advance to the next table (#3 winners go to #2, #2 to #1, and so on) while losers remain in their seats. Before the next round, players at the new table must swap partners; no player should have the same partner twice in a row.

In the second round (begun by the bell at the head table), players earn one point for their team with each 2 they roll. In the third round, 3's earn points, and so on. Rounds continue up through 6 and then back down to 1 again for a total of eleven rounds.

Points can also be earned by two other types of throws. A throw of three of a kind that are **not** the number for the round (e.g., three 4's in round two) earn six points, and the player keeps rolling. A throw of three of a kind that **are** the number

for the round (e.g., three 5's in round five) is called a Bunko, and earns an automatic 21 points (an automatic win at the head table). The player who throws a Bunko yells it out ("Bunko!") and records it on his or her personal score card. Personal cards should also record each game won by the player's team.

At the end of the game (eleven rounds) three prizes are awarded:
1. To the last team to win at the head table.
2. To the player with the most (personal) Bunkos.
3. To the player with the most wins.

PERSONAL SCORE CARD

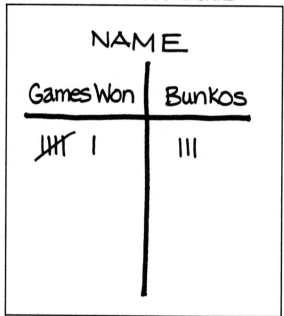

TABLE SCORE CARDS

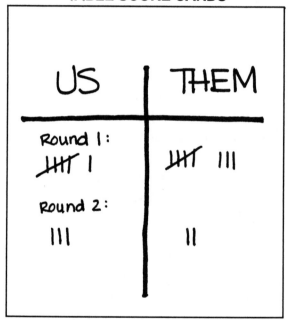

(Contributed by Dick Gibson, St. Petersburg, FL)

Buzzards and Eagles

This is a good game for camps, where you have a large group and play area. Divide players into four teams and give them names like "Buzzards," "Eagles," "Turkeys," and

other bird names. Then designate a headquarters for each team that is an equal distance from what will be called the "Central Nest." The object of the game is for each team to transport eggs from their headquarters to the Central Nest. Each egg is worth 1,000 points.

Give the teams an equal number of eggs—real ones or the plastic-colored eggs available at Easter. Each team will also need a "portable nest" —that is, a common bathroom plunger! Finally, every player needs a feather or a strip of cloth which is tucked into the waist as in flag football. Don't allow kids to tie them to their jeans or tuck them in so far that they're hidden.

Once each team has their eggs at their own headquarters, they may on your signal begin transporting them to the Central Nest, but only in the "portable nest"—no other way. Obviously, several trips back and forth will be required for each team, since the portable nest will only hold a few eggs.

Players may try to keep other teams from transporting their eggs by "plucking" them—that is, by pulling their flags, flag football style. Anyone who is plucked must report to the bird hospital and see the vet for five minutes before returning to play.

If players pluck someone who is carrying a portable nest with eggs, they can take those eggs to their own headquarters and use them to score points for their team. However, players cannot steal another team's

portable nest or break it. Players are also forbidden to enter another team's headquarters. To keep this game from getting too rough, you should rule out tackling or holding players down in order to pluck them.

Besides the score for eggs, you can award a team additional points each time they pluck someone. Just have the plucker and the "pluckee" report in.

If you're at camp with a large staff of counselors, designate them as "buzzards," whose only job is to run around plucking "eagles" and to make them drop their eggs as they run for the Central Nest. In this case, there would be only two teams.

(Contributed by Teen Valley Ranch, Plumtreee, NC)

Chewing Gum Relay

This is a relay race for two or more teams using sticks of chewing gum, work gloves, and shopping bags. Individual sticks of gum (wrapped)

are placed inside the shopping bags, and each team is given a pair of work gloves. The idea is to put on the gloves, run down to the bag, pull out a piece of gum, unwrap it and chew it (with the gloves on), run back, and then pass the gloves to the next person. The team that finishes first is the winner. (Contributed by Jeffrey Collins, Lexington, MA)

Commercial Squirts

Have the group sit in a circle and give one person a squirt gun. Ask that person to fill in the blank or identify the product advertised in a quote from a TV commercial in the list below. If the player knows the answer, he or she gets to squirt the people sitting on either side (once each). If not, the squirt gun is passed on to the next person, and the quote is repeated. If no one gets a quote right after three tries, go on to another quote. Add others to the list if you like.

"It's not a car, it's a _____." (VW)
"Double your pleasure with _____." (Doublemint gum)
"How do you spell relief?" _____ (R-O-L-A-I-D-S)
"It's a good time for the great taste of _____." (McDonald's)
"Brush your breath with _____." (Dentyne)

"Oh what a feeling, _____!" (Toyota)
"Those O's will help keep you on your toes." _____ (Cheerios)
"Melts in your mouth, not in your hands." _____ (M & M's)
"Have you driven a _____ lately?" (Ford)
"Who said you can't take it with you?" _____ (Pepto Bismol)
"It couldn't be anything else but _____." (Maxwell House Coffee)
"Nothing beats a great pair of _____." (L'eggs)
"You work hard, you need _____." (Right Guard)
"The choice of a new generation." _____ (Pepsi)
"Like a good neighbor, _____ is there." (State Farm)
"Trust the _____ touch." (Midas)

Another variation is to play using questions from a trivia game. (Contributed by Ed McClellan, Cross Plains, TN)

Dice Dive

Here's a wild living room game for small groups. For larger groups, divide into smaller groups and get several games going at once.

Have players sit in a circle and number off 1–2–1–2 so that every other player is on the opposite team. Place a pile of marbles in one big mass on the floor, in the center of the circle of kids. There should be about six to ten marbles per player.

Begin with any player. He or she throws a pair of dice onto the floor. If the total is **even**, nothing happens. But if the total is odd, everyone must dive for the marbles and grab as many as possible until all of them are gone. Points are totaled (one point for each marble grabbed by your team), and the marbles are returned to the pile.

Now a player on the opposing team throws the dice. Turns alternate between team members this way until everyone has had a chance to throw. Then the game is over, and the team with the biggest total wins.

If anyone grabs the marbles when the dice throw is **even** (it will happen frequently), all marbles grabbed must be deducted from the offending team's total at that point. The game gets rather frantic as players try to anticipate the roll of the dice, so it's a good idea to have players clip their fingernails before the game to avoid scratches. Also, it's a good idea to draw a line around the marbles, and have everyone stay behind that line until the dice hit the floor. (Contributed by Phil Blackwell, West Columbia, SC)

The Dough-Tongue Shuffle

This is a relay game in which the young people are divided into two equal groups. Each group lines up, with players one behind the other. Then the first person in each line is given a large donut (preferably plain). On a signal, the first person in each group must run up to and around a given obstacle while holding the donut by sticking his or her tongue through its hole—no hands allowed. (This usually requires that the head be tilted back and the tongue pointed upward.) After running around the obstacle, the runners must go to a designated area where a judge is waiting. Then each runner must eat his or her donut. The donut must be completely eaten (to the satisfaction of the judge) before the runner can receive in his or her **hand** another donut from the judge. The runner then carries this second donut to the next person in the relay line. The first runner places the donut in position on the next runner's tongue, and the relay continues. The first team to complete the relay by running all its members shouts "THE DOUGH-TONGUE SHUFFLE!" and wins. (Contributed by Joe Harvey, Fort Myers, FL)

Every Second Counts

This game is based on the T.V. show of the same name. Divide the group into three teams, and allow the teams to come up with a good team name. You'll need a scorekeeper and a blackboard as a scoreboard. The object of the first part of the game is to accumulate seconds by answering questions correctly. The accumulated seconds are then used in the second part of the game.

To begin, each team sends up one person to be on a "panel." One at a time, these panelists must answer a series of questions asked by the master of ceremonies. Every correct answer is worth two seconds to the team of the player who is answering. If the player answers incorrectly, then that player is "frozen out" for the remainder of that series of questions, and the next panel member gets a try.

After each series of questions on a given topic, the panelists change so that every team member gets a chance to participate.

Here are some sample questions. Make up your own, as easy or as difficult as you choose:

1. **NEW TESTAMENT OR OLD TESTAMENT**
   Tell whether the following books are in the New Testament or Old Testament. Answer **New Testament** or **Old Testament**.

Matthew	Genesis	Hosea
I Samuel	Revelation	Ruth
Ezekiel	Titus	Psalms
Jude	Exodus	Proverbs

2. **BIBLE NAME OR MADE-UP NAME**
   Many Bible characters had strange and unusual names. Tell which of the following are real Bible names and which are made-up names.

Isaiah	Caiphas	Porcelona
Uzayuh	Syntyche	Naaman
Mephibosheth	Metamucil	Neawomen
Sapphira	Rahab	Adarondak

3. **PAUL OR OTHERS**
   Many of the books of the New Testament were written by the Apostle Paul. Tell which of the following were written by Paul, and which were not. Answer **Paul** or **other**.

Acts	John	I Peter
Galatians	I Thessalonians	I Corinthians
Ephesians	Revelation	Titus
Romans	Philippians	Colossians

4. **LOVERS OR ENEMIES**
   The Bible is filled with many famous pairs. Tell which of the following pairs were lovers or enemies. Answer **lovers** or **enemies**.

Adam and Eve   Jezebel and Ahab   Jeroboam and Rehoboam
David and Goliath   Elijah and Jezebel   Aquilla and Priscilla
Samson and Delilah   Ruth and Boaz   Rebekah and Jacob
Mary and Joseph   God and the Devil   Cain and Abel

5. **JESUS**

Tell which of the following facts about Jesus are true and which were made up. Answer **true** or **false**.

Born in Jerusalem
Born of a virgin
Born in Bethlehem
Baptized as an infant
Raised from the dead
Lived on earth 40 days after His resurrection
Made a living as a shepherd
Was betrayed by Judas
Taught in the temple at age 12
Was merely a mortal man
Was man and God
Crucified in Nazareth

During the second part of the game, each team is given a pad and pencil. In their alloted time (the total number of seconds they have accumulated from the first part of the game), they are to list as many books of the Bible as they can. All three teams should do this simultaneously, stopping when their time runs out (timekeepers can stop them). The winning team is the team with the most books of the Bible on their list. (Contributed by John Gates, Welcome, NC)

Family Confusion Game

Here's a great game for family events when you want to get parents and kids interacting and having fun. Distribute photocopies of the game sheet on the next page and have extra pencils ready for those who need them. Then give the group a designated amount of time to complete the activities described. You may want to talk about the results afterward. (Contributed by David C. Wright, Vienna, VA)

Find Me If You Can

This game is simply a version of indoors "Hide-and-Seek," with one important difference: You play it at night in the dark.

Divide into two teams of equal size, called hiders and seekers. Specify whether hiders are to hide individually, in pairs, or in threes (alternate to make it more interesting). Then give them three

FAMILY CONFUSION!

1. The Woo-Woo Mixer
To find five others who were born in the same quarter of the year as you, identify yourself by making the appropriate sound as indicated below:

January/February/March: "Woo!"

April/May/June: "Woo-woo!"

July/August/September: "Woo-woo-woo!"

October/November/December: "Woo-woo-woo-woo!"

After all the folks in your group have found one another, hold hands, make a circle, and play "Ring Around the Rosies." Then have one of your group members initial here: _____.

2. Family Vacation
Form a group with three other people so that it includes a dad, a mom, and two kids. Create a "train" at one end of the room, each person with his or her hands on the hips of the person in front, and with "Dad" at the head of the line. He leads the train across the room, zig-zagging back and forth from one end to the other. In the meantime, the kids should complain about how long it's taking, ask when they'll get there, and demand a stop for food or the bathroom. Then have your other vacationers initial here:

_____ _____ _____.

3. Family Cooperation
Find any two other people. Sit on the floor back to back and with arms linked. In this position, the three of you must attempt to stand up together. After you've been successful, have a group member initial here: _____.

4. Sneak a Date (kids only)
Walk across the room with a member of the opposite sex without being spotted by your parents. If they spot you, you must try again later. Have your "date" initial here: _____.

5. Family Dinner Time
Form a group of five that includes both parents and kids (at least one of each). Sing together the commercial jingles for three or more fast food restaurants. Have a group member initial here: _____.

6. Family Communication Practice
Find a kid if you're a parent, or a parent if you're a kid, and one extra person with a watch that times seconds. Cover your ears, face your "parent" or "child," and shout your favorite kid or parent lines for a full ten seconds. Sample kid lines: "You never listen to me!" "All my friends get to do it!" "You don't trust me!" Sample parent lines: "When I was your age ..." "I don't care who does it!" "As long as you're living under my roof ..." Have the time keeper initial here: _____.

minutes to hide while the seekers are secluded in a room behind closed doors. You might want to declare certain areas off-limits in a church building, like the pastor's study, the baptismal font, or the oven in the kitchen!

When hiding time is up, turn off all the lights and let the seekers loose. Anyone found must go to the room where the seekers were secluded.

Give the seekers a maximum of 15 minutes; when time is up, turn on all the lights and end the round, even if not everyone has been found. Then have the teams switch roles. Play as many rounds as you like. The winning team is the one that finds the most players of the opposite team (total of all rounds). (Contributed by Vernon Edington, Manchester, TN)

Food, Glorious Food

Here's another version of the "Confusion Game," with a food theme. Use it at your next banquet or food event. It could also be used as part of a "Planned Famine" or other food/hunger awareness service project. (Contributed by Daniel Harvey, Portland, OR)

FOOD, GLORIOUS FOOD

1. Find two other people born in your same group of months by making the appropriate sound of your food group.

Jan/Feb/Mar	—BREAD	—"I've got the eaties for my Wheaties!" (sung)
Apr/May/June	—MEAT	—"Oink, oink, oink!"
July/Aug/Sept	—VEGETABLES	—Shout the name of your least favorite vegetable, e.g., "Beets, Beets, Beets!"
Oct/Nov/Dec	—DAIRY	—"Moo!"

2. Once you have formed your group of three, together name six edible objects that begin with the letter "S." Have one of the group initial here: _____

3. Find a partner from somewhere in the room and quickly shout together "Smorgasbords are disgusting!" seven times. Have your partner initial here: _____

4. Locate someone who likes liver and have him or her initial here: _____ (gag!)

5. Grab a new partner and count each other's teeth. Write the # of teeth your partner has here _____ and have him or her initial here: _____

6. Say to a new partner you don't know the "two all-beef patties, special sauce, lettuce, cheese, pickles, onions on a sesame seed bun" line three times. Have that person initial here: _____

7. Get another partner and see if you can "pinch an inch." If you can, tell that person he or she should eat more Special K.

8. Have someone lift you off the ground and guess your weight. If the person guesses too low, wink at him or her. If the person guesses too high—slap him or her. Initial here: _____

French Charades

This game is played like "Elephant Pantomime" in **Ideas #1–4**, but since you don't restrict the act to any one theme, it can be played as often as you like with the same group. Divide into teams of five to seven people. Have the members of one team leave the room while the others think of a situation which can be acted out without words. Then bring in one person from the team that was sent out of the room. Explain the situation he or she will be acting out.

Now bring in a second person from that team. Without saying a word, Person #1 must act out the assigned plot for Person #2. Person #2 may or may not understand the charade, but he or she must subsequently act out the same situation for a third member of the team. Person #3 performs the charade for Person #4, and so on. The last person must guess the original story line.

Remember, all this is done in complete silence. Even the simplest charade can undergo a thorough metamorphosis after being passed down several times. If the last person cannot guess the charade, Person #1 should perform it again and let the last person guess once more.

Here are some classic French Charade situations to spur your creativity.

Charade 1:

You are a high school beauty pageant contestant, anxiously awaiting the announcement of the winner. Suddenly, you hear your name! You now step forward to receive your crown and roses. Then comes your victory walk down the aisle. As you proceed down the aisle, waving to the crowd, you encounter several misfortunes. First, you are allergic to roses so you begin to sneeze, but you keep on going, waving and sneezing to the crowd. Then, on the way back up the aisle, your high heel breaks and you finish the walk with one heel missing!

Charade 2:

You are a pregnant mama bird about to give birth! You must fly around the room gathering materials for your nest. Once you make your nest, you lay your egg. Then finish the charade by hatching the egg and finding a worm to feed your new baby.

French Charades works best with older teens and college-age groups.

(Contributed by Teen Valley Ranch, Plumtree, NC)

Frisbee Attack

Here's an exciting new version of Frisbee Tag. To play, you'll need a playing area with a radius of about 40 feet. The game is best played with five to ten players. One person is chosen to be "It," and another is chosen to be the "Frisbee Thrower." "It" is free to move around, while the Frisbee Thrower must stand in the middle of the bounded area, preferably on a chair or table. You will also need at least three Frisbees (or other flying discs).

The object of the game is for "It" to get the other players out by hitting them with a Frisbee. As the game begins, "It" has all the Frisbees in his or her possession, and tries to hit the other players with them. If a player is hit, he or she is "frozen" and can no longer move. If "It" misses, the Frisbee can be captured by anyone who wants to run after it. When a Frisbee is captured, the player who has it can try to get it to the Frisbee Thrower in the middle of the field, either by carrying it or throwing it. This is important, because only the Frisbee Thrower is able to "unfreeze" players who have been frozen by "It." The Frisbee Thrower accomplishes this by throwing a Frisbee to one of the frozen players, who must catch it before it hits the ground. In catching the Frisbee, the frozen player may only move one foot. If he or she moves both feet, the throw is invalid. If the player

becomes "unfrozen," he or she may give the Frisbee back to the Frisbee Thrower to release another frozen player.

Meanwhile, "It" is still scrambling around trying to hit players with Frisbees, intercept captured Frisbees, and so on. The game ends when "It" has frozen everyone and the Frisbee Thrower has no more Frisbees to throw. As more players are added, more "Its" can also be added. It's not too difficult to find the right balance so that the competition stays even.

Allow everyone a chance to be "It," and give a prize to the one who can freeze everyone in the game in the shortest time. You might want to set a time limit for each "It." (Contributed by Harold Atterlei and Dan Young, Lake Oswego, OR)

Frisbee Bowling

A number of people can play this game, and very little skill is required. To set up, all you need is a table, ten paper cups, and three Frisbees (flying discs). The cups are stacked in a pyramid several inches away from the far edge of the table (see photo). From a distance of about 20 feet, each player gets three attempts to knock as many of the cups as possible onto the floor, by hitting them with a Frisbee.

Each cup is worth one point. You can call each round a frame as in regular bowling, with a game consisting of as many frames as you like. If more than five people are playing, keep a pencil and paper handy to keep track of the score. To keep the game moving, players can take turns throwing the Frisbees, retrieving them, and restacking the paper cups. (Contributed by Deborah Cusson and Sean Mahar, Monson, MA)

Fruit Basket Fly-By

In this game, each team has two baskets, one filled with fruit at one end of the room, and the other empty at the other end of the room. Teams must compete to see who can be first to get all the fruit from one basket to the other. The trick, however, is that the fruit can only be transported by "fruit flies" who fly by having their teammates carry them aloft and over a barrier of chairs or tables across the middle of the room.

Each team divides into halves. Then one-half goes to the side of the room with the full basket, and one-half to the side with the empty one. On a signal, one player from each team on the side with the full basket becomes a "fly." They must tuck a piece of fruit under their chins,

118

hold their arms out like wings, and be carried by their teammates up to a row of chairs or tables which separate them from the other side. There, the fly is carefully passed to the other half of the team waiting on the far side of the barrier. (After passing the fly over, carriers can crawl under or climb over the barrier to help carry the fly on the other side as well.)

Teammates on the other side then carry the fly to the empty basket, into which he or she drops the piece of fruit. The fly is let down, and immediately a new fly must be chosen to carry another piece of fruit, and so on until all the fruit has been transported. If necessary, after all the players have served as flies, some can repeat the role. If a piece of fruit is dropped en route, the fly must "land," pick it up, tuck it under his or her chin, and take off again as before. Team to complete the task first is the winner. (Contributed by Lee Strawhun, Piqua, OH)

Gag-A-Napkin

Here's a "quickie," just for fun. This game will really liven up even the most boring banquet. Each person opens up a paper napkin and places a corner of it on his or her tongue. Then have a race to see who gets the complete napkin in their mouth first. (Contributed by Mark A. Nelessen, New London, WI)

Garbage Bag Ball

For this game, take a large plastic garbage bag and fill it full of balloons (blown up). Tie it with a twist-tie. You now have a "garbage bag ball." Here's an exciting game that makes good use of it:

Have all but ten of the kids form a large circle on their knees. The remaining ten kids then form a "pinwheel" formation in the center of the circle, lying on their backs, heads toward the center. Everyone should have their shoes off for best results.

The garbage bag ball is then tossed into the circle. The object is for the kids on their backs to kick or hit the ball out of the circle, over the heads of the kids in the outer circle. The outer circle tries to keep it in play. If the ball is kicked over a player's head in the outer circle, then he or she must take the person's place in the inner circle who kicked it. Play for as long as you wish. (Contributed by David Washburn, Brockport, NY)

Grab & Guess

Give each person a pencil and sheet of paper numbered 1 through 30. Have someone stand behind a blanket hung up to form a curtain, with a bag that contains the items listed below. That person will take one item out at a time and allow the rest of the group to take turns (five seconds only) touching the object with their hands. No one, however, is allowed to see the items behind the curtain. After each object is touched, players return to their seats and write down what they think the object is. The player with the most correct guesses wins.

1. flashcube
2. dime
3. key
4. glass
5. coffee stirrer
6. pen
7. cassette tape
8. crayon
9. paper clip
10. spoon
11. stuffed animal
12. guitar pick
13. comb
14. envelope
15. rubber band
16. Band-Aid
17. spool of thread
18. postage stamp
19. billiard chalk
20. calculator
21. light bulb
22. bobby pin
23. safety pin
24. extension cord
25. flashlight battery
26. clock or watch
27. toy car
28. bagel
29. thimble
30. cotton ball

(Contributed by Valerie Stoop, Fleetwood, PA)

The Great Pew Race

If your church has bench-type pews in the main building, here's a way to put them to good use.

Divide your group into small teams of three or four kids each. Have them all gather at one end or the other of the church (whichever has the most room). On signal, the kids all (at once) dive under the first pew, and must crawl all the way to the other end of the church and back, under the pews.

The first team to have all its players return is the winner. (Contributed by Tracey Werner, Metmora, IL)

Improved "Human Foosball"

The game "Human Foosball" (as described in **Ideas #32**) is much better controlled if everyone in a given line is required to join arms as shown in this illustration:

This forces each line to act (as is the case in genuine "Foosball") as a unit. It also makes it harder for players to break the rules (such as stepping outside the lines). (Contributed by Steve Perisho, Boise, ID)

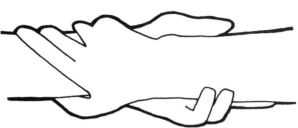

Indoor Murderball

Here's an indoor game for two teams. You need at least five on a team, but you can play with a lot more, depending on the size of the room you have. You need a room that is nearly indestructable, with space to run.

Two teams of equal size line up

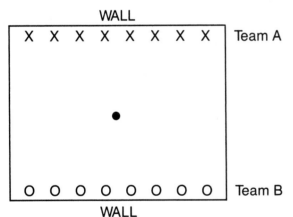

on opposite walls, about 3' from the wall. Team members then number off.

A ball is placed in the middle of the room. (Any large ball will work.) The leader calls out a number, and the two players with that number (one from each team) run out to the middle and try to hit the opposite team's wall with the ball. The team standing in front of the wall tries to prevent that from happening.

Players attempt to get the ball to its goal any way they can—carrying it across, throwing, kicking, rolling, whatever. Anything is legal. (Contributed by Ralph Gustafson, Green Bay, WI)

Indoor Obstacle Course

This relay game is best played by two or more teams. Because of the time necessary to complete the obstacle course, it's best to limit each team to six players or less.

Set up the course as shown in the diagram. Each player is given a soda straw. On the signal to begin, the first player from each team goes to the starting position to pick up one of five kernels of corn from a paper plate. The only way they can move the corn, however, is by sucking on the straw and creating a vacuum that holds the kernel while they walk over to a foam cup on the near side of a table five feet away. Once they reach the cup, they drop the kernel in it and go back for the next one, continuing until all the kernels have been moved. If a corn is dropped en route, the player may pick it up again (using the same method) and continue.

Once all five kernels are in the cup, players must blow the cup across the table (the wider the table, the better) and make it land in a box placed on the floor underneath the table's far edge. If the cup or any of the corn misses the box, the cup must be refilled by a designated assistant from the player's team and then replaced on the table's edge. The player keeps trying until the cup and corn all fall into the box at once.

Next, players crawl under the table, grab a jump rope on the other side, and jump with it over to a spot 20 feet away, where a pile of uninflated balloons is waiting. They must blow up one balloon till it bursts, then run to a tape mark on the floor five feet away (see the diagram). There they must pick up two plastic rings from the floor and toss them around a can three feet away. (Empty bread crumb cans work well for this.) When the players have made a successful toss with both rings, they crawl back under the table and tag the next person (and probably collapse). The first team to complete the relay wins.

The game is as much fun to watch as it is to play, so kids who don't

want to run the course may enjoy acting as assistants. Besides helping out with unsuccessful cup-blowing attempts, the assistants must also replace the cup on the table and the corn on the plate after the player has succeeded in that part of the relay.

As a variation you can use a stopwatch and allow individual players to compete against the clock. (Contributed by June L. Becker, Reading PA)

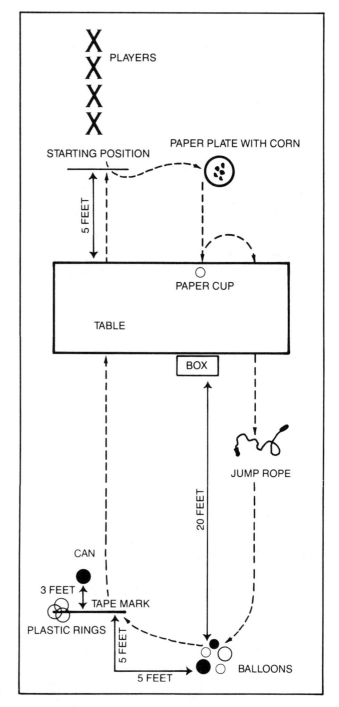

Innertube Baseball

Similar to softball, this game utilizes an innertube. The "batter" picks up the innertube at home plate and rotates seven times, heaving the innertube into the field on the seventh rotation. The batter's team may count out loud as the batter rotates to help him or her keep track of when to release the tube. Although there are three bases as in softball, there is no out of bounds, so the innertube may be released in any direction once seven rotations have been completed.

Players are only "out" when tagged with the innertube. There are no force outs or "pop flies." Defensive players may tag a base runner by touching the runner with the tube or throwing the tube at the runner. Any time the base runner comes in contact with the tube, he is out (unless he is on base, of course).

There is one penalty in this game called "jamming." Jamming occurs when a defensive player tries to "cream" a base runner with the tube (unnecessary roughness). This is a judgment call on the part of the umpire. Award the offended team with a run and allow the base runner to advance to the closest base. Without this rule some players will attempt to start another game called "Maul Ball" which is not recommended for most amateur Innertube Baseball players.

The last rule is: the umpire can add or subtract any rules at any time to make the game fun and exciting. All umpire rulings are final unless the umpire receives sufficient financial reimbursement, thus influencing the outcome of the game.

If you wish, have several size innertubes available so kids can choose a tube appropriate for their size. You may wish to have a large tube for guys, a small tube for girls. (Contributed by Steve Smoker, Morehead, NC)

Jello Bob

This game is very messy, but lots of fun to watch. Make a big batch of jello in a large 10- to 15-gallon container. Strawberry or cherry works best. After the jello has a chance to set a little bit, put several whole strawberries in it.

Now, choose some volunteers to "bob" for strawberries. Time each contestant with a stopwatch. The person with the best time wins; and, of course, the prize is a free bowl of jello. For added fun, make sure there is one less strawberry in the pot than there are contestants—but don't let the contestants know! (Contributed by Thomas Robertson, Honesdale, PA)

License Plates

Here's a take-off on a game most folks have played while traveling in a car. List on a blackboard, overhead, or handout the following state nicknames (and others you may know) from auto license plates. Then have your group divide up into teams to identify the correct state for each name. The team that correctly identifies the most states wins the game. You can play the game several times by only using ten states at a time. If the game seems too difficult for your age group, provide the state names as well (out of order) and make it a matching game. (Contributed by Bill Williamson, Los Angeles, CA)

First In Flight	(North Carolina)	Land of Lincoln	(Illinois)
The Empire State	(New York)	The Sunflower State	(Kansas)
The Aloha State	(Hawaii)	The Great Lake State	· (Michigan)
The Grand Canyon State	(Arizona)	The Bluegrass State	(Kentucky)
The Keystone State	(Pennsylvania)	The Silver State	(Nevada)
Land of Opportunity	(Arkansas)	The Bay State	(Massachusetts)
The Vacation State	(Maine)	Land of 10,000 Lakes	(Minnesota)
The Centennial State	(Colorado)	The Magnolia State	(Mississippi)
The Volunteer State	(Tennessee)	The Show-Me State	(Missouri)
The Constitution State	(Connecticut)	The Ocean State	(Rhode Island)
The Land of Enchantment	(New Mexico)	The Garden State	(New Jersey)
First State	(Delaware)	The Lone Star State	(Texas)
The Golden State	(California)	The Peach State	(Georgia)
The Hoosier State	(Indiana)	The Heart of Dixie	(Alabama)
The Sportsman's State	(Louisiana)	The Sunshine State	(Florida)
The Hawkeye State	(Iowa)	America's Dairyland	(Wisconsin)

Life-Size Bible Trivia Pursuit

Here's a good youth group version of the popular board game "Trivial Pursuit." The object is to collect all the pieces of the "cross" (or any other substitute for the "pie" in "Trivial Pursuit") and to return to the starting point successfully. Pieces of the cross are collected when a player lands on a space in the playing area that has a cross marked on it, and answers a question correctly.

There should be no more than four players in the game at once. So the best way to play is to have the group divide into four equal teams, and appoint one team member to be their representative in the game. The team as a whole tries to come up with the correct answers to the questions. There should be one referee, who asks the questions.

The playing area should be laid out on the floor, using sheets of construction paper taped down to form the game board. The papers should be large enough for a player to stand on. Category titles and crosses can be written on them.

Alternate categories along the board, and remember to include "roll again" spaces. Some suggested categories are Old Testament facts, New Testament facts, the life of Christ, the letters of Paul, men of the Bible, women of the Bible. You will need to prepare 20 to 25 questions per category before the game begins. There are several Bible trivia games on the market with questions that can be used, or you can get good Bible questions from Bible quiz books. Or, of course, you can just write your own questions.

You will also need a large die for the teams to roll in order to determine moves. A large foam die from a toy store or novelty shop would work great. You can also

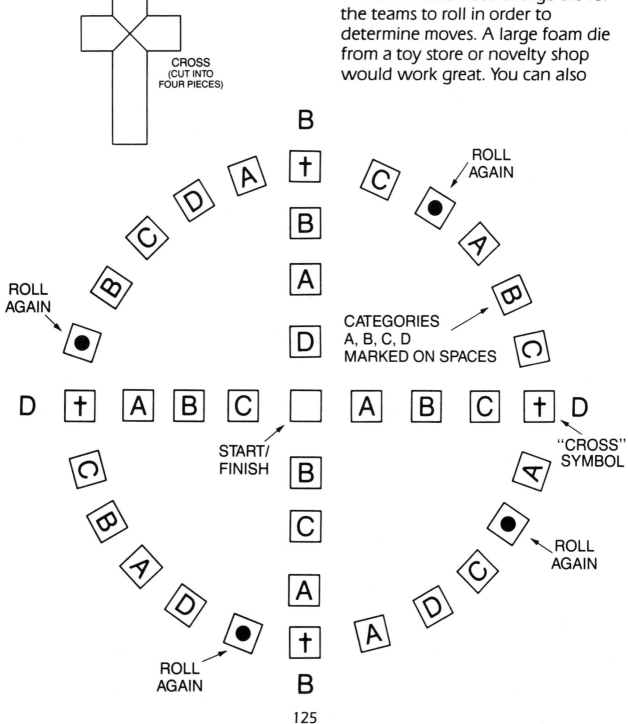

CROSS
(CUT INTO
FOUR PIECES)

ROLL
AGAIN

ROLL
AGAIN

CATEGORIES
A, B, C, D
MARKED ON SPACES

START/
FINISH

"CROSS"
SYMBOL

ROLL
AGAIN

ROLL
AGAIN

make your own using a square box or a block of styrofoam.

To play: Choose your teams, and have each team select the player who will represent them on the game board. Each team is responsible for providing answers, rolling the die, and instructing their player how to move on the board. Only the player on the board can give the official answer to the referee; therefore, the team must arrive at a consensus and communicate their answer to their player. In addition, the player cannot move on the board unless the team tells him or her where to go. When the player lands on a space marked with a category, the referee will ask the team a question from that category. The team has 30 seconds to come up with the correct answer and to communicate it to their player, who gives the answer to the referee. The referee can have a timer on hand to make sure that the time limits are kept. If an answer is correct, the team rolls again; if not, the next team rolls.

When a team has collected all the pieces of the cross, they move the player to the center space by rolling the die. The player can only enter the center by an exact roll. The team must continue to answer the questions as in normal play until the player reaches the center. Once a player has landed in the center space, the opposing team(s) will choose one of the available topics from which the referee must ask that player a question. If the question is answered correctly, the team wins; but if not, the player remains in the center until it is his or her team's turn again and another question is asked. Play continues until someone wins.

This is a great way to test kids on their Bible knowledge and to provide them with a fun way to learn Bible facts. It also emphasizes teamwork, making it a good group-building activity. This version of "Trivial Pursuit" can be played within an hour, assuming that the questions are not too difficult. (Contributed by Dr. Gary D. Cecil, Glenshaw, PA)

Lottery Volleyball

This off-beat brand of volleyball adds as a special element—the thrill of the unexpected. Divide into teams and position players as in conventional volleyball. The referee should stand a few feet out of bounds near mid-court with a container of "lottery tickets" numbered 1 through 9 (have several of each number, and mix them up so that they can be drawn at random).

As the server serves, the referee draws out a ticket and calls out the number. The team receiving the ball must hit the ball that number of times (no more, no less) before returning it over the net. If they are successful, the serving team must do the same. Play continues requiring the same number of hits per play until a team fails. On the serve for the next round, a second ticket is drawn out and read, and play continues as before according to the number of hits required by the new ticket. Excitement will build on each play as team members count out hits, and you'll especially enjoy the groans when the referee calls out the dreaded number 1.

All other conventional volleyball rules prevail, but you might want to liven things up by using water balloons instead of a ball, or by playing flamingo style (on one leg). (Contributed by Mark A. Hahlen, Louisville, KY)

Mega Volleyball

Here's how to play volleyball with an extra-large group (24 players or more at a time). You need three volleyball nets, four standards, string or lime (tape for indoors) to mark the boundaries, two volleyballs, and a ref.

Place one pole in the center and the other three around it, so that the nets are stretched out from the center like spokes in a wheel (see the diagram). Make the boundary a circle so that each segment of the court is shaped like a pie slice (the three sections should be equal).

Play is similar to regular volleyball, except that the ball is not returned across the net to the serving team. Instead, it advances to the third team, who sends it on to the first team, thus moving either clockwise or counterclockwise around the circle. In the diagram shown, A serves to B, who volleys to C, who must get the ball back to A, and so on. To keep the game fun, don't allow spikes. For added excitement, get two balls going at once!

As in the regular game, errors include misses; out-of-bound volleys; more than three contacts with the ball by the same team before it crosses the net; and more than one contact with the ball in immediate succession by the same player. Scoring, however, is different from regular play in that 25 points are given for every **error**. Thus the team with the **lowest** score wins.

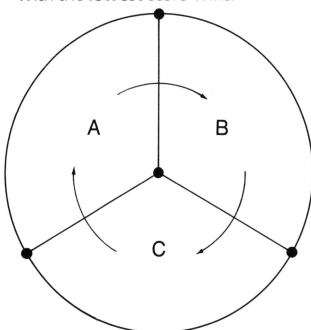

(Contributed by Ed Weaver, Ontario, OR)

Mega-Bar Volleyball

This is a good variation on conventional volleyball to prevent an "I'm too cool to play" attitude.

Purchase about six large candy bars or some other favorite munchie. Display these where teams can see them as they play.

Form two teams and play as usual, but with two exceptions. First, when you rotate, move the server out of the game and move a new player in next to him or her. Second, award a mega-bar to any **server** who fulfills one of the following requirements:

1. Serves five points in a row.
2. Serves two aces in a row (an ace is when no one else touches the ball).
3. Serves the final point.

Play 11-point games so that excitement about the last point builds more quickly. Kids usually can't wait to get a chance to serve. (Contributed by Todd Capen, Lodi, CA)

Missionary

In this game, each team must guide its "missionary" safely through a field of "headhunters" (the other team). You'll need to divide into two teams of equal size.

The first team, the missionaries, choose one of their members to travel through a dangerous "mission field." That player must put a paper bag over his or her head and move across the playing field from a starting line to a finish line while trying to avoid being touched by any of the headhunters. Teammates guide the missionary across the field by shouting directions to him or her, but they must coordinate the directions and shout them in unison to avoid confusion. Teammates cannot walk with the missionary.

Meanwhile, the other team, the headhunters, spread out over the playing field at random. They will attempt to impede the progress of the "missionary" by touching him or her. They cannot, however, move from their original positions on the field, except **once** during each round, when they may take three giant steps in any direction. But any contact with the missionary must be made while a headhunter is standing still, so these steps must be planned carefully. The headhunters may also shout false instructions to the missionary, but silence is often a better strategy.

Each team has one chance to guide a missionary and one chance to be headhunters. The missionary is timed from the starting line to the finish line, with a penalty of 20 seconds added for every contact with a headhunter. The team with the lowest time wins. (Contributed by Ray Wilson, Watertown, SD)

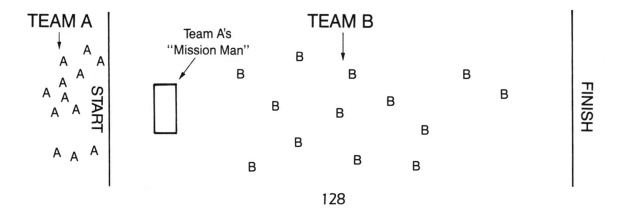

128

Musical Sponge

This game is just like musical chairs, but with a few minor changes. There should be the same number of chairs in the game as there are players. As the players circle the chairs, they hold onto the shoulders of the person in front of them. They are all blindfolded.

Before the music stops, the leader places a wet sponge on one of the chairs. The unfortunate player who sits on the wet sponge when the music stops (or when the whistle blows) is out. (Contributed by David Rasmussen, Edmonds, WA)

Paper Chase

This one's for warm weather. Two people are chosen (or volunteer) to be chased by the rest of the group. They are given an old catalog and sent out from a designated starting place **after dark**. These two leave a page of the catalog on the ground every 20 to 30 feet as a trail for their pursuers. Then, 30 minutes after they begin, they hide in the general vicinity of the last piece of paper.

After a 15-minute head start by the pair, the paper chasers set out from the appointed starting place with flashlights in hand. They follow the trail of paper (picking up each one) until they come to the last sheet. This may take place an hour or two later, because the two they're looking for have run as quickly as they could while the group moves much slower along the typical trail through weeds, woods, cemetery, barn lots, creeks—any and everywhere.

Once the pursuers find the last piece, they must hunt for their hidden friends. This isn't as easy as it may sound—in fact, they may not be able to find them at all. If the two aren't located by a prearranged time, they must come back to the church building or starting place to rendezvous with the paper chasers. (Contributed by Ron Payne, Ingraham, IL)

Parliff

This is a gym game for 16 or more kids, played with a basketball. One team spreads out across the court while the other goes up to "bat" next to one wall of the gym. The batter takes the ball and either punts or throws it in any direction (no boundaries). Immediately he or she then runs to the far wall, touches it, and runs back to touch the "home" wall. Meanwhile, the team in the "field" is chasing down the ball and passing it to a designated shooter under the goal next to their own home wall.

If the shooter can make the basket before the batter touches the home wall, the batter is out. If the batter makes it home first, his or her team wins a point for the "run." Allow three outs, and then the opposing team is up. Highest score after nine innings wins. (Contributed by Chris Thompson, Birmington, AL)

People Trivia

To help your group get better acquainted with one another, try this variation of the popular trivia games. Distribute a questionnaire to your kids with questions they must answer about themselves. Make the questions correspond to the categories in the trivia game you plan to use. For example, for "Entertainment" you can ask for the person's favorite TV show; for history, you can ask for his or her birthplace. Also use miscellaneous questions such as "What was the most embarrassing moment of your life?"

Next, prepare question cards for the game that combine the "official" questions with questions about your group members, such as "Who was born in Hogsback Mountain, Montana?" "Whose favorite TV show is Lawrence Welk?"

Play the game otherwise as usual—and prepare for some fascinating "trivial" revelations about your group. (Contributed by Bob Machovec, Chesterland, OH)

Pew Races

A simple but fun game for the church sanctuary. Have all the contestants sit along the middle pew (equal distance from front and back). Give each one a penny, which they flip on signal. Whoever gets heads goes forward a row; those with tails go back a row. Play continues in this way, as quickly as players want to move, but they **must** flip in order to move each time. Players who reach the back row stay there until they get heads. The winner is the first one to reach the front row and **then** get heads. You may want to stipulate that players must either crawl under

the pews or walk around them. (Contributed by Randy Wheeler, Colorado Springs, CO)

Pie Tin Toss

For this game, you will need to secure the use of six high hurdles, like those used at a track meet. If you can't get real ones, just improvise. Line the hurdles up as in a regular hurdle race.

Team members run with a pie tin filled with shaving cream. When they come to the hurdle, they must throw the pie tin up, go under the hurdle, catch the pie tin on the other side, and continue until they have gone under all six hurdles. That person then runs back and tags the next team member in line, who does the same to form a relay.

Each team is timed, and the best time wins. If a runner drops a pie tin, he or she must go back to the beginning and try again. (Contributed by Linda Thompson, Molalla, OR)

Pin The Collar On The Pastor

If you have a big shopping mall near you, chances are good that it has a place which makes life-sized computer photos from a snapshot. Have one made of your pastor's face (from the shoulders up), and play "Pin the Collar (or necktie) on the Pastor." Your kids will love it! (Contributed by Gary McCluskey, Colorado Springs, CO)

Ping Pong Polo

For this exciting indoor game, have team members make their own "polo sticks" out of rolled-up newspaper and masking tape. Several sheets of paper should be rolled up lengthwise, and then taped along the edge.

The object of the game is for team members to knock the ball (a ping pong ball) with the "polo stick" into their team's goal. An excellent way to set up goals is to lay two tables on their sides (one table per goal), with the top of the table facing into the playing area. When the ball hits the face of the table, it will make a "popping" noise, indicating that a goal was scored.

Each team should have one goalie who will guard the table. The goalie can use any part of his or her body to protect the table.

To make the game even more like real "polo," have the kids "ride" broomsticks like horses while they play the game. It's always advisable to have a few extra ping pong balls on hand. (Contributed by Cindy Fairchild, Fair Oaks, CA)

Plunger Ball

Here's another great variation of baseball your kids will love. To play, you need a large rubber or plastic ball (not too heavy) and a good old

American toilet plunger. This game can be played indoors or out.

Divide into two teams. One team is in the field and the other is "at bat." The team which is up bats with the plunger by poking at the ball with the rubber part on the end. The runner runs to first, and all the normal rules of baseball or softball apply.

You can change the rules as you see fit. For example, it's usually best to have four or five bases rather than the customary three. They can also be closer together. Boundaries can be adjusted and positions in the field can be created spontaneously.

Players can be put out by hitting them with the ball. You can have five outs per inning, rather than three. (Contributed by Lee Strawhun, Pique, OH)

Poopdeck II

Here are some additional "decks" you can add to the "Poopdeck" game described in **Ideas #21–24** to complicate things further:

Second Deck	Bridge Deck
Third Deck	Flight Deck
Fourth Deck	Hanger Deck
Promenade Deck	Upper Deck
Boat Deck	Forecastle Deck
Sun Deck	Cabin Deck

If you like, add special activities to each area, such as having kids flap their arms while in the Flight Deck. In addition, the following commands, if interspersed with the deck commands, can generate a great deal of playful confusion:

"Hit the Deck!"
(Participants must drop to a prone position.)

"Clear the Deck!"
(Participants must step completely outside the marked area and may not step back in, no matter what other command may be issued, until they hear "On Deck!")

"On Deck!"
(Participants are free to step back inside the marked area.)

(Contributed by Steve Perisho, Boise, ID)

Rattle Tattle

Have your kids bring a dollar's worth of change with them to youth group, and start things off with this version of "Bingo." Give each person a game sheet like the one on this page. Then have the group mingle and find people who have coins as described on the sheet, or who can answer the questions correctly. Five in a row—up, down, or

A nickel minted between 1970 & 1975	A game token	A penny made before 1950	What does "E Pluribus Unum" mean?	A half dollar
Exactly 37¢ in change	A dime minted between 1981 & 1983	A quarter with a small "D" on it	What is the name of the building on the penny?	Four quarters
A quarter more than 25 years old	Whose picture is on the quarter?	A foreign coin	A nickel minted between 1951 & 1955	A 1983 penny
Seventeen pennies	Five dimes	Which president is on the dime?	Exactly 63¢ in change	A penny, a nickel, a dime, and a quarter
Six coins all the same	A silver dollar	No quarters	A 1972 quarter	Someone who can flip "heads" three times in a row

diagonally—wins.

The game can also be played individually by allowing players to use only the coins in their possession to fill in the spaces. Adapt to make it harder or easier, according to your situation. (Contributed by Rick Jenkins, Laurel, MS)

Skate Night

Here are some great games that can help turn the most ordinary "skate night" into a successful special event. Check with your local roller rink for permission to play these games on skates:

1. **Dipsy Doodle Trio:** Any combination of three players can take to the floor to form a team except for three guys. Each trio must join hands and skate in a line together. Every time the

whistle blows, all teams must begin skating the opposite direction! What results is a floor full of people playing crack-the-whip as they try to do a joint about-face. The last team standing wins.

2. **Pop In, Pop Out:** Couples take to the floor to skate. Whenever a guy wants to "cut in" and skate with a girl, he gets a small lunch sack from you, goes out on the floor, blows it up, and pops it behind the couple he wants to cut in on. Make sure to have a trash can centrally located on the skating floor so the popped bags aren't littered everywhere. Alternate with times when the girls cut in.

3. **Rotation:** This game gives kids a good chance to get acquainted. Everyone gets a partner; then the couples begin skating in a circle, with guys on the outside.

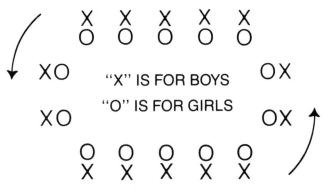

X X X X X
O O O O O

XO   "X" IS FOR BOYS   OX

XO   "O" IS FOR GIRLS   OX

O O O O O
X X X X X

No passing is allowed. Every time the whistle blows, the guys advance up to the next girl in the line. Give couples a few minutes to introduce themselves while skating, and then blow the whistle again.

4. **North, South, East, West:** Designate each corner of the rink as north, south, east, or west. Kids skate until the music stops, at which time they must head for the nearest corner. You then call out one of the directions, and those standing in that corner are eliminated. Keep going until only one or two are left, and give them a prize from the concession stand.

(Contributed by Steve Smoker, Morehead City, NC)

Slip And Slide Relay

For this exciting summertime game, use a commercial "Slip 'N' Slide," or create a homemade one out of a heavy plastic sheet. Divide into teams and give each team member a cottage cheese container full of water. Each person then runs and slides on the wet surface, holding the cottage cheese container full of water with one hand over his or her head. After sliding, the water from the cottage cheese container is poured into a bucket at the end of the plastic sheet. The team that can get the most water in their bucket within a given time limit is the winner. (Contributed by Linda Thompson, Mollala, OR)

Speed Trivia

Divide the group into 2 to 4 teams. In the center of the room place a row of 10 chairs for each team and number the chairs from 1 to 10. A representative from each team sits in the first chair of their team's row of chairs.

```
                  X = Chair
Team 1 X X X X X X X X X X
Team 2 X X X X X X X X X X
Team 3 X X X X X X X X X X  GOAL
Team 4 X X X X X X X X X X
Chair # 1 2 3 4 5 6 7 8 9 10
```

Take a box of Trivial Pursuit or Bible Trivia cards (or any kind of trivia questions) and read off a question to Team #1. They have 15 seconds to come up with the correct answer and relay the answer to their team representative in the chair. The only answer you will accept will be the one given by the person in the chair. The team cannot shout out the answer but must have one person run up and tell the answer to their teammate in the chair. If they give the correct answer, their representative moves up to chair #2. Play continues with Team #2, then Team #3, etc. Each team, of course, receives a different question.

If a team gives an incorrect answer, their representative moves back a chair (unless, of course, they are sitting in chair #1).

The first team to get their representative to chair #10 wins the game.

An alternative version of this game is to let all the teams play at once. You read out a trivia question and the first team to give their representative the correct answer is allowed to move up a chair. All incorrect answers moves a team back one chair. (Contributed by Lynn Pryor, Snyder, TX)

Sports Toto

This game has its origins in Europe. It's fun and adds the element of chance to some wild and crazy games.

To play, divide your group into 4 teams of equal size. It doesn't matter how many are on each team. Each team should have a team name, and a team captain who will also act as scorekeeper.

To begin the game, the leader asks each team to send one of its members out to the center of the room. After all 4 players (one from each team) are selected, the leader introduces each one. ("This is Jim Darby, representing Team #1!").

After the players are introduced, each team huddles together and "votes" on which player they think will win the yet unnamed event about to be announced. Teams don't have to vote for teammates. They can vote for any of the four players out on the floor. Each team must decide on a single person to receive their vote.

After each team has voted, the leader draws an "event" or task out of a hat. It can be anything. Here are some examples:

1. Blow up a balloon and sit on it until it breaks.
2. Peel a potato with a blunt table knife.
3. Blow a table tennis ball from one end of the room to the other.
4. Drink a can of warm soda pop and burp.

When the whistle is blown, the players begin competing, and the 4 teams cheer for the one they voted for. The winning player then earns a point for any team that voted for him or her.

You can add even more excitement by having teams guess who will win, place (come in second), and show (come in third). Bonus points can be awarded for guessing the correct order, 1-2-3.

Make sure that the events are things anyone can do. In fact, you should have a number of events which favor non-athletic kids, like trying to solve a rather complicated mathematical problem, or guessing the number of beans in a jar. If you use a little creativity, your kids will ask to do it over and over again. (Contributed by Eileen Thompson, Java Center, NY)

Superhero Relay

Here's a game you can play next time you're doing a lesson on heroes. You'll need 2 "phone booths" (be creative; a couple of refrigerator boxes will work); 2 dolls; several tables; 2 masks; and 2 pairs of high-topped tennis shoes.

Divide the group into 2 teams. Line them up about 50' away from the phone booths. The first 2 kids on each team run to their team's phone booth, go inside, and put on the mask and the "super-powered" shoes. They can run to another room where they save a baby (doll) from a burning building. Next they take the baby to a hysterical mother, put hand over heart, and say the "Pledge of Allegiance" to the flag (while the mother hums a patriotic tune). From there, they tunnel under the earth (crawl under the tables) and "fly" back to the phone booth. (This is

done by having four people carry each contestant in the flying position.) Finally, they change back into their street clothes and leave the masks and shoes in the phone booths for the next 2 players. (Dolls must be returned immediately to the other room.) The first team to finish is the winner.

(Contributed by Rick Wheeler, Lubbock, TX)

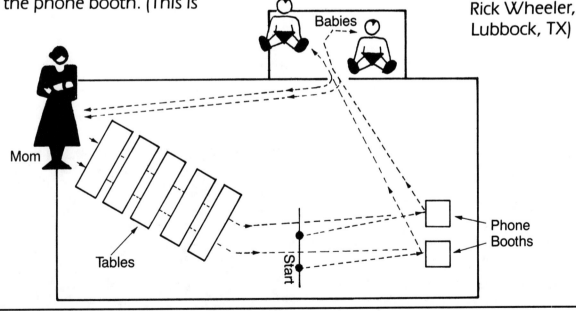

Swedish Baseball

This variation of baseball is most effective with 25 or more participants. Teams are divided equally with one team out in the field and the other at bat. No bats or balls are used. All you need is a Frisbee.

The batter comes to the plate and throws the Frisbee out into the field. The fielding team chases down the Frisbee and tries to return it to a garbage can which is next to home plate. The Frisbee must be tossed in rather than simply dropped in. Meanwhile, the batter runs about 10 feet to the two bases, which are about 8 feet apart, and begins to circle them. Every lap is one point for the batting team, and the runner continues until the Frisbee is in the can. All the players on the batting team get to be "up" each inning. There are no "outs."

After 2 or 3 innings, the score can get quite high. You'll need to have a scorekeeper who can keep track of all the points.

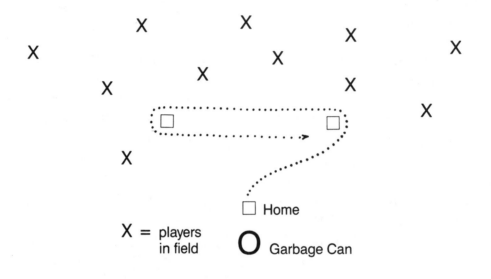

X = players in field

□ Home

O Garbage Can

(Contributed by David Rasmussen, Edmonds, WA)

Tardy Trap

Here's a great game that is well worth the effort required to set it up. It's played like a board game in that players move from one space to the next, competing to be the first to arrive at the final destination.

You can lay out the game on the floor (see diagram) using half-inch masking tape. Two rolls of tape

should be enough. Use colored tape to indicate the red (+) and yellow (–) penalty marks. The die or dice can be made from a square box painted white with black dots, or from foam rubber. Some toy stores sell oversized dice.

For the "Boys' Room," find an old toilet that the kids must sit on. (It's really funny to see the kids' reactions when they're sent to the Boys' Room.) You'll also need to provide pillows for the "duel" that is required when two players are occupying the same space.

In addition, you'll need to make the game cards as indicated. They can be any size.

Here are the instructions for "Tardy Trap," which can be passed out or read to the kids:

As usual, you are late for school. The situation is desperate—one more tardy slip, and you're on detention. Fortunately for you, your homeroom teacher is Mrs. Ima Blindbatt, who wears glasses made from Coke bottle bottoms. If you can get to homeroom without getting caught, you'll be safe. Unfortunately, getting to homeroom is not all that easy because it's on the third floor at the far end of the building. Each floor is infested with tattletale, nerdo hall monitors (seeking whom they may devour), and sadistic detention-crazed teachers (who slap detention slips on roaches if they're caught in the halls during class period).

But you've got a fighting chance. You can hide in lockers, purchase counterfeit hall passes, and find refuge in the Boys' Room. Be careful, though, because just when you think it's safe to go back into the hall…

The Rules:
1. Each player moves forward by the roll of the dice.
2. As a player lands on the red or yellow mark, he must do as indicated by the corresponding game card.
3. To get out of Detention Hall, you must roll an even number on your turn, up to three turns. Three detentions and you're out of the game.
4. If another player is sent to the Boys' Room and you are presently occupying that position, you are automatically "relieved" and may go back to the starting floor you left.
5. Two players cannot occupy the same space (except for the = sign just before entering homeroom). If a player lands on a space already occupied, a pillow duel decides who stays. The loser must go back to the starting floor. The duel is fought by two players standing only on one leg and holding the other leg off the ground. The free hand is then used to wield the pillow. The winner is the first one to make his or her opponent lose balance and fall over.
6. To enter homeroom, you must roll a "6" on your die.

TARDY TRAP GAME CARDS
(can be made any size)

RED   ## YELLOW

The principal is waiting for you at the door!
YOU'RE CAUGHT!
GO TO DETENTION HALL.

Sharky Johnson black-markets counterfeit hall passes. Meet him in boys' room.
LOSE ONE TURN!
GO TO THE BOYS' ROOM.

GO TO THE NEAREST STARTING FLOOR

MOVE BACK 2 BLOCKS

You were just spotted by a Hall Monitor, but you play it cool and show him your counterfeit hall pass. Does he believe you?
ARE YOU KIDDING?!
GO TO DETENTION HALL.

BLAME SOMEONE ELSE—
Mrs. Aulfulitch, the home ec teacher, caught you in the hall. She demands your name for Detention Hall. You give her someone else's.
BLAME SOMEONE!
SEND THEM TO D.H. FOR ONE TURN.

MOVE BACK 3 BLOCKS

GO BACK TO YOUR STARTING FLOOR BLOCK

Elmo Nerdo sees you sneaking around in the hall. He has a hall pass but you don't and he knows it, 'cause he knows everything and reports you to the principal.
YOU'RE CAUGHT!
GO TO DETENTION HALL.

You were just spotted by a Hall Monitor, but you play it cool and show him your counterfeit pass. Will he pass you?!
YES, BUT ... THE PASS IS FOR THE BOYS' ROOM.

GO BACK 3 BLOCKS

GO BACK 2 BLOCKS

You were just spotted by the Hall Monitor, but you play it cool and show him your counterfeit pass. Will he pass you?
YES!! YOU LUCKY DOG!

A Hall Monitor suddenly pops out of nowhere. The only place to hide is the boys' room.
LOSE ONE TURN!
GO TO THE BOYS' ROOM.

GO BACK 1 BLOCK

GO FORWARD 3 BLOCKS

The Hall Monitor was hiding in a locker!
YOU'RE CAUGHT!
GO TO DETENTION HALL.

You hear footsteps coming, so you quickly jump into a locker. It was only the janitor, but the locker locked and you are stuck!
LOSE ONE TURN!

GO FORWARD 2 BLOCKS

GO TO THE NEAREST RED BLOCK

140

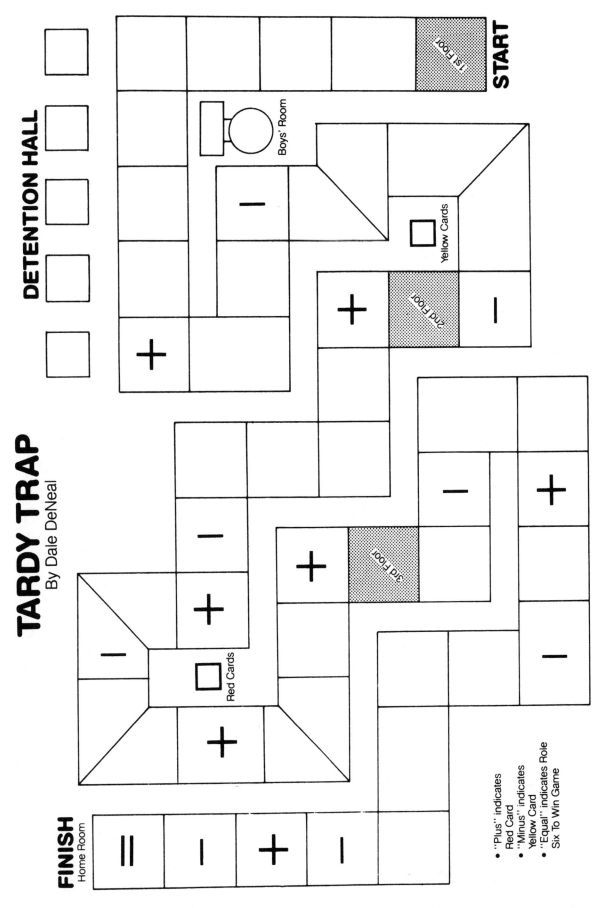

TARDY TRAP
By Dale DeNeal

START — 1st Floor

DETENTION HALL

Boys' Room

Yellow Cards

2nd Floor

Red Cards

3rd Floor

FINISH — Home Room

- "Plus" indicates Red Card
- "Minus" indicates Yellow Card
- "Equal" indicates Role Six To Win Game

(Contributed by Dale DeNeal, Louisville, KY)

141

Tennis Ball Golf

Here's a spin-off from the game "Frisbee Golf." Set up a golf course using boxes (big ones for amateurs, small ones for "pros") in a park or some other large open area. Golfers toss a tennis ball, attempting to get it inside the box for each hole. Boxes should be numbered 1 through 9 (or 18).

You can make this game as easy or as difficult as you want, depending on the location of the boxes, and how the ball is tossed. You can require that all tosses be underhand, or through the legs, over the shoulder, bounced, or however you wish. Usually a player will put the ball into the box only to watch it bounce out. (Contributed by Dave Mahoney, Columbus, IN)

Time Warp Tag

Here's another crazy version of the most famous of all games. You simply play a regular game of tag but at the blow of a whistle, each player (including "It") must slow down to a speed equal to a sports replay "Slo-Mo." In other words, they must do everything in slow motion. Kids will soon get the hang of it and become very exaggerated in their motions.

Make sure the kids do everything in "Time Warp" state, even talking and shouting. The game can be played in total Time Warp, or you can blow the whistle for start/stop intervals. Limit the size of the playing area so that several players have a chance to become "It." (Contribute by Mark A. Simone, Ravenna, OH)

Trip Trivia

Here's another "Trivial Pursuit" spinoff. On your next extended outing, put someone in charge of gathering little bits of trivia, like "What cabin number did the sponsors sleep in?" or "What is the first letter on the church bus license plate?" or "What was the last word the youth director said before he was thrown into the pool?" Use your imagination—nothing is too far out. Then put all the questions together and during your next meeting, see who can be the "Youth Trip Trivia Champ." This is an excellent way to reminisce and to set the stage for an evaluation time for any activity or trip. (Contributed by Rod Rummel, El Sobrante, CA)

Two-Ball Volleyball

This game is played like regular volleyball, with the following exceptions:

1. Two balls are used.
2. Each team serves a ball at the same time, and play continues

until both balls are misplayed.

3. Two points are scored for each volley. A team doesn't have to serve to score, so both points can be scored by the same team on one volley.

(Contributed by Merle Moser, Jr., Berne IN)

Volleybowl

This fast-paced game is exciting for all ages, but especially for younger kids. You need two volleyballs, two bowling pins, and a large playing area (indoors or out).

Divide into two teams of equal size and have each one choose a "pin keeper." Then have each team line up, all facing the same direction, in two parallel lines about 15 feet apart. Set up a pin about ten feet in front of the first person in each line, and have a pin keeper for each team stand behind his or her team's pin. Then give a volleyball to the first person in each line.

Team A	X X X X X X X
Team B	O O O O O O O

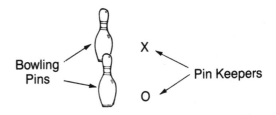

When a signal is given, the first person in each line attempts to knock down his or her team's pin, either by rolling or throwing the ball at it. If the pin is knocked down, the team gets a point. Then the pin keeper must set the pin up again and return the ball to the next person in line for play. If the pin is missed, no point is earned, and the pin keeper must return the ball to the next player in line. After each attempt, the player goes to the end of the line. Team members keep rotating in this way as fast as possible until the pre-determined period of play (usually five minutes) is up. Team with the most points wins.

The excitement of the game is heightened if team members shout out their score after every successful attempt and when the two-minute and one-minute warnings are given. To add a wrinkle, use half-inflated balls or two balls for each team (a headache for the pin keepers); or have players throw the ball between their legs by bending over forward.

(Contributed by Mark A. Hahlen, Louisville, KY)

Wall Hockey

This is an indoor game that can be played by groups as small as six or as large as 50. It's similar to "Snatch" (Steal the Bacon) in **Ideas #5–8**, but it uses hockey sticks and a ball or puck instead of a handkerchief.

The playing "field" should be bounded on two sides by walls, where the players must line up in two equal teams, one team along each wall (see the diagram). At the other two ends of the play area goals are set up, using street hockey nets, boxes, or chairs. The object of the game is to score the most goals by hitting the puck or ball into the opponent's net.

Players must count off in order, numbering themselves in one direction on one team and in the opposite direction on the other team. Each team is given a hockey stick (a broom will do if you use a larger ball). To begin play, all players must place one hand on the wall behind them, and **keep** a hand on the wall at all times during the game. Players on each team next gather to place their free hand on the hockey stick. Once everyone is holding the stick, the leader calls out a number, and the player from each team with that number takes his or her hand off the wall, grabs the stick, and goes out to face the opponent in the center of the "field." The rest of the team members release the stick but must keep a hand on the wall. Failure to do so costs a player's team one point.

To make the game more interesting, call out other numbers during a play. The two players in the center must then drop their sticks where they are, return to their lines, and put a hand on the wall before the next player can go out. This also helps keep more kids in the game. With large groups of 50 or more, you may want to divide up into four teams—one pair with letters and one with numbers—and then call out numbers and letters alternately.

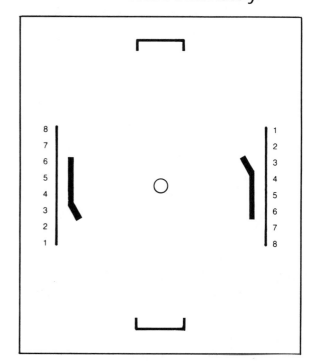

(Contributed by Brian Fullerton, Wenatchee, WA)

Water Baggies

The water balloon is an indispensable ingredient in youth ministry games. But how many hours do youth leaders spend filling balloons for the group?

One alternative is to have buckets of water ready and a supply of plastic sandwich bags, of the fold-lock top variety. As the game gets underway, the participants fill the bags by holding them under water and closing the top. The result is an instant, very temporary, water balloon substitute. Another advantage is that cleanup is easier than with regular water balloons. (Contributed by Tim Gerarden, Iowa City, IA)

Water Wars

Water Wars is similar to "Capture the Flag," but not nearly as dry! Divide your participants into two teams. Each team has their own territory, set up as shown in the diagram with the following features:

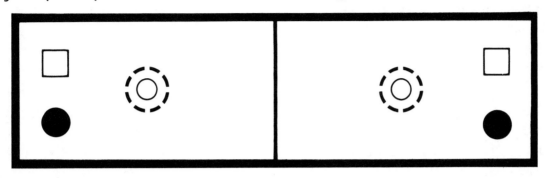

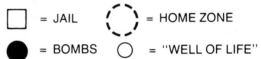

1. A large plastic garbage can filled with water. This is the "Well of Life."
2. A large plastic garbage can filled with 300 to 350 water balloons. The balloons are "bombs."
3. A bucket to throw "Well of Life" water on teammates and captives.
4. A jail to hold prisoners. This is a square area marked with chalk, large enough for several players to stand inside.
5. A source of water for each team to refill their "Well of Life."
6. A home zone. This is a chalk circle marked around the "Well of Life."

The object of the game is to tip over the other team's "Well of Life." To accomplish this goal, each team has at least 300 water balloons. They go fast, so the more water balloons, the longer and better the game will be.

Players may enter enemy territory to attack opponents only when armed with a bomb. If opponents are hit with a bomb in their own territory, they are declared "dead" until someone from their own team throws a bucket of water on them from their own "Well of Life."

If players are hit in enemy territory, they are taken prisoner and put in jail. The only way to escape jail is for a teammate to bring a bucket of water from his or her own "Well of Life" all the way across enemy territory, and throw it on the prisoner(s). In order for all players in jail to be released, they must be holding hands, or else all of them must get wet.

A player may not tip over the opposing team's "Well of Life" while armed. The home zone may **not** be guarded from within the white line. If an attacking player is hit with water **before** tipping the "Well of Life," he or she becomes a prisoner and must go to jail. If a player moves successfully through enemy territory without getting wet and tips the opposing team's "Well of Life" over, his or her team wins. This game can go very quickly, so it's best played in a series of five or seven games. (Contributed by Dave Hall, Ralston, NE)

Wheel of Fortune

Here's a modified version of the T.V. game show that can be played with your youth group. The biggest difference is that you don't use a "wheel" and that the phrase to be guessed is a Bible verse. You will need:

1. A container (paper sack, coffee can, etc.)
2. Posterboard (or stiff paper) squares (one inch square) with point values written on some and "lose turn" written on others. These go in the container above and are drawn out by the players.
3. An overhead projector and screen, or a blackboard.

Note: *You should have one "lose turn" square for every four point value squares. For example, if you have 100 squares, 80 of them should be point values and 20 "lose turns". You may want to include 3–5 "lose money" squares.*

Divide into two teams (A and B). Have the blanks for the Bible verse written on the overhead or blackboard. For example, if the verse is "Pray without ceasing," then this is how it should look:

_ _ _ _ _ _ _ _ _ _ _

_ _ _ _ _ _ _.

Let's say the first player on Team A draws out a square worth $50 (keep each square that is drawn out of the container until play is turned over to Team B) and he/she guesses the consonant "T". You fill in all the "T"s

and give Team A 100 points (2 "T"'s multiplied by 50 pts.). The board now should look like this:

_ _ _ _ _ _ T _ _ _ T

_ _ _ _ _ _ _.

The play proceeds to player #2 on Team A. This process continues until 1 of 3 things happen:

1. A player draws a "lose turn" or "lose money" square. Action goes to Team B and all the squares that Team A drew are put back into the container.
2. A player chooses a consonant that is not in the verse. Action goes to Team B and write that consonant on the bottom of the board/screen. Again, put all squares drawn back into the container.
3. Team A solves the puzzle/verse.

When a player draws a point value square, he or she can only guess a consonant. Teams can **buy** vowels for $100 each. That amount is then subtracted from their point total.

It is usually a good idea to choose a verse or phrase that has between 50–75 letters in it. Proverbs 12:25, Romans 12:9, I Corinthians 15:33, and James 3:8 are all good examples.

When a team thinks they can solve the puzzle, they must do it immediately following their turn. They only get one guess. The first team to correctly recite the verse is the winner. (Contributed by Jim Wing, Niles, MI)

SERVICE

Admission for Missions

To help collect needed supplies for a mission hospital supported by your church or denomination, charge "admission" to your weekly youth group meetings for a month. Each kid attending must bring one of the following items to get in:

Aspirin—baby and adult
Multivitamins—with or without iron
Iron pills
Antibiotic ointments
Adhesive tape
White cotton thread
Sturdy plastic cups and margarine tubs
Containers for the children's ward
Hand soap
Instant soup
Baby cereal
Scrub brushes
Sanitary napkins
Twill tape
Hand towels
Razor blades (old-fashioned type)
Sheet blankets
Nursing uniforms (specify colors, sizes, and fabric types)
Men's uniform tops

Adjust the list to fit your own mission hospital's needs. (Contributed by Tommy Martin, Ellensburg, WA)

Bringing in the Sheaves

Here's a simple, low-cost way to line up food and provisions for a work camp or service project. Just make up your menu, prepare a shopping list, and post the items needed on a sign-up sheet in your church. Include instructions about when and where to leave donated items. This is a practical approach to stretching a tight service project budget.

1 large potato salad _____
2 dozen hamburger buns _____
1 small jar mustard _____
1 large onion _____
2 heads lettuce _____
2 packages chips _____
2 packages chips _____
2 gallons milk _____
2 gallons milk _____
2 loaves wheat bread _____
2 loaves white bread _____
2 loaves French bread _____
4 dozen eggs _____
10 lbs oranges _____
5 lbs bananas _____
2 boxes cold cereal _____
2 packages lunchmeats _____
2 packages lunchmeats _____
1 12-oz pkg cheese slices _____
1 12-oz pkg cheese slices _____
1 quart jam _____
2 dozen sweet rolls _____
2 large cans vegetable soup _____
hot cocoa mix _____

(Contributed by Mike Stipe, The Dalles, OR)

Dessert Desert

"Dessert Desert" is a fun service project for your group. Have the kids line up several cream pies to be donated by people in the church. Then let them deliver the pies to the doorsteps of elderly people or shut-ins, by ringing the doorbell and running. The recipient opens the door to find a pie and a little note as shown in the illustration. Try one on the steps of the police department!

(Contributed by Jim Halbert, Atascadero, CA)

Dear: _____
You have just become a victim of **"Dessert Desert."** The youth group from the Church of the Nazarene thought you might enjoy a delectably delicious pie made by some of our very own people in the church.
Enjoy and God Bless!

Missions Scavenger Hunt

Collect items for mission organizations or other charitable groups your church supports by having a Missions Scavenger Hunt. Kids are sent out in teams to go door-to-door asking for specific items from a list of toiletries, household necessities, packaged dry foods, clothes, books, or whatever is needed. Points are awarded for every item collected; team with the most points wins.

The following sample "Missions Scavenger Hunt" combines this service project with a fun puzzle-solving game. The answers provide the scavenger hunt items.

MISSIONS SCAVENGER HUNT

1. Yankee Doodle went to town riding on a pony, stuck a feather in his hat and called it _____.
   The photographer who took Yankee Doodle's picture told him to smile and say, "_____."
   I'm sure that Yankee Doodle went to lunch and had _____ & _____.

2. It comes in a can: You can fry it or bake it!
   You can slice it or dice it!
   It's name rhymes with ham.
   It is not a yam.
   You know what it's called ... It's called ___ ___ ___ ___.

3. If mother nature didn't help you out.
   Don't sit there and pout.
   Just knock on their door.
   And ask for two not four.
   Ask for <u>FALSE EYELASHES</u>.
   **Category #1: YOUR MOTHER HAS SAID,
   "DON'T SLURP YOUR _____."**

4. This is commonly thought of as a vegetable but is a fruit
   — — — — — — —.

5. A room full of oatmeal would be called a ___ ___ ___ ___ room.

6. Why did the ___ ___ ___ ___ ___ ___ ___ cross the road? To get away from the Colonel.

7. A game is played where you sit in a circle and pass an object that is hot. what is it? A ___ ___ ___ ___ ___ ___.

8. Every relish dish has this:
   Is not red but it is green,
   If you eat enough you'll stay LEAN
   — — — — — — —.

9. You will see a smile on their faces.
   When you ask for a pair of <u>red shoelaces</u>.

10. What do Chun King, Princess Diana, Prince Charles, and Uncle Ben all have in common? ___ ___ ___ ___

Category #2: EVERY MOTHER INSISTS THAT HER KIDS EAT THEIR
___ ___ ___ ___ ___ ___ ___ ___ ___.

11. ___ ___ ___ ___, porridge hot,
___ ___ ___ ___, porridge cold,
___ ___ ___ ___, porridge in the pot nine days old.

12. ___ ___ ___ ___ ___ ___, ___ ___ ___ ___ ___, the musical fruit,
The more you eat the more you toot!
The brown ones are too drab you see,
So bring back ones of color to me!

13. Unusual in its packaging . . . It comes on something that rhymes with knob. ___ ___ ___ ___ on the ___ ___ ___.

14. Bugs Bunny wouldn't give these up for anything. I hated them. What's Up Doc? ___ ___ ___ ___ ___ ___ ___

Category #3:
Knock, knock,
Who's there?
Banana.
Banana who?　　*Knock, knock,*
　　　　　　Who's there?
　　　　　　Banana.
　　　　　　Banana who?　　*Knock, knock,*
　　　　　　　　　　　　Who's there?
　　　　　　　　　　　　Orange
　　　　　　　　　　　　Orange who?

(Orange you glad I didn't say banana!)

15. –18. COLLECT FOUR TYPES OF THIS CATEGORY:
_____

19. A green zipper. (for no good reason)

20. This will take the gum out of your hair if you dare a dab there.
___ ___ ___ ___ ___ ___ ___ ___ ___ ___ ___ ___ ___

(Contributed by Sam Crabtree, Brooking, SD; Craig Carlson, Sioux City, IA; and Kathy Ahlschwede, Minneapolis, MN)

Nursery Renovation

It's difficult to find a service project that all the members of a youth group tackle with enthusiasm, but you may strike oil with this one. Most of the kids in your group probably babysit, and many of them may help keep the church nursery at various times during the week. If so, they would probably be eager to do something for the little tykes (and their parents). If the church nursery leaves a few things to be desired, why not let the teens renovate it?

Devote a work day or lock-in to clean the windows, paint the rocking chairs, scrub and repair the mattresses, clean and disinfect the toys, wash the walls and woodwork, make colorful cushions and matching curtain valances, and shampoo the carpet. If the walls are drab, paint them or put up bright posters.

The congregation will be convinced that the youth really care about the church and the little kids. And the youth will be proud that they've done something that's tangible and practical. (Contributed by Robin Garrett, Crestwood, KY)

P.E.T.S.

Form a P.E.T.S. team (People Encouraging Through Service) of young people to serve specially-targeted groups in the church. Meet one night a week to perform services according to these priorities:

1. Hospital Calls—Make and deliver poster-size get well cards for church members and acquaintances in the hospital. Spend ten minutes or so with the patient, putting the poster on the wall, chatting, and praying together. If you can, give a bouquet of balloons as well.

2. Absentee Calls—If no one's in the hospital, check the youth group attendance records for names of kids who have been absent four straight weeks or more. Make posters covered with faces and the message, "We Miss Your Face!" Then take it to their homes. They usually come the next week!

3. Birthday and Anniversary Calls—If no one's in the hospital or on the "critically absent" list, check the church roles

for birthday and wedding anniversaries. Make and deliver poster cards accordingly.

4. Encouragement Calls—When no one's in categories 1 to 3 on a particular night, make posters for anyone who could use an uplift.

Pay them a short visit.

This program scatters around lots of joy, gives the kids a sense of ministry, and provides great P.R. for the youth program. (Contributed by Randy Wheeler, Colorado Springs, CO)

Saturday Servants

To give your youth a regular chance to serve church members with special needs, designate occasional Saturday mornings (9:00 a.m. to noon) as the time for "Saturday Servants." Use a bulletin insert announcing the project two weeks before so church members who need assistance can call the church ahead of time with their requests.

"Saturday Servants" focus primarily (though not necessarily exclusively) on performing chores for the elderly, shut-ins, widows, divorced persons, and single parents in the church. Jobs to be done might be anything from yard work to child care, car maintenance to furniture moving. It's a good idea to ask the people being served to provide the necessary equipment and cleaning supplies (if possible).

Your youth will find that their sacrifice of time and energy on a Saturday morning can provide a significant and practical ministry to many members of the church. (Contributed by Gary Wrisberg, Columbia, MO)

Servant Search

Here's a service project that will challenge your kids to creative servanthood. Divide your large group into small groups of two or three. Tell them they have exactly one hour to penetrate the community and serve it in some fashion. The goal is to serve as many people as possible in any way possible. Be creative: Some students will sweep the sidewalks, others will go door-to-door asking to wash windows or pull weeds, and others will pick up trash in a local parking lot or field. Some may even go to a local gas station and pump gas for people at the self-serve islands. (No one is allowed to receive money for the services.)

At the end of the hour, the students return to tell about their experience. Award prizes for the most creative, hardest workers, most people served, and so on. Give lots of affirmation to each team. It will help build self-esteem in your students and encourage them to be self-starters. (Contributed by Alan Hamilton, Long Beach, CA)

Smoke Alarm Ministry

Here's a service project that could literally save lives. Have your youth install battery-operated smoke detectors in the homes of the elderly of your community.

First, decide how detectors will be purchased or donated. Around Christmas many department stores will sell minimum quantities at wholesale. Better yet, the local Fire Marshall's office usually has connections to suppliers who will donate the detectors if the group doing the installations will make a list of persons serviced.

Second, prepare a list of elderly people who might need the service. Then perform a phone survey asking these persons if they would welcome the group in their home to install, for free, the smoke detector. If so, arrange a time (usually an entire Sunday afternoon) when they would be home to receive the service team.

Third, find out if the Fire Marshall can also provide slides, films, or volunteer speakers who will come in a week before the project to sensitize the youth to general fire safety practices, as well as to the specific risks facing the elderly. Because a disproportionate number of fires occur in the homes of older people, this project could mean the difference between life and death. (Contributed by Mark Forrester, Madison, TN)

Soup Kitchen Support.

If your church wants to help feed the hungry, but you're in an area where there would not be enough needy people to warrant a soup kitchen, try this idea. Set up a "market table" in the fellowship hall or a Sunday school room where church members bring produce from their own gardens for other members to buy. Items can be purchased for a freewill donation rather than a set price.

The money raised from this project can then be sent to help support a soup kitchen in another area. Though the market table involves only a minimum of preparation and organization, it can generate a useful sum for ministry to the hungry. (Contributed by Frank Billman, Woxall, PA)

Towel Award

Here's a meaningful way to thank a youth group member who performs acts of service without seeking recognition. Present him or her with the "Towel Award," a monogrammed towel set. This award should be given as a high honor and only to those who have consistently performed acts of service without having been asked, and without calling attention to themselves.

The towel, a symbol of service in John 13, will remind everyone of the true meaning of servanthood. (Contributed by Rick Brown, San Angelo, TX)

Used Bible Drive

Have you ever counted the number of Bibles you have in your home? Many families have several that are never read. Why not try a Used Bible Drive to put those extra bibles to good use? Announce to your congregation that you'll be collecting used Bibles and other Christian reading material to be sent to people who have none. Then send them to World Home Bible League in South Holland, Illinois, which collects used Bibles and distributes them to other countries where they can be used. For more information about the League's program, write World Home Bible

League, 16801 Van Dam Rd., South Holland, IL 60473; (312) 331-2094. (Contributed by Dawn Cahill, Mountain Home, AR)

Visitation Leaders

To help your youth group have more meaningful visits to shut-ins, hospitals, and nursing homes, appoint one young person to each of the following four areas of responsibility:

Area #1: Prayer. Find volunteers for:
  a. the opening prayer;
  b. the closing prayer;
  c. other prayer (if appropriate).

Area #2: Scripture. Find someone to:
  a. choose a passage;
  b. comment on it before reading it;
  c. state one point of the passage (after reading it) and discuss it.

Area #3: Music. Locate people who will:
  a. choose appropriate songs;
  b. take enough songbooks
  c. find a musician(s);
  d. perform some special music.

Area #4: Gift(s). One person should:
  a. obtain an appropriate gift(s);
  b. obtain an appropriate card;
  c. have the card signed and present the gift and card with a kind word on behalf of the group and the church.

(Contributed by Daniel C. Broadwater, Catonsville, MD)

Vitamin Boxes

If someone in your youth group (or one of their friends) is confined for a long illness, have the other group members each bring an inexpensive gift (already wrapped) to your next meeting. Place the gifts in a large box marked "Once-A-Day Vitamins." Deliver the box to the patient with instructions to open only one gift each day. The idea is to give him or her something to look forward to besides treatments. (Contributed by Ralph Bryant, Alvin, TX)

Widow and Widower Dinner

To get your kids together with the older folks in your church, have the youth group plan, prepare, and serve (at the tables, not buffet style) a dinner for the widows and widowers. After the meal, provide entertainment: old movies, group singing, games. Whoever isn't part of the entertainment can take care of cleanup. The people served will be so grateful, and the kids will have so much fun, that it just might become an annual event! (Contributed by Dawn Cahill, Mountain Home, AR)

CHAPTER SIX

SPECIAL EVENTS

Aggressive Dinner

For this variation of the old "Progressive Dinner," load up in cars or vans and eat each course of your meal in a different city. For example, go to a McDonald's in one town and have french fries; go to a Burger King in another town and have hamburgers; and then head for yet another town and have sundaes at Dairy Queen. Of course, this assumes that there are other cities within driving distance. Kids will enjoy the "trip" aspect of this one. (Contributed by Kay Jorgenson, Kent, WA)

Banana Night Strikes Again!

Just what you've been waiting for! Here are some banana games to add to all the other "Banana Nights" found in previous volumes of **Ideas**.

1. **Barbie Banana Beauty Contest:** All you need are a few naked bananas and some paper doll dress-up clothes. Each person dresses his or her banana to enter the beauty contest. You can use clothing out of magazines and department store catalogs if you don't have paper doll clothes readily available.

2. **"All My Bananas" Soap Operas:** Have the kids make up their own soap opera using their beauty contest bananas. Limit them to 3 minutes, and have teams compete for the most gripping dramatic presentation.

3. **Custom Banana Hot-Rod Show:** This is a wild one. Give each "bunch" (team) a model car kit to customize their banana. They then enter the Custom Banana Hot-Rod Show; or if their banana car will roll, they can enter the "Banana Hot-Rod Grand Prix." Let each team roll their cars down an incline. The champ is the one that reaches the bottom first (or goes the farthest).

4. **Banana Videos:** Use video cameras, and have each group make a real video using their bananas as puppets. The bananas can "lip-sync" their favorite record.

5. Banana Air-Band Contest:
Have the kids lip-sync records using bananas as instruments. This can also be taped on video.

6. Tip Banana Toe:
This game is messy. You need a floor that is easily cleaned, or you can do it outside. Line up chairs so as to create an aisle which you strew with banana peels. Contestants are then blindfolded and must walk down the aisle without stepping on a banana peel. Chances are they won't make it.

7. Banana Power Munching:
This is just a good old "see who can eat the most bananas in a certain period of time" game.

8. Banana Feet Relay:
Kids line up facing one direction, then sit down, lined up. The first person has to pick up the banana with his or her feet and then roll over, straight-backed, and hand off (feet off, that is) the banana to the next person, who takes it from that person's feet using only his or her own feet. The last person in line then has to peel the banana and eat it (yuk!). If done with teams, the first to finish is the winner.

9. Capture the Banana:
Just like "Capture the Flag," but use bananas instead of flags.

(Contributed by Mark Ziehr, St. Petersburg, FL)

Bon Appetit!

Next time you do a "candlelight dinner" at McDonald's or Burger King, try this approach. Have the kids dress up and go to the fast food restaurant of your choice. Then divide into table groups (four to a table) and give each group a bag which includes a tablecloth, linen napkins, silverware, centerpiece, and menus.

After the tables are set, a "waiter" can come around to each table and collect the menus. These should be filled out and signed by each patron. The front of the menu can include instructions, including the fact that they are limited to one hamburger, one order of fries or onion rings, and one drink per person. The waiter also serves the food when it's ready. Here's how the menu should read:

(Contributed by Tim Smith, Fresno, CA)

155

Bowling Awards

Does your youth group enjoy bowling? If so, here's how to make an average bowling night much more interesting. Print up some awards like the one pictured here, and give them for categories like these:

Most strikes
Low game (male/female)

Most expressionless bowler
Greatest hope for the pro tour
Most creative shot of the night
Best form (male/female)
Most gutter balls
High game (male/female)
Sore loser award
(Contributed by Paul E.B. Gruhn, Anderson, IN)

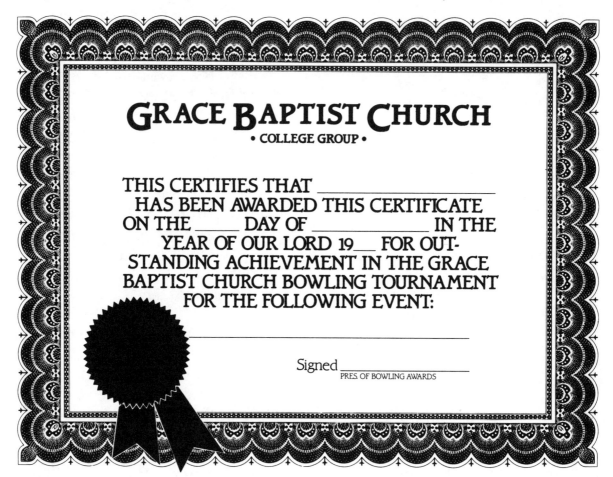

GRACE BAPTIST CHURCH
• COLLEGE GROUP •

THIS CERTIFIES THAT _____
HAS BEEN AWARDED THIS CERTIFICATE
ON THE _____ DAY OF _____ IN THE
YEAR OF OUR LORD 19__ FOR OUT-
STANDING ACHIEVEMENT IN THE GRACE
BAPTIST CHURCH BOWLING TOURNAMENT
FOR THE FOLLOWING EVENT:

_____

Signed _____
PRES. OF BOWLING AWARDS

Church Zoo

Here's an all-church event that the youth group can organize. Have everyone bring a pet to church and set up a "church zoo" for a few hours. All can show their pets, demonstrate any "tricks" the critters might be able to do, and compete for an award presented to the pet which looks the most like its owner. This could be tied in with a lesson for the children on Noah's ark. Encourage everyone to participate. Any pet is allowed (yes, even goldfish). Make sure people bring leashes and cages when necessary. (Contributed by Gary N. McCluskey, Colorado Springs, CO)

Crossword Car Rally

This is a great car rally or scavenger hunt idea which incorporates the completion of a crossword puzzle in order to win. You will, of course, need to create your own puzzle, but it's not too difficult to do. Divide into teams (or car loads), and give each one a printed copy of the puzzle, with clues similar to the ones below.

DOWN

2. What is guaranteed at Frank's Nursery, 49th St. and 54th Ave. N.?
3. "Rustlers _____" is playing at the Garden Drive-In, Tyrone and Park.
4. What is located at 6980 54th Ave. N.?
5. Who was Northeast High School's opponent for football homecoming in 1985? 54th Ave. N. and 16th St. N.
6. What kind of products are sold at the Chevron Food/Gas Mart at 34th St. and 9th Ave. N.?
8. What type of trees are free at 33rd Ave. N. and Park St.?
10. What is free on the Shopping Center Construction Company sign at 49th St. and 9th Ave.?
11. Opposite of yes.
12. Greeting.
13. Laugh sound.
16. Who is going out of business at 34th St. N. and 16th Ave. N.?

17. Whose cottage is at 2605 50th Ave. N.?
18. Whose creamery milk is sold at 34th St. and 62nd Ave. N.?
19. What type of new homes are at 49th St. and 16th Ave. N.?
20. What type of puppies are sold at 49th St. and 3rd Ave. N.?

ACROSS

1. What position did John J. Murphy hold that is listed on the bronze plaque at 30th Ave. N. and 80th St. N.?
7. How many flavors does the Twistee Treat sell at 54th St. and 58th Ave. N.?
8. What night is Bingo played at Holy Cross Church, 54th Ave. and 79th St. N.?
9. What is sweet at 62nd St. and Haines Road?
10. What does Lou sell at 34th St. and 32nd Ave. N.?

(Contributed by Dick Gibson, St. Petersburg, FL)

Decoder Scripture Scavenger Hunt

Here's another great scavenger hunt idea. Divide into groups (or car loads) and give each group a sheet of instructions like the one below. On the sheet is a "mystery phrase" (a Bible verse) which must be deciphered by filling in the letters in the spaces provided. The letters are found by going to the various places on the scavenger hunt list.

Rules of play: Each group will have 1 hour and 15 minutes to complete their search. The winner will be the first group to return to the church and read the correctly deciphered scripture to Dick. Incorrect guesses do not disqualify you from continuing in the hunt but they do use up part of your allotted time. You are not required to stop at each clue location if you can decipher without it. If no group is able to complete the verse within the time limit, the group with the most complete words will win.

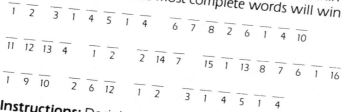

```
__ __ __ __ __ __ __ __   __ __ __ __ __ __ __ __
1  2  3  1  4  5  1  4    6  7  8  2  6  1  4  10

__ __ __ __   __ __   __ __ __   __ __ __ __ __ __ __ __
11 12 13 4    1  2    2  14 7    15 1  13 8  7  6  1  16

__ __ __   __ __ __   __ __   __ __ __ __ __ __
1  9  10   2  6  12   1  2    3  1  4  5  1  4
```

Instructions: Decipher the coded scripture verse by finding the missing letters from the clues below:

1. Most repeated letter in name of Rutland Bank Branch Office at 34th Street North and 22nd Avenue North.
2. First letter on back of stop sign at 66th Street and 4th Avenue North.
3. First letter of repeated word on sign at Budget Exhaust Center on Fifth Avenue North and First Street.
4. First letter in phone number for information on bus to Bucs games, listed on light pole close to Firestone at Tyrone Mall.
5. First letter missing from "St. Petersburg" city sign attached to AMTRAK Station.
6. Missing letter from Crossroad Center sign at Tyrone and 21st Avenue North.
7. Leaning letter at 1401 Fifth Avenue North.
8. Last letter of boat registration on Sh-Boom II at 1825 Elm Street Northeast.
9. Missing letter at Golden Dragon Restaurant sign close to 34th Street and Fifth Avenue North.
10. Tilted letter on First Banker sign at 5885 Central Avenue.
11. First letter on building behind Social Arts building at St. Pete J.C.
12. Unusual letter at 5047 Central Avenue.
13. Final letter in serial number of air conditioning unit for Room 3-1 at Bear Creek Elementary, 61st Street South and Third Avenue South.
14. First letter in name of man for President at stop sign at Snell Isle Blvd. and Coffee Pot Blvd. N.E.
15. First missing letter on shingle store front at 6297 Central Avenue.
16. Last letter on inside of dumpster lid behind Crossland Savings at First Avenue North and 34th Street.

(Contributed by Dick Gibson, St. Petersburg, FL)

Fantasy Island Night

This is a special event which requires adequate preparation and publicity. Have people come dressed in a particular role they would like to play or as a famous person they fantasize being like. Perhaps they have a career or a goal in life they would like to achieve, or maybe it's just a make-believe fantasy, like being a contemporary celebrity or historical figure. Prizes can be given for categories such as "Most Imaginative and Creative," "The Reachable Star," "The Impossible Dream," "The Weirdest," "The Best Overall Fantasy." Have someone dress up as "Mr. Rourke" in a white suit to be the host for the evening. Allow each person to describe his or her fantasy for the rest of the group. Decorations and refreshments can have an "island" theme. (Contributed by Jeffrey Collins, Lexington, MA)

Giant Monopoly

This event combines the standard game of "Monopoly" with a car rally. In "Giant Monopoly," the whole youth group plays "Monopoly" using **real houses** around the community as the "properties" on the game board. Here's how it works:

First, line up enough homes around town to be all the properties on the game board ("Baltic Avenue," "Boardwalk," and so on). If you want to cut down on the number of houses you use, have one house represent all the properties of the same color on the board. On the day or evening that the game is played, all the owners of these houses will need to be at home and know what to do. You will also need to arrange cars and drivers for each team.

To play, use a regular "Monopoly" game. Divide into teams of four or five kids per team. (They must all ride in the same car together.) Distribute "Monopoly" money to each team as follows:

6 x $500 bills	15 x $10	
6 x $100	15 x $5	
6 x $50	15 x $1	
18 x $20	(Total: $4,500)	

Place $1,000 in the middle of the board. Roll the dice to see which team goes first. Most of the regular Monopoly rules will apply, like collecting $200 every time you pass "Go."

But here's where the game really differs: If you're the first one to land on a property, you may either buy it or (if you choose not to buy) allow it to go to the highest bidder. If someone owns the property you land on, then your team must get in the car and go to that property and pay the fee. The owners at the home will collect the fee and give you a receipt. Then you return to the game so that you can roll again. While you're gone, the other teams can continue to play until they also have to leave for whatever reason. When there are other teams present at the game board, you must take your turn in order, but if no one else is there, you may roll more than once at a time. Other rules:

1. **Chance or Community Chest:** You must pick a card and do what it says.
2. **Railroads:** You must get in the "train car" and go for a train ride—one mile out and one mile back. Then you must pay the conductor (driver).
3. **Utilities:** You must go to the house designated as the utility office and pay.
4. **Jail:** You must go to jail if you land on the "Go to Jail" space or draw the "Go to Jail" card. The jail can be a room in the building. You can get out of jail by paying $100, rolling doubles on your next turn, or sitting in jail for three minutes.
5. **Free Parking:** Landing on this gives you all the money in the middle of the board.
6. **Luxury Tax:** You pay $75 to the middle of the board.
7. **Income Tax:** You pay $200 to the middle of the board.
8. **Mortgages:** These are administered by the bank.
9. **Out of money:** If you are running short on cash, you can take your title deed to your owner's house and collect your money (if there is any) any time.
10. **Selling property:** You may sell to another group or trade with them as you choose.

The game is over at the end of the designated time. At that time, each team must gather up all its money and assets and turn them into the bank. The team with the most money and accumulated property value wins.

Obviously, this event will need to be carefully planned and well thought out before you do it, but it's worth the effort. The idea of playing a "Monopoly" game with the whole town as your board is crazy enough to generate a lot of enthusiasm and participation. (Contributed by Scott Welch, Wilmore, KY)

Great And Glorious Goofy Golf Getaway

Here's a new twist to a special event featuring an evening of miniature golf. Have the kids meet at the "clubhouse" (church) wearing their favorite golfing garb. While kids are arriving, you can provide putters and golf balls for some "putting around" on the carpet or lawn. Get some automatic ball returners and putting cups for this.

You can begin your evening of fun with some games at the church featuring golf balls. Many of the relays and races from the **Ideas** books involving ping pong balls, eggs, and so on can be adapted for use with golf balls. For example, you can play the "Spoon and Golf Ball Relay," with kids holding a spoon in their mouths with a golf ball in it while they run around the "flag" and back. Another appropriate game would be "Down the Drain," in which kids roll marbles from one person to the next using those long plastic tubes that come in golf bags.

Following the games, serve some food, featuring the following "One-Course Menu":

Club Sandwiches
"Chip Shots" (potato chips)

Iced "Tee"
"Golf Balls" (donut holes)
"Holes-in-One" (donuts)

Above the trash can, post a sign that says "Putt trash here." Perhaps you can think of other golf "puns" to use throughout the evening. After the kids have eaten, head for your local miniature golf course and let the kids play a few rounds. Give awards for the best scores, holes-in-one, and other achievements. (Contributed by John O. Yates, Welcome, NC)

Hallelujah Hoedown

Depending on which part of the country you're from, your young people may enjoy an event centered around the theme of "hillbillies." You could call it a "Hallelujah Hoedown and Hayride" (if you include a hayride, of course).

Activities can include the

following:

1. **Hillbilly Fashion Show:** Have the kids come dressed as hillbillies, and award prizes to the best-dressed hillbillies.
2. **The "Corn-fusion" Game:** Use the game "Confusion" from **Ideas #13–16**, but adapt it to a

hillbilly theme.

3. **The Barnyard Game:** From **Ideas #1–4**. Kids make the sounds of barnyard animals and get into groups.

4. **Hayride:** Check around your area for possibilities. If you can't use a real hay wagon, perhaps you can use trucks, or even a **bus** filled with hay!

5. **Hillbilly Talent Competition:** Have the kids come prepared to compete for prizes. Talent must be "authentic" hillbilly talent, like banjo-playing, yodeling, cow-chip tossing, hog-calling, singing through the nose, knee slapping, spitting, etc.

6. **Outdoor Cookout:** Have a Bar-B-Q and serve good ole country vittles like corn on the cob, black-eyed peas, mashed potatoes and gravy, biscuits, and the like. You might even have a few ice-cream churns ready to crank up as well.

Decorate with a "country" motif—bales of hay, etc., and some country or bluegrass music playing in the background. You can close with some country gospel songs, like "Will the Circle Be Unbroken." (Contributed by Randy Nichols, Sumter, SC)

Ice Cream Social On The Roll

This event is a lot of fun and delicious, too! Divide your crew into groups of four or five, and give each group a one-pound and a three-pound metal coffee can (with plastic lids). Provide each group a copy of the recipe below, and let the fun begin.

1. In the one-pound can, mix together:
   1 slightly beaten egg
   1 cup milk
   1 cup whipping cream
   ½ cup sugar
   dash of vanilla

2. Put the one-pound plastic lid on tightly. Place the one-pound can inside the three-pound can. Pack with crushed ice and ¾ cup rock salt. Put a three-pound plastic lid on tightly. Roll the can on the floor for 15 minutes.

3. Drain the water and stir the ice cream. Pack with ice and rock salt. Roll for 5 more minutes.

Add bowls and your favorite toppings, and you'll have some ice cream sundaes that will make a treat hard to beat. (Contributed by Tom Baker, Florence, KY)

Long Distance Party

Kids grow up and move away, go to college, or are just away at special times. One way for the "dear departed" to maintain contact with the old gang back home is to send them a Long Distance Party. It's simple. Just buy a cake mix, frosting, sprinkles, a party hat and some decorations; put it all in a box; and mail it to those far-away friends, along with letters of greeting from the group. This is especially appreciated by college students who really miss the support group back home.

Any occasion is suitable, but it would be most appropriate around a birthday. Instructions should be included, explaining that the group wanted to celebrate with them, but distance wouldn't allow it. (Contributed by Mark A. Simone, Ravenna, OH)

Music Video Night

If you have someone in your group or church with a video camera, here's a special event your youth group will love: Let the kids create their own music videos.

Before you have your Music Video Night, divide into small groups (or "bands") and allow them a week or so to plan their show and assemble their props. They can put anything they want on their video (within reason, of course). They can perform their music live, or they can lip-sync a record.

On the night of the event, have the groups meet in separate rooms to plan and rehearse their videos. After this, let your cameraperson videotape each group one at a time. Arrange the filming so that each group can perform in isolation, without the other groups watching. Then, at the conclusion of the filming, have everyone meet together and show all the videos.

Arrange some snacks and things to do for the kids who are waiting while others are filming. To speed things up, tell the groups that they only get one "take." It's a lot of fun to see what everyone comes up with, and the bloopers will be great! (Contributed by Steve Gladen, North Hollywood, CA)

Out-Of-School-For-The-Summer Party

Most kids would enjoy a year-end party that celebrates no more school and the beginning of the summer. Games could include:

1. **A Dunce Relay:** Divide into teams. One player on each team runs to the blackboard and writes "teacher is a dunce," and then returns to his or her seat and tags the next player on the team. The game continues in relay, and the first team to finish wins.

2. **Unspelling Bee:** Just like a regular spelling bee, except each word must be misspelled, but still recognizable. Give an award for the most creative entry.

3. **Unlearning Contest:** Each team comes up with the most creative way to forget anything learned during the school year they still happened to remember.

4. **Excuse List:** Each team tries

to write the most excuses for not getting an assignment in on time.

5. **Bubblegum Blowing Contest:** The "teacher" (sponsor) turns his or her back to the class. Each "student" is given bubble gum, and then begins blowing bubbles behind the teacher's back. When the teacher turns to face the "class," the biggest bubble seen by the teacher wins.

6. **Shootout at the O.K. Corral:** This is a historic reenactment of "My Final Day in High School." Each member is armed with a squirt gun and is mounted piggyback to have a shootout in the school library.

7. **Class Notes Bonfire:** Have all the kids bring any class notes they don't want to save and send them up in flames. (Contributed by Dan Van Loon, Clear Lake, IA)

Reservations Only

If your normal youth group activities suffer from poor attendance on those long holiday weekends (like Memorial Day and Labor Day), this idea might help.

Hold a "reservations only" dinner at the church, complete with linen tablecloths, lighted candles, music and good food. This would be an excellent opportunity to utilize members of your church of different ethnic backgrounds who can cook exotic foods. Afterwards, have dessert and perhaps show a video movie at someone's house.

Send out invitations in advance (two to three weeks) and give the event a sense of special importance. Make it an "R.S.V.P." deal and you'll find that the kids will respond in a very positive way. Some people are just looking for something good to do on the long weekend, and if you make a tradition out of it, you'll find that it will grow in popularity. It's a creative and effective way to let your kids know that their local church remains active during holiday weekends. (Contributed by James Wilson, Midwest City, OK)

Scavenger Hunt Teams

Next time you do a scavenger hunt with teams, try this. Link the teams together, either inside a hula-hoop or by safely tying them together with a rope or string (not around the necks). This will add some excitement to the scavenger hunt, and it forces the team to stick together. It can be funny as well as frustrating when the team members want to go in several different directions at once. It forces them to reach some kind of agreement.

(Contributed by David Rasmussen, Edmonds, WA)

School Lunch Hamburger Special

If you ever want to hear your kids use some of their more "descriptive words," ask them about their school lunches. Since the subject usually brings out all sorts of moans, groans, and weird expressions, why not get to the bottom of the problem once and for all? Have a contest to find out which school in your area has the absolutely worst hamburger.

If you have kids from a variety of schools in your youth group, create at atmosphere of school spirit and competition. Have a representative from each school take a container to school (provided by the youth group) and bring back to the youth group an actual hamburger, purchased in the school lunchroom.

Then, let your panel of judges go to work. One at a time, they can examine, scrutinize, smell, taste, and perform chemical tests on each hamburger in front of the group. With a lot of creativity and some terrible cold and soggy hamburgers, this can be a lot of fun.

Promote it ahead of time, let the kids spread the word, and it will certainly generate a lot of interest, enthusiasm, and disgust. (Contributed by Janice Kibbe, Waco, TX)

Super Bowl Bash

If your group is into watching professional football, have a party on Super Bowl weekend featuring some football films, refreshments, and games like these:

1. **The Super Bowl Bible Quiz:** Divide into 2 teams. Prepare a list of Bible questions ahead of time. The object of the game is to score touchdowns by answering 8 questions correctly. Each question is worth 10 yards. Teams on offense start on the 20-yard line, and have 80 yards to go for a touchdown. You keep the ball as long as your team answers questions correctly. When you answer incorrectly, the ball goes to the other team, and they begin

where they left off on their last possession. After each question, the team can "huddle" and then make their play (answer the question). When a team scores, then both teams start over on their 20-yard lines for the next series of downs. Play for as long as you like.

2. **Coin Flip Football:** This game is played by two people. Have the kids pair off, and give each pair a "gridiron" printed on a piece of paper. It should look like this:

		1	0	2	0	3	0	4	0	5	0	4	0	3	0	2	0	1	0	
		1	0	2	0	3	0	4	0	5	0	4	0	3	0	2	0	1	0	

Coin Flip Football
Two Player Game

The rules should also be printed on the page. They are:
- Flip a coin to see who receives first. Start on your 20.
- Advance the ball 10 yards for every "head" you flip.
- Lose ball to other player if you flip a "tails" twice in a row.
- Kick ball 40 yards if you change offense to another player.
- The first player to score 2 touchdowns is the winner.

3. **Super Bowl Bingo:** Distribute Bingo games similar to the one shown below. Write your own questions in the spaces, incorporating the current Super Bowl teams as much as possible. Then have kids mill about the room, asking people to answer the questions on their sheets. Whenever someone knows (or thinks they know) the answer, they give that person their

166

answer and sign their name in the space. The first person to get 5 in a row wins, but they automatically lose if their 5 people cannot correctly answer the questions they have signed.

Super Bowl Bingo
Two Player Game

What was the '84 Super Bowl Score?	How many games did the 49ers win in their regular season?	What is Walter Payton's Football Jersey Number?	Who is in today's Super Bowl?	What emblem do the Bears have on their helmets?	Who is the 49er quarterback?
How many games did the Dolphins win in their regular season?	Who is the Chicago Bears Head Coach?	Which NFL team has had a perfect season?	Which team did Joe Namath win a Super Bowl with?	What city is today's Super Bowl being played in?	Name a defensive player for Miami.
What NFL team has the most famous cheerleaders?	What team plays in Indianopolis?	Put your own name here!!	How much does 1 min. of commercial time cost for this Super Bowl?	Who is the Dolphins quarterback?	Name a defensive player for the 49ers.
Who is the 49ers' coach?	Which team is going to win the 1986 Super Bowl?	Who is the Dolphins' coach?	Name four other Bowl games.	Where is Dan Marino's former college?	Where was last year's Super Bowl played?
Where die Joe Montana play college football?	Name 3 coaches for the Bears team— past or present.	Who won last year's Super Bowl?	Who won the 1984 Super Bowl?	Who is the Cowboys' coach?	Which four teams were left in the NFL Conference Championships?

(Contributed by Tim Borgstrom, St. Charles, IL)

Tater Night Two

Here are some more games to add to the "Tater Night" special event in **Ideas #35**.

1. Mr. Potato Head Race:

Everyone is put on a team, with the number of teams being equivalent to the Mr. Potato Head games you have available (check your local toy store). The object of the game is for each team to put together their Mr. Potato Head successfully. They line up single file about 20 feet away from Mr. Potato Head, and each person on the team runs to him blindfolded and adds one more part. The first team to finish, or whichever team has the best Mr. Potato Head at the end of the time limit, is the winner.

2. **Baked Potato Scramble:** Write on a blackboard or a large piece of butcher paper the words "baked potatoes." Have the kids pair off and see which pair can come up with the most words using only the letters in "baked potatoes." Each letter can only be used as many times as it appears in these two words.

3. **Potato Push:** Have the kids push a potato along the ground in a figure eight course. Using only their heads (or noses, chins, foreheads). Rather than doing it as a relay (one person at a time), give each person a potato, and have them do it all together all at once, in a line. It's really fun to watch.
(Contributed by Bill Williamson, Los Angeles, CA)

Telephone Scavenger Hunt

Here is another variation on the old Scavenger Hunt or Car Rally that injects some life into the theme.

Divide your group into teams. Since each of these will be traveling together, group sizes will be determined by your vehicle capacities. Each group begins with an equal amount of change (such as 20 dimes) and a card with the church telephone number on it. After the designated start, all teams depart to find the first available pay telephone. They are to call the church and choose a number from 1 to 20. They will then be given the information question bearing the number chosen from a list of questions you have collected. Examples of these might be:
1. What is the name of the manager at the Tyrone Square McDonald's?
2. What is the price of a Biff Burger?
3. What is the number of the manhole cover at the corner of Center and 34th St.?
and so on.

The groups are to find the answer to their question, find a second phone booth, and call in their answer. If correct, they can request another question. If incorrect, they must call again with the right answer before receiving another.

You can play for as long as you like, but you should designate a certain time after which no more questions will be given out. Winners are determined by the team who successfully answers the most questions. In case of a tie, the group who returns the most of their original phone money will win.
(Contributed by Dick Gibson, St. Petersburg, FL)

Watermelon Olympics

Here's a good event for the summer. Have a "Watermelon Olympics" for the whole family. Each family brings one watermelon and a picnic lunch. There are a variety of watermelon games already in the **Ideas** library (see **Ideas #13–16** for several), plus you can try these:

1. **Watermelon Grab:** Hide all the watermelons (similar to an Eastern egg hunt) and then divide into two groups—the "grabbers" and the "taggers." The grabbers go out and try to locate and bring back a watermelon to "home base" without being tagged by the taggers. If they are tagged, they must put the watermelon down on the spot where they were tagged and "go to jail" for three minutes. Grabbers can only be

tagged while carrying a watermelon. See how many watermelons can be successfully brought into home base within a given time limit; then switch sides.
2. **Watermelon Sack Race:** This is just like a regular sack race, only the contestants must carry a watermelon along with them as they hop along with both feet in the sack.
3. **Watermelon Balance:** Each team is given a watermelon and a tennis racket. Players must carry the watermelon on the head of the racket to a goal and back. Players can hold the racket any way they want, but they cannot touch the watermelon with any part of the body.
4. **Speed Seed Eating and Spitting Contest:** Cut the watermelons into wedges and place them on a table. Each team gets a styrofoam cup. On a signal, teams start eating watermelon and spitting their seeds into the cup. The team that fills up its cup with seeds first is the winner.

(Contributed by E.J. Nusbaum, Ft. Benning, GA)

CHAPTER SEVEN

YOUTH GROUP LEADERSHIP

Brownie Taste Test

Announce in the church newsletter or bulletin that the youth are sponsoring a "Brownie Taste Test" at their next meeting. Members of the church are asked to submit a batch of their favorite brownie recipe for judging. On the night of the taste test, let the youth taste the different batches and select the best recipe. The kids will love to eat all those goodies, and the adults will enjoy showing off their favorite recipes. Be sure the group sends thank you notes to everyone who submits an entry. (Contributed by Suzanne W. Rushworth, Chattanooga, TN)

Card Groups

You can use a deck of common playing cards to divide a larger group into smaller groups at random. First sort the deck into suits (hearts, spades, diamonds, clubs), using as many suits as you want to have groups. Then arrange each suit in ascending order (from 2 to ace) and place in a separate stack. Now create one stack by taking the top card from each stack, then the next card from each (in the same order), and so on through the deck.

As kids enter the meeting place, hand each one a card from the top of the deck and ask them to hold on to them until time to divide up into groups. To form groups, have all the people with the same suit come together. (Contributed by John Larson, Cottage Grove, OR)

Do-It-Yourself Fog Machine

Here's how to make your own dry-ice "fog machine," which can be used for all kinds of things: dramatic or musical productions, haunted houses, photo sessions, or whenever you want to create an "eerie" effect.

You'll need the following items:
1. A 3- to 5-gallon bucket
2. Some heavy-duty cardboard
3. An electric hair dryer
4. About six feet of dryer vent hose (4" diameter preferred)
5. Duct tape
6. Hot water and dry ice

Everything listed above except the ice is easily obtainable at home or at a hardware store. You can find the dry ice outlets listed in the telephone directory under "Ice."

To build your fog machine, follow these instructions: First, place the bucket upside down on the cardboard and trace around the bucket. Cut the cardboard to make a lid for the bucket. Next, cut holes in the top of the lid for both the hair dryer nozzle and the dryer vent hose (a little smaller than the hose, so the hose can be twisted into the hole and will stay). Use duct tape to seal the cardboard lid around the top edge of the bucket.

Once the lid is sealed and the hose attached, you're ready to make fog. Here's how: Fill the bucket (through the hair dryer hole in the top—be careful) with HOT water. You might want to use a large funnel to avoid getting water on the cardboard lid. Or you can fill the bucket with hot water before you seal the lid onto the bucket.

Chop dry ice with an ice pick into small enough pieces so that it can be dropped through the hair dryer hole. After the ice is in, turn on the hair dryer and place it into the hole. The fan in the hair dryer will force the resulting "fog" out the other hole, through the hose. You can use the hose to direct the fog wherever you want it. The longer the hose you have, the farther you can spread the fog. It works!

Warning: Be sure to wear gloves when handling the dry ice, and avoid inhaling the carbon-dioxide fog. (Contributed by Dan Craig, Littleton, CO)

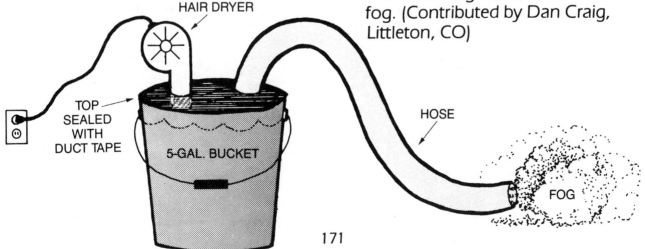

HAIR DRYER

TOP SEALED WITH DUCT TAPE

5-GAL. BUCKET

HOSE

FOG

171

Flunk Your Youth Sponsors!

Here's a good way to let your kids see how smart (or not-so-smart) their youth sponsors are. The kids get to play the role of "teacher" and the sponsors become the "students." It's all done in fun.

Have all the kids in your youth group come up with one question each from any subject they choose. After collecting all the questions, they can then be typed onto one sheet and given to the youth staff. A time limit is set (depending on the number of questions). The results are then announced at the next meeting. Chances are good that most of your sponsors will flunk. But your kids will love it.

You can tie this idea in with your Sunday School curriculum or Bible study as well. Have the kids create questions based on what they've learned during the course of study. The teachers and sponsors must then answer the questions.

Most of you are agonizing your way through final exams this week. **Here is your chance** to turn the tables, vent your frustration, and

FLUNK YOUR YOUTH SPONSORS!

You are about to write a test that **we** will have to take. So make your question as difficult as you possibly can! Here are the instructions:

1. Write a test question (one per person) in one of the five following forms:
   a. True/false
   b. Matching (no more than 5 pairs, please)
   c. Multiple choice (no more than 5 choices, please)
   d. Fill-in-the-blank (must require a specific answer—no essay questions)
   e. Identification (able to be answered in a sentence or two, and allowing for some subjectivity)
2. The test question must come out of your knowledge of the various subjects you have been studying this past semester. Write out your question below, and write the answer **on the back** of this sheet.

(Contributed by Steve Perisho, Boise, ID)

Focus on Youth Leadership

To demonstrate that you take youth leadership seriously, try giving some visibility to the officers in your group (if you have them). You can do this in two ways:

1. Draw up and circulate a list of specific job descriptions for each position. The list will help your leaders know what's expected of them, and will make others aware of how much they do for the group. See the sample descriptions given below.

2. Have a yearly dedication service on a Sunday morning when youth group officers are installed and honored in the presence of the whole congregation. The service described below should give you some ideas. (Contributed by Victoria J. Roark, Orlando, FL)

JOB DESCRIPTIONS FOR YOUTH GROUP OFFICERS

PRESIDENT. Presides over entire Youth Department and sees that each group is functioning. Works with each chairperson in his or her work area. Participates with all age levels. Consults with grade level representatives. Available to represent the youth at church meetings and functions.

VICE-PRESIDENT. Assists the president of the Youth Department in aiding the three grade levels. Presides when the president is unavailable.

SECRETARY. Responsible for taking minutes during Youth Council meetings. Sends birthday cards monthly and "miss ya" cards quarterly. Takes care of correspondence. Calls all officers for meetings.

TREASURER. Responsible for the group's financial matters and works closely with all fund-raising. Collects Sunday night snack supper money.

GRADE LEVEL REPRESENTATIVES (one for each grade). Works with the counselors, Sunday school teachers, class projects, and program suggestions. Makes all necessary announcements, phone calls, and visits in his or her grade concerning activities. Represents his or her grade on the Youth Council. Takes roll during meetings.

WORSHIP CHAIRPERSON. Plans the spiritual life of the Youth Group. Acts as executive officer of the Spiritual Life Retreat. Responsible for the spiritual aspects of each program, project, or party, and works closely with the Youth Director. Participates in planning youth-led worship services.

MISSIONS CHAIRPERSON. Makes recommendations to the Council for mission projects that may be undertaken by the group. This includes a summer mission trip as well as other projects throughout the year.

PROJECTS CHAIRPERSON. Makes recommendations to the Council for all other projects that may be undertaken by the group. This includes work projects for fund-raising and social services, as well as church-wide projects.

SOCIAL CHAIRPERSON. Plans social activities, which also include afterglows. Sets up for the socials and the snacks. Also responsible for holiday parties, dances, and hayrides.

RECREATION CHAIRPERSON. Plans recreation for occasional group recreation nights. Responsible for recreation at retreats and afterglows. Also plans special Sunday recreation outings for two Sunday afternoons a quarter.

NEWSLETTER CHAIRPERSON. Sees that the monthly newsletter, "The Writing on the Wall," is published. Assigns youth to write articles, chooses pictures for the publication, and gets the bulk mail out.

PUBLICITY CHAIRPERSON. Responsible for "getting the word out" through telephoning, posters, and the hall bulletin board.

MUSIC CHAIRPERSON. Keeps the music department, Sunday school, and youth group calendars coordinated. Helps choose youth choir music and leads singing in informal settings.

DEDICATION SERVICE FOR YOUTH OFFICERS

I. New officers are called to the altar.

II. Prayer for Continued Service:

Instill within the hearts of these, who have been chosen to lead their fellow youth, the true spirit of love, understanding, and a genuine concern for the work of your Kingdom. Instill within the hearts of those who have chosen them the spirit of devotion and loyalty, and a desire to serve as co-workers in your Church and Kingdom. Lead us now, Lord, as we listen to you and bless those accepting these great responsibilities. AMEN.

III. Charge to the Officers (see text below).

IV. Charge to the Parents:

As parents of these youth, you have been called to be supportive in the responsibilities they have accepted. Guide them and work as a family in serving Christ and His Church! Will you pledge to follow these guidelines?
RESPONSE: With God's help, I will.

V. Charge to the Congregation:

These young people are the future of Christ's Church. They are young leaders and need your devotion, loyalty, cooperation, guidance, and prayers. Will you pledge to support them in all these ways?
CONGREGATIONAL RESPONSE:

We pledge to support these officers, as well as all of our youth, through devotion, loyalty, cooperation, guidance, and prayer. We also pledge to live as examples for them to follow in growing as young Christians into adulthood.

VI. Officers kneel for prayer of dedication.

VII. Words to live by (from the pastor).

VIII. Altar prayer time.

IX. Benediction (all):

The Lord bless you and keep you;
The Lord make His face to shine upon you,
and be gracious unto you;
The Lord lift up His countenance upon you,
and give you peace. AMEN.

Numbers 6:24-26

CHARGE TO THE OFFICERS

You have been called to the office of PRESIDENT. Work toward the goal of Christ's high calling for this office. Will you carry out your responsibilities of this office as outlined by the Youth Council?
RESPONSE: *With God's help, I will.*

You have been called to the office of

VICE-PRESIDENT. Live up to this high calling of Christ and be a leader and example of Him. Will you carry out your responsibilities of this office as outlined by the Youth Council?
RESPONSE: *With God's help, I will.*

You have been called to the office of TREASURER. Be responsible with the finances and be dependable when called upon. Will you carry out your responsibilities in this office as outlined by the Youth Council?
RESPONSE: *With God's help, I will.*

You have been called to the office of WORSHIP CHAIRPERSON. You have the responsibility to see that worship is a central part of this youth program. Will you carry out that responsibility as outlined by the Youth Council?
RESPONSE: *With God's help, I will.*

You have been called to the office of MISSIONS CHAIRPERSON. Help the group to be aware of the needs of people in our world and how we can minister to them. Will you carry out your responsibilities of this office as outlined by the Youth Council?
RESPONSE: *With God's help, I will.*

You have been called to the office of PROJECTS CHAIRPERSON. Your leadership will help the group to set goals and priorities to serve God better through mission and service. Will you carry out your responsibilities in this office as outlined by the Youth Council?
RESPONSE: *With God's help, I will.*

You have been called to the office of PUBLICITY CHAIRPERSON. Work diligently at your job. The group's plans will not reach many people without your help. Will you carry out your responsibilities in this office as outlined by the Youth Council?
RESPONSE: *With God's help, I will.*

You have been called to the office of NEWSLETTER CHAIRPERSON. You have the responsibility of publishing the monthly newsletter, "The Writing On the Wall." Will you carry out your responsibilities in this office as outlined by the Youth Council?
RESPONSE: *With God's help, I will.*

The Golden Apple Award

Proverbs 25:11 says that "a word fitly spoken is like **apples of gold** in settings of silver." So why not recognize your youth workers periodically with "The Golden Apple Award?" From time to time, present a real golden apple (you can usually find them in nice gift shops) to one of your workers for faithful service in youth ministry. Let the young people themselves make the presentation during a Sunday morning worship service, then follow up with an announcement and congratulations in the church newsletter or bulletin. Such recognition not only honors your staff; it also encourages them to continue and increases your ministry's visibility. (Contributed by Phil Haas, Wichita, KS)

Graffiti Rules!

If you have a meeting room which is used exclusively by your youth group, give the kids one or two walls to "graffiti" with anything they want. Provide paint, spray paint, and brushes, and let the kids be creative.

You might want to make one rule about public decency; but otherwise, let the kids say what they want. You can always paint over it later and try again. (Contributed by Steve Gladen, North Hollywood, CA)

G.Y.M. At Church

Sometimes the success of a group has a lot to do with its name. Here's an idea for one. Call your youth group "G.Y.M.," which stands for "Great Youth Meeting." Then capitalize on the acronym in your events and organization. Your meeting place can now be called the

"GYM-nasium," your youth sponsors can be called "coaches," your activities can be called "work-outs." Your weekly newsletter can be entitled "Gym Shorts." You can carry out the theme as far as you wish. It's an idea that's "no sweat." (Contributed by Jim Mitchell, Klamath Falls, OR)

In-Transit Occupation Opportunities

Here's a good way to make those long, boring bus trips to a camp or special activity a fun experience for

everyone. Make up a list of "job opportunities" for every person on the bus. Then mail the list to all the kids before the trip and give them the chance to apply for the positions on a first-come, first-served basis. Here's a sample list:

SECRETARY. Keeps track of pertinent information from odometer orator, timekeeper, driver, personnel secretary, and others, to work at writing "The Story of Our Workcamp Experience." Will keep and collate all information from others upon trip's end.

BUS ATTENDANT #1. Checks oil, adds if necessary; inspects for underhood leaks or malfunctions; assists in gassing the bus; checks front lights and safety signals.

BUS ATTENDANT #2. Checks tires, rear lights, and safety signals; assists in gassing the bus, records gallons/liters and cost.

PERSONAL SECRETARY. Keeps track of humorous and interesting stories of our activities to, from, and during our trip.

ENVIRONMENT CONTROL TECHNICIAN #1. Ensures that center aisle and right side of the bus (facing the front) are kept free. Ensures that all windows on the right side of the bus are closed at end of the trip. Periodically passes wastebasket to messy passengers.

ENVIRONMENT CONTROL TECHNICIAN #2. Ensures that center aisle and left side of the bus (facing the front) are kept free of debris. Ensures that all windows on the left side of the bus are closed at the end of the trip. Keeps track of the messiest person, who must help clean the bus when we get home.

SECURITY ENGINEER #1. Makes sure the bus is not tampered with at rest stops. Stands guard while Security Engineer #2 is pursuing necessary comforts.

SECURITY ENGINEER #2. Makes sure bus is not tampered with while Security Engineer #1 pursues necessary comforts.

SOUND TECHNICIAN #1. Supervises the operation of the tape deck—volume, balance, tone, rewind.

SOUND TECHNICIAN #2. Supervises the selection of tapes, relying on passenger input and sensitivity. Checks tapes for backlash, sees that they are placed in proper cases. Assists Sound Technician #1 with any complex operational procedures.

INTERIOR RECREATION ASSISTANT #1. Assists Recreation Director in leading games and coordinating resources for activities. Reports on non-participants of group games for public embarrassment later. Right side of bus only.

INTERIOR RECREATION ASSISTANT #2. Same as #1, but left side only.

TIMEKEEPER. Keeps track of time from departure to arrival. Clocks the amount of time spent at rest areas, food establishments, etc.

ASSISTANT TIMEKEEPER. Assists timekeeper by arranging chronological particulars, and helps timekeeper with simultaneous timings of who spends the most time in the bathrooms, who sleeps the most, etc.

OFFICIAL NOSE COUNTER. Counts noses to make sure no one has more than one, and reports directly to the driver when all noses are accounted for. We do not discriminate against people without noses, but we ask that you please wear one (plastic acceptable) in order to be counted.

ODOMETER ORATOR. Records odometer readings of miles traveled, and reports them to the timekeeper for recording. Lets us know how many miles between rest stops, food stops, gas stops, and on the entire trip, start to finish.

ASSISTANT TO THE DRIVER. Assists driver with map reading, conversation, conveying messages to passengers. Receives a portion of all snacks to feed the driver. (It is very unfair to smell chocolate and not receive any!) Also enforces the NO TACO OR CORN CHIPS rule. (Taco and corn chips stink in a hot bus!)

RECREATION DIRECTOR. Keeps our ride from getting boring by being prepared to involve us periodically in recreation activities, games, quizzes, skits, etc.

All persons shall be employed as Stupidity Discouragers. Read here what is stupid!
1. It is stupid to litter inside or outside the bus.
2. It is stupid to be so loud on the bus that everyone gets a headache.
3. It is stupid to stick anything out the bus window (arms, legs, heads, hands, friends).
4. It is stupid to bring soft drinks on the bus (ice water okay).
5. It is stupid to buy big gulps, slurpies, or gallon-size drinks because no one's bladder is large enough to contain them.
6. It is stupid to do anything unsafe.

You'll find that kids will take pride in their jobs and do them with enthusiasm. At gas stops, for example, kids will act as a regular pit crew, jumping out of the bus, taking care of all its vital functions, and recording information. If you need to accommodate more people, you can come up with a few "creative" jobs, like "chief tire thumper," "on board photographer," "visual perception technician" (cleans windshield at rest stops), or whatever. (Contributed by Doug Bretshneider, Jenison, MI)

Invite A Drama Group

Most high school drama classes put on a play or two during the course of the school year. Usually these drama students work for months rehearsing their lines, creating costumes and building sets. Then they put the play on for the student body or their parents, and it's all over.

Most drama classes would welcome the chance to find another audience for a production in which they've invested so much time. Find out what plays your high school drama group plans to put on this year, and if the play sounds acceptable for a Christian youth group meeting, invite the group to present their production to your group. They could even use the youth group for a "dress rehearsal."

Often you can use the play as the basis for a talk or devotional (many plays deal with values), and it will serve as a great introduction to the youth group for many of the drama kids. (Contributed by David C. Wright, Vienna, VA)

Jigsaw Mixer

If your group is like most, you'll usually have a few kids who always come early to your meetings. Often they sit around and act bored, or they run off somewhere and wind up being late when the meeting actually starts.

To remedy this, provide a big jigsaw puzzle on a table in the back of the room which can be worked on by anyone who comes early. A 400- to 600-piece puzzle should keep kids busy for weeks. When the puzzle is finally finished, it can be made into a poster using "puzzle saver" glue, and hung up in the room or given to someone as a gift. This activity is creative, group-building, thought-provoking, and decorative, all at the same time! (Contributed by Keith Curran, Huntingdon, PA)

Money Mania

Want your youth to be obsessed with giving? Try "Money Mania" at your next week of camp or Vacation Bible School. Ask everyone to bring a certain kind of coin each day or night you take up an offering, according to the following plan:

Monday: "Dime Night." Each person gives one dime for every member of his or her family.

Tuesday: "Nickel Night." One nickel for every letter in the giver's name.

Wednesday: "Penny Night." One penny for every pound the giver weighs.

Thursday: "Quarter Night." One quarter for every foot of the giver's height.

Friday: "Dollar Night." One dollar for each heart the giver has! You can use this system to raise an offering for practically any need. One variation is to take the offerings every Sunday for five weeks.

Make sure you have plenty of coin wrappers. You'll be surprised at how much everyone will enjoy giving in this way. (Contributed by Tommy Baker, Florence, KY)

---

101 Ways to Choose A Group Leader at Random

When your youth divide up into small groups for discussion, all too often the same people in each group end up answering all the questions and leading all the conversations. One way to help kids choose a wider range of leaders or spokespersons is to select from the following list a different criterion for leadership every time you need a "volunteer" or break into groups. This will not only spread around leadership opportunities; it will also teach you things about your young people you never knew before. (Contributed by Tommy Baker, Florence, KY)

101 Criteria for Randomly Choosing a Group Leader

1. The person who has visited in the most states in America.
2. The person from the largest family.
3. The person whose birthday is closest to the youth pastor's.
4. The person who is seated closest to the youth pastor.
5. The person who has never been to Disney World/Land.
6. The person who lives farthest from the church.
7. The tallest person.
8. The person with the smallest shoe size.
9. The person with the most blue on.
10. The person who has employed the most modes of travel (boat, car, train, plane, etc.)
11. The person in your group who loves spinach the least.
12. The person wearing shoes that don't lace.
13. The person with the darkest hair.
14. The person who weighed the least at birth.
15. The person who stayed closest to home on his or her last family vacation.
16. The person who has been in the most weeks of church camp.
17. The person who has used an outhouse the most number of times.
18. The person with the least number of letters in his or her full name.
19. The person with the most first cousins.
20. The person who has had the most boyfriends/girlfriends.
21. The person who has made the most A's in school.
22. The person who has most recently kissed on the first date.
23. The person who uses Crest toothpaste, or has used it the longest.
24. The person who has to get up the earliest for school or work.
25. The person with the most pets.
26. The person with the biggest hand.
27. The one with the most syllables in his or her full name.
28. The one with the most jewelry on.
29. The person with the youngest sibling.
30. The person who uses Dial soap.
31. The person who lives farthest from the hospital.

32. The person who watched Saturday morning cartoons most recently.
33. The person who has worn braces the longest.
34. The person whose family has the oldest model car.
35. The person who has eaten most recently.
36. The person who has attended the most professional basketball games.
37. The person who has had the most broken bones.
38. The person who has been to the dentist most recently.
39. The person with the most vowels in his or her full name.
40. The person with the youngest mother.
41. The person with the most buttons on.
42. The one who got the least amount of sleep last night.
43. The person who learned to ride a bicycle at the earliest age.
44. The person who has the most older siblings.
45. The person who learned to swim at the youngest age.
46. The person who has eaten at the most fast-food restaurants in the past week.
47. The person with the most fillings.
48. The person who has been in the most car accidents.
49. The person with the most M's in his or her full name.
50. The person who has been shopping most recently.
51. The person whose birthday is closest to Ground Hog's Day (Feb. 2).
52. The person with the shortest hair.
53. The person who was the longest at birth.
54. The person to go on vacation most recently.
55. The person with the most uncles.
56. The person who most recently did *not* kiss on the first date.
57. The person from the smallest family.
58. The person with the largest shoe size.
59. The person with the lightest hair.
60. The person who has never flown, or who has flown the least.
61. The shortest person.
62. The person who lives closest to the hospital.
63. The person who has visited the fewest U.S. states.
64. The person whose birthday is closest to Jesus' birthday (Christmas).
65. The person who weighed the most at birth.
66. The person who has had the braces off his or her teeth the longest.
67. The person who ate the most for breakfast this morning.
68. The person who ate most recently at McDonald's.
69. The person who can play the most instruments.
70. The person who learned to ride a bicycle at the latest age.
71. The oldest person.
72. The person who gets up the latest for school or work.
73. The person with the smallest hand.
74. The person with the fewest syllables in his or her full name.
75. The person whose birthday is closest to today's date.
76. The person with the most grandparents living.
77. The person with the oldest sibling.
78. The person who most recently purchased an album.
79. The person who has had the most part-time jobs.
80. The person who has lived in the most houses or apartments.
81. The pickiest eater.
82. The person who watched the most T.V. in the past week.
83. The person who has traveled the farthest around the world at any one time.
84. The person with the most letters in his or her full name.
85. The person who has had the most stitches.
86. The youngest person.
87. The person who learned to swim at the youngest age.
88. The person with the most younger siblings.
89. The person who lives closest to his or her school.
90. The person who is wearing the most red right now.
91. The person with the most black on.
92. The person who got the most sleep last night.
93. The person with the most S's in his or her full name.
94. The person with the longest little finger.
95. The person with the fewest vowels in his or her full name.
96. The person with the youngest father.
97. The person whose family owns the smallest car.
98. The person with the most aunts.
99. The person who went away the farthest on his or her last vacation.
100. The person who was shortest in length at birth.
101. The person with the longest hair.

(Contributed by Tommy Baker, Florence, KY)

Parent Questionnaire

At your next parents meeting, have those who come fill out the questionnaire on the next page. It will help you recruit volunteer help and give you some insight into the parents' perspectives on your program. Be sure to add at the bottom your name, address, phone number, and typical weekly schedule. (Contributed by Denny Finnegan, Honolulu, HI)

Pinpointing

Here's a simple idea that helps kids feel important and also promotes outreach. Get a large city or area map, mount it on a corkboard or bulletin board, and display it in your youth room. Then place map pins

PARENT QUESTIONNAIRE

I. Personal Information
1. Name _____
2. Phone No. _____
3. Children in youth program:

Name	Age	Grade	School

II. We need your help!
1. If you could provide transportation once in a while, please check here. _____
    How many could you transport? _____
2. If you could provide refreshments one to three times this year, please check here. _____
3. If you'd be willing to offer your home as a place to meet once or twice this year, please check here. _____
    How many people would fit comfortably? _____ Uncomfortably? _____
    What are some special features about your home that might be of interest in planning a meeting (e.g. swimming pool, game room, wide screen TV). _____
    _____
4. If you'd be willing to assist in one of our youth retreats, please check here. _____

III. We also want to help you! Rank the discussion topics below according to how helpful they would be to you as a parent (#1 would be most important, and so on).

_____ Parent-teen relationships   _____ Christian models in the home
_____ Conflict resolution   _____ On being a parent
_____ Family devotions   _____ Resources available to parents
_____ Pressures on youth today   _____ Building a Christian home
_____ Christian education in the home   _____ Other _____
                                                                           _____

IV. Evaluation of the Youth Program. Please answer honestly.
1. The one thing I like best about the youth program is _____
    _____
2. The one thing I dislike most about the youth program is _____
    _____
3. How do you feel about the youth leaders? _____
    _____
4. What one goal do you most want to see the youth program accomplish? _____
    _____

V. Please complete the following sentences:
1. God is _____.
2. The Bible is _____.
3. Our family is _____.
4. The most important thing for a family to have is _____.

VI. Are there any other comments you'd like to make?

(the little ones with the round colored heads) on the map where all your youth group members live. When visitors come, have them place a pin on the map where they live. This will have a positive impact on both members and prospects.

To use this idea for outreach, give each group member a couple of different-colored pins and have them place the pins on the map where two of their non-Christian friends live. Later, maybe once a month, have the kids go visit some of these prospects and invite them to a youth activity. (Contributed by Rick Allen, Uvalde, TX)

Poster Registration

Keeping track of who was present at a major event can be rather difficult with a larger youth group. Here's a solution. Make a special poster and attach to it a pen on a string, then encourage everyone to write his or her name on it. Ask visitors to write the name of the person they came with as well as their own name. This will give you the opportunity to contact them later. After the event is over, the poster can be used to decorate the youth group meeting room. (Contributed by David Rasmussen, Edmonds, VA)

Put-down Covenant

Put-downs (negative comments made by one person about another) can seriously undermine relationships in a youth group if they're allowed to go unchecked. Here's one way to help stem the tide.

Spend some time with the youth group discussing the subject of put-downs and how important it is to be careful about what we say to each other (Ja. 3:2–12).

Following this study, have the kids create a "Put-Down Covenant" similar to the one on the next page. You might pass out a sample, and allow the kids to modify it or add their own thoughts to it. Then have everyone sign it and post it in the meeting room as a constant reminder that put-downs are unacceptable in the youth group by their own agreement.

Put-down Potty

If you're having trouble with kids who constantly put each other down in youth meetings and activities, try this. Get a child's "potty seat" and label it the "put-down potty." Then, whenever a member of the group (youth or sponsor) puts another person down, the culprit must pay a fine (10 cents). The fine can be collected in the potty, and the money collected can be sent to a worthy mission project.

This approach helps to call attention to the problem without being heavy-handed about it. You will discover that the increased awareness will result in fewer and fewer put-downs. The amount of the fine can be set at any level you feel will be most effective and fair to all. (Contributed by Hal Evans, Pueblo, CO)

Put-Down Covenant

We would like our youth group to be a place where everyone can come, feel accepted, and feel good about themselves.
We know that put-downs and criticisms make people feel rejected, hurt, and bad about themselves.
We also know that hurting others in any way is wrong before God.

Therefore, we promise, with God's help, to:
1. **Stop putting others down ourselves with words or actions.**
2. **Remind others in the group of their responsibility not to put others down.**
3. **Ask forgiveness from God and from others when we fail.**
4. **Forgive others when they fail.**

_____   _____
Signed   Date

(Contributed by David C. Wright, Vienna, VA)

Short Stories and Scripture

The modern short story can be a creative and effective tool for communicating scriptural truths. Oscar Wilde's "Happy Prince," for example, can be used to introduce social concerns to youth; Nathaniel Hawthorne's "Young Goodman Brown" may spark a lively discussion of the human condition.

Most public and university libraries subscribe to **The Short Story Index**, a periodically-updated, topical index to short stories in anthologies. If you're interested on a short piece on peace making, for example, you would check each volume of the **Index** under "peace," "non-violence," "pacifism," and related topics, noting the short stories listed there and the anthologies in which they appear. Then you would simply check the library card catalog to locate copies of the anthologies, and review them to find the most promising story for your purposes.

Needless to say, each story should be critically evaluated for its appropriateness as a reading for Christian youth. Though many of the pieces indexed will not present viewpoints which are biblically informed, they can serve by way of contrast as starting points for discussing what a biblical perspective would be. (Contributed by Steve Perisho, Boise, ID)

T-Shirt Solidarity

Having special T-Shirts printed for your group builds a sense of group identity. Find someone who will prepare an attractive design for your group name, and then have the design printed onto good quality T-Shirts. This can be done commercially or silk-screened by hand, if you know how to do it. Chances are good that you can find a T-Shirt shop in your city to do it for you at a reasonable cost.

To make the most of your shirts, throw a Back-to-School Party and tell the youth to come wearing their school colors. Toward the end of the evening, give out the shirts. Then note that as school starts, they'll probably become involved in many other activities; but you hope the shirts will be a reminder that they'll remain a special part of your group, and that you hope to see them throughout the year. Let everyone put on the shirts and take a group

picture, and then have copies made for everyone. (Contributed by Suzanne W. Rushworth, Chattanooga, TN)

Thank You Notes

Do you ever have trouble getting your group to write thank you notes? Try this approach: provide a single sheet of white paper, give each kid a different color pen or marker, and let each person write a brief note of appreciation on it to someone who deserves a thank you note. Tell them they can write in any direction, add doodles, and liven it up any way they like. The youth will enjoy the chance to be creative, and the recipient of the note will appreciate their thoughtfulness. (Contributed by Suzanne W. Rushworth, Chattanooga, TN)

Treasure Chests

To collect memories of their years in your youth group, give each new member a large, sturdy cardboard box. The kind that are used to ship eight reams of typing or photocopying paper are especially suited for making a "treasure chest," because they're reinforced and have removable lids instead of flaps.

Encourage the kids to use these boxes for collecting all kinds of youth group memorabilia: photos, programs, ticket stubs, camp schedules, Bible study notes, trip logs, or whatever (but nothing perishable). The outside of the boxes can be decorated with items glued on to form a collage.

Over the years these treasure chests can become a reminder of how much their owners have grown, and a good source of laughs. To make them even more meaningful, you can build a yearly program around presenting the boxes to new members, with the "vets" sharing some items from their own collections. (Contributed by Mark A. Simone, Ravenna, OH)

Visitation To Go

If your church or youth group encourages "visitation"—that is, small groups who visit new prospects in their homes—here's a way to get those new prospects involved in the youth program immediately.

Plan a special event or an outing of some kind around your visitation program so that they occur on the same day. This could be an ice cream social, a roller skating party, or just about anything. Then, when you visit new prospects, don't just ask them to come to church or youth group some time in the future; invite them to go with you right then and there. You'll be surprised at how many will come if the visiting group is enthusiastic and a little persistent. If they need time to get ready, just tell them you'll come back to pick them up in half an hour or so. Use the special event as a way to meet these new kids and to expose them to the youth program of the church. (Contributed by Russ Porter, Rosenberg, TX)

Welcome to the '80s

To help new adult sponsors break the ice with the youth at the beginning of the year, have them recruit a young person to introduce them while playing in the background a popular record from their own teenage years. As the Beatles, the Mamas and the Papas, or the Supremes sing a golden oldie, the sponsor should appear in the style of clothes they wore when they were in high school. After they've had a chance to show off their go-go boots, granny glasses, Nehru collars, and flowered ties, another young person recruited from the group should shout, "Hey, you guys, this is the '80s!"

Next the sponsors can explain that their experiences are different from those of the kids, and that their ideas about youth groups come from a different decade, but that they intend to have a great program with the help of the youth themselves. The group should be ready to respond enthusiastically to a follow-up brainstorming and planning session immediately after the introductions. (Contributed by Karen Carpenter, Memphis, TN)

You Deserve A Break Today

If you have access to your kids' school(s), you can offer them a great alternative to the cafeteria lunch. The idea is simply to cater a free lunch from a nearby fast-food place for a few lucky students. One week prior to the event (which should be highly advertised on school bulletin boards), place several lottery boxes around campus, and pass out tickets during lunch each day. At a time which has been previously announced, hold the drawing and announce winners over the intercom.

Then, on the designated day, set up an elegantly-decorated table in the cafeteria and serve the lucky winners royally. Besides being lots of fun, this event provides great publicity for your ministry. (Contributed by Chuck Behrens, Washington, PA)

Youth Worker Job Bank

List every conceivable role or task in your church's youth ministry, right down to such mundane details as transportation to the car wash. Then make a "volunteer youth workers questionnaire" like the one shown. Distribute the form to the entire congregation—perhaps as a church bulletin or newsletter insert—and wait for the response. Approach the volunteers for the tasks you need done immediately, and file the rest in a job bank for future reference.

This approach has two important benefits. First, it broadens your base of volunteer participation. Second, you may find people willing to take on limited or short-term responsibilities who were unable to help before because only a long-term, all-or-nothing involvement was possible. (Contributed by Dave Mahoney, Columbus, IN)

YOUTH WORKERS QUESTIONNAIRE

With all the activities our youth group has going, we need help in a number of roles and tasks. Would you be willing to volunteer for at least one (more if you can) of the following areas? If so, please complete this form and place it in the collection plate, turn it in at the church office, or give it to the youth pastor. Thanks!

Name _____

Address _____

Phone _____

I'd like to work with the following age group (rank first to last):

_____4th, 5th, 6th grade   _____7th, 8th   _____9th, 10th   _____11th, 12th

I'd like to work in the following area(s) with this group:

BIBLE SCHOOL TEACHER _____

CAMPS AND RETREATS
   Chaperon _____
   Food _____
   Recreation _____
   Group leader _____

PUBLICITY
   Make fliers and ads _____
   Make phone contacts _____

MISSION TRIP
   Chaperon _____
   Helper _____

DRAMA
   Costumes _____
   Director _____
   Make-up _____
   Stage Crew _____

MULTI-MEDIA
   Photography _____
   Slides _____
   VCR _____

PRAYER BREAKFAST
   Cook _____
   Leader _____

EVANGELISM
   Calling youth _____
   Transporting youth _____

MID-WEEK BIBLE STUDY
   Host _____
   Leader _____

YOUTH MEETINGS
   Chaperon _____
   Coach _____
   Refreshments _____

HOLIDAY IDEAS

Balloon-O-Lanterns

If you'd like to have a pumpkin-carving contest, but a roomful of the "real thing" would cost too much, use orange balloons and felt tip markers instead. Have the kids inflate the balloons (save your breath) and be as creative as they like in drawing faces. Give prizes for the ugliest, the scariest, the funniest, or whatever. (Contributed by Russ Porter, Rosenberg, TX)

Bobbing For Pickles

Fill a large tub with ice water. Along with apples, add some smaller items such as pickles, olives, and grapes. Allow each person 30 seconds to bob for as many items as possible, giving each "catch" to a partner who collects them on a paper plate. Use the following point system for scoring: apple = 1 point; pickle = 2; grape = 3; olive = 4. Give prizes to the person with the highest score. (Contributed by Marge Clark, Sanford, FL)

Bone Hunt

For a Halloween activity that leads into a discussion about the body of Christ, purchase the inexpensive little "coffins" which contain candy "bones" of a human skeleton, one coffin for each hunting team (four players per team). Remove the bones and wrap them in separate packets, and then hide the packets around the church building and grounds. Replace each bone in the coffins with a clue about where it has been hidden, written on a slip of paper cut to resemble that particular type of bone.

Give each team a coffin and send them out searching for the parts of their skeletons. They are not to open the packets until they return with all of them (though some of them probably will, eating what they find). Once the group comes back together, each team should assemble its skeleton.

Form one big circle and place the finished products in the middle. Read 1 Corinthians 12 together and talk about how the body of Christ is incomplete if any part is missing (illustrate with the skeleton of any team that ate a bone ahead of time). You can also discuss what it means to have diverse gifts and to recognize Christ as the Head of the Body.

End the evening by taping together the hands of the people sitting beside each other in the circle, and placing some snacks in the middle. They won't be able to eat unless they cooperate by feeding each other. (Contributed by David Washburn, Brockport, NY)

Cantastic Can Circus

To raise canned goods for distribution to needy families at Thanksgiving, hold a "Can Circus" one evening in mid-November. Kids bring canned goods with them for admission to the circus, then compete in teams for "cantastic" prizes in several events:

1. **Can Collection**—Each team is awarded a point for every can its members brought with them.
2. **Can Castle**—Each team vies to construct the best castle (or tallest tower) using only the cans they brought in.
3. **Can Quiz**—See which team can identify the most items from the following list (all the items begin with "can"). Use the dictionary to add some of your own as well.
   1. America's northern neighbor (Canada).
   2. A Native American craft (canoe).
   3. A heavy cloth (canvas).
   4. A mid-Western state (Kansas).
   5. A yellow bird (canary).
   6. A long, narrow valley (canyon).
   7. Someone who would love to have you for dinner (cannibal).
4. **Bowling Cans**—For each team, set up ten empty cans like bowling pins, and roll softballs to see which team can rack up the highest total score (each team member gets one roll).

5. **Can Crash**—Set up a pyramid of five empty cans for each team, and let them throw wiffle balls to see how many they can knock down (each team member gets one throw).
6. **Can Soccer**—This is a relay race, with players "dribbling" a can as they would a soccer ball—down around a chair and back.
7. **Can the Penny**—Another relay race, where players put a penny between their knees, waddle across the room to an empty can, drop the penny in the can using only their knees, and return to their team.

8. **One-Hand Can Wrap**—One contestant from each team must gift wrap a can using only one hand (the other remains behind his or her back). Award points for the best job.

9. **Can Rolling**—Each member of a team gets one chance to roll a can toward a target, which is simply a small square of masking tape on the floor. The team wins a point for each can that rolls in the square and remains there.

10. **Can-I-Ball**—This is played just like "Steal the Bacon," but use a can for the bacon.

11. **Fetch the Can**—Put all the cans at one end of the room. Have players line up relay style and race down one at a time to bring a can back to their team. The team that has fetched the most in two minutes is the winner (only one can must be carried at a time).

Any number of games can be adapted to utilize the cans your group brings in. A great way to turn food collection into fun! (Contributed by Terry O. Martinson, South Weymouth, MA)

Creative Costume Scavenger Hunt

Have your group go out Halloween night begging, not for treats, but for items to make a costume. Meet at the home of one of your staff or youth and divide the group into teams, assigning each one a different street in the surrounding neighborhood. Then let each team choose one of its members to be their "model." Teams must go door to door, asking at each home for one or two items they can use in creating a costume for their model. At one place they may get an old hat, at another some lipstick, at another a wig, and so on. Set a time limit, and when teams report back to home base, hold a competition for the best costume. (Contributed by Randy Lanford, Fort Worth, TX)

Costume Bingo

Here's a great mixer for a Halloween party, or any party in which all the players are in costume. Print up Bingo cards like the one shown, and have kids get signatures of people who match the descriptive phrases. As in regular Bingo, five in a row wins. Keep playing until you have several winners. (Contributed by Vernon Edington, Manchester, TN)

Costume Bingo

Instructions: Sign your name in the blank marked "own name."
Find other people who match the squares and get their signatures.

Own Name	Someone whose mom told them how to dress for this party	Someone wearing facial make-up for the first time	Someone who waited until the last hour before deciding what to be
Someone who wishes Lady Godiva would have shown up	Someone who's giving up a favorite TV show to be here	Someone who's glad to have the chance to show off their legs	Someone who has to explain to everyone who they are
Someone whose hat keeps slipping off	Someone who plans to eat one of every dessert	Someone whose costume is uncomfortable	Someone who would rather **not** have their picture made right now
Someone who wishes they could really be who they are dressed as	Someone who borrowed more than two items for their costume	Someone who wishes we had a costume party every year or so	Someone who can't get to where it itches

Halloween Tunnel

This year, try a tunnel instead of a spook house. You can construct it out of boxes from refrigerators or other large appliances. Use masking tape or a staple gun to fasten them together end to end, and run the tunnel like a maze throughout the church building. Include trap doors and dead ends to make the trip more confusing, and decorate throughout with the scary items usually found in a spook house. You can even have them crawl through cooked noodles and wet bread!

For some great thrills, cut a few holes in the tunnel wall in several locations so that masked faces and rubber-gloved hands can thrust through to clutch at victims as they pass by. End the tunnel with a slide by rigging up carpeted plywood over some stairs. Then have someone on hand to issue a cardboard "toboggan" for the final ride. Station another person at the bottom to assist in landings, where the fall can be broken by a few old mattresses. It's a journey they'll long remember! (Contributed by June Becker, Reading, PA)

Holy Halloween

Try offering your kids an alternative celebration on Halloween night this year. You can preserve the pleasure of dressing up by having the kids put together elaborate and authentic costumes. But limit them to characters related to the Scripture or the Church: biblical heroes like Esther or Paul; famous figures from church history like Luther or Wesley; evangelists, preachers, or missionaries; and maybe even a couple of seraphim and cherubim!

Party decorations should reflect the same themes, with Bible scenes and characters. Tell Bible stories instead of ghost stories, and hold a contest for the **prettiest** (rather than scariest) jack-o-lantern face. If you normally have a haunted mansion, try a Bible mansion with "live" Bible scenes instead.

Take the kids out as a group and travel through the neighborhood singing hymns or praise songs. Instead of asking for treats, leave a small gift at each home you visit— perhaps some fruit or a pocket New Testament—and give them a tract or a packet of information about your church. (Contributed by Doug Newhouse, Florence, KY; Mark Reed, Decatur, IL; Richard R. Everett, North Haven, CT; and Ron Camblin, Orlando, FL)

Horror Hay Ride

Combine the fun of a traditional autumn hayride with the chills and thrills of a Halloween haunted house. Plan a route that will take them out in a lonely, spooky area at night, and have a cast of ghouls and goblins in costume waiting there to moan, groan, threaten, and attack unexpectedly from clever hiding places. You should have the only flashlight on the ride so you can control what they're able to see.

Your actors can have a planned script which includes a truck breakdown at the most desolate point on the route, a kidnapping, and a wrestling match with a monster; or let them haunt spontaneously. A night your group will never forget! (Contributed by Phil Blackwell, Charleston, SC)

Pin The Nose On Jack

This is a Halloween version of "Pin the Tail on the Donkey." The rules are the same as for that game, but instead of a donkey picture, use a drawing of a jack-o-lantern minus the nose. Then, instead of a tail, have blindfolded players pin or tape on individual noses created from pictures of noses which have been cut out of magazines and glued on to yellow construction paper triangles. Each person's nose should be unique, and can be taken from any person or animal: an elephant's trunk, pig's snout, bird's beak, or whatever. (Contributed by Warren and Linda Waddell, Oshkosh, WI)

Pumpkin Party

Have an entire evening of activities centered on that most familiar of autumn symbols—the pumpkin. Try some of these games, and invent your own:
1. **Pumpkin Patch Pick**—Like an Easter egg hunt, only you search for hidden pumpkins (which are admittedly a little more difficult to hide than eggs).
2. **Pumpkin Pushovers**—Teams or individuals go bowling with pumpkins instead of balls. Mark off alleys with masking tape, and use plastic two-liter soft drink bottles as pins. Pumpkins should all be similar in size.
3. **Pumpkin Puzzle**—Have teams choose from a large selection of pumpkins the one they think comes closest to weighing 40 pounds without going over that amount.
4. **Pumpkin Pie Pig**—Each team chooses an eater and a feeder to be seated across from each other at a table. The eaters must keep their hands behind their backs, and the feeders must keep one hand under the table. Feeders are given a pumpkin pie and a spoon, and are blindfolded. On the signal, feeders begin stuffing the eaters with the spoon or fingers, whichever is preferred. First team to have their eater finish eating the entire pie wins.

This evening is cheaper if you have your group plant some pumpkins ahead of time so that you'll have your own patch in the fall. (Contributed by Elizabeth Power, River Glade, NB, Canada)

Scary Scavenger Hunt

Have the kids find, **not** the following items, but instead objects that could serve as **substitutes** for these items. For example, red poster paint might take the place of blood. Limit the hunt to the church building and grounds.

Witch's eye
Bat's wing
Voodoo doll
Pumpkin
Fur from a black cat
Ghost footprint
Blood
Count Dracula's teeth
Pumpkin pie
Left hand of a mummy
Old bone
Green slime
 (as in "Ghostbusters")

(Contributed by Robert Summers, Durand, MI)